RE: WRITING
Strategies for Student Writers

RE: WRITING

Strategies for Student Writers

Frances Kurilich
SANTA MONICA COLLEGE

Helen Whitaker

Rd. 74 - 77

Holt, Rinehart and Winston, Inc.
New York   Chicago   San Francisco   Philadelphia
Montreal   Toronto   London   Sydney   Tokyo

Library of Congress Cataloging-in-Publication Data

Kurilich, Frances.
    Re: Writing   Strategies for student writers / Frances Kurilich,
Helen Whitaker.
     p.   cm.
    Includes index.
    1. English language—Rhetoric. I. Whitaker, Helen. II. Title.
III. Title: Re: Writing Strategies for student writers.
PE1408.K84 1988
808'.042—dc19   87-30787
                                      CIP

ISBN 0-03-004632-7

Requests for permission to make copies of any part of the work should be mailed to:
Permissions
Holt, Rinehart and Winston, Inc.
111 Fifth Avenue
New York, NY 10003
PRINTED IN THE UNITED STATES OF AMERICA

8 9 0 1 016 9 8 7 6 5 4 3 2

Holt, Rinehart and Winston, Inc.
The Dryden Press
Saunders College Publishing

PREFACE

Underlying *Re: Writing* are several key assumptions about people and about the writing process:

- that beginning writers need to develop a sense of writing as a unique activity.

- that structure allows individual ideas to take form in a way that is communicable.

- that writers become "good" with practice in a variety of writing situations.

- that good writing is difficult and challenging and that in rising to meet that challenge, we do indeed grow in confidence, skill, and understanding.

In addition to highlighting a basic sequence of activities to guide writing, the text also provides direction and guidance for the various writing projects. Why? The leap from theory to practice is an important one, and any measures which help a person to bridge that gap effectively are welcomed by both student and instructor.

The *process* of writing this text has been an educational one for us. During the past several years, we have been fortunate to receive help and advice from a number of sources. First, to the English 81 and 21 students of Santa Monica College, the greatest thanks of all, for virtually all of the writing assignments and exercises have been class-tested and studied with respect to student reactions. To Dick and Corinne Dodge, our thanks not only for help with the original form of the text but for their good advice and support. A particular note of thanks to Alice

Dubiel, who drew the graphics for the original version of the text and who has supplied her own support and suggestions for *Re: Writing*.

We are indebted to the following reviewers who have provided useful criticism and valuable insight: Joan Brand, Cincinnati Technical Institute; Aleeta Christian, Austin Peay State University; Walter Cmielewski, County College of Morris; Deborah Core, Eastern Kentucky University; Barbara Craig, Del Mar College; Mary Foege, Gateway Technical Institute; Carol Joyce Fokine, Portland State University; Ann Green, Jackson Community College; Jacqueline Griffin, Essex County College; Chris Henson, California State University; Nancy Herzfeld-Pipkin, Grossmont College; David Hopkins, Rio Hondo Community College; Deborah Larson, University of Missouri (St. Louis); Lorraine Lauria, Onondaga Community College; Nancy Martinez, University of New Mexico; Phyllis Pickens, Burlington County College; Maureen Potts, The University of Texas at El Paso; Muriel Rada, Metropolitan Technical Community College; Philip Tetrault, Dean Junior College; Susan Yaeger, Monroe Business Institute.

Our special thanks to the staff of Holt, Rinehart and Winston: Charlyce Jones Owen, Associate Publisher for English; Kate Morgan, Developmental Editor; Sondra Greenfield, Senior Project Manager; Bob Kopelman, Design Supervisor; and Nancy Myers, Production Manager.

Finally, to two special husbands, many thanks for their patience, encouragement, and understanding of this production.

F.K./H.W.

TO THE STUDENT

We hope that you will remember that books of all sorts are your greatest educational allies. *Re: Writing* is designed to help you master the writing process. By no means the last word in this area, the text has been developed from the kind of classroom situation you find yourself now in as a college student.

Try to make this text yours in a number of ways. First, examine the table of contents to get a feel for what is inside. Any part of the book which interests you can be read even before your instructor reaches that point in class. In fact, it is sometimes impossible to cover an entire text in a quarter or semester, so by all means read frequently and often. As your instructor returns papers to you, check any notations that relate to problems or errors, and use the table of contents to locate the material that will help you avoid the problem on your next paper.

Although the modern world provides many inventions to make our lives easier, such as the word processor, it is not essential to use a computer in order to learn to write. With a desire to learn, a willingness to set aside time for reading and thinking about your reading, and plain old-fashioned practice, you will gradually come to absorb the basic principles of writing. And you will have accomplished this task through the use of your most powerful tool: your mind.

Every process, including writing, involves a journey. We hope this book gets you on your way.

CONTENTS

RE: WRITING
Strategies for
Student Writers

UNIT I

Getting Started

- **BEGINNING A WRITING PROJECT**
- **CLARIFYING THE WRITING PROCESS**
- **USING PREWRITING TO GET STARTED**
- **PREPARING FOR THE ROUGH DRAFT**

OVERVIEW

Beginning a Writing Project *emphasizes understanding the assignment and the pressure of time.*

Clarifying the Writing Process *focuses on writing as a special activity and dynamic process directed to an audience.*

Using Prewriting to Get Started *highlights that stage of the writing process when ideas are generated and focused.*

Preparing for the Rough Draft *considers the task of organizing prewriting material into reasonable order.*

Introduction

As a college student, you will find yourself faced with many activities, one of the most critical being *writing.* If your writing is clear and well organized, you will have mastered the primary academic form of communication: the written word. If you could *tell* your literature instructor what you know about Shakespeare's sonnets or *talk* to your biology instructor about cell division, your job would be much easier, and this text would be unnecessary! But because writing forces a person to make choices and organize ideas into coherent statements, it plays a key role in forming an educated mind.

This first unit provides you with a basic writing strategy that emphasizes what to do to get started in an efficient and potentially successful manner. Unit I also provides an overview of writing as an activity requiring special care and attention. As your awareness of the components of good writing increases, so will the quality of your individual writing efforts.

BEGINNING A WRITING PROJECT

The beginning stages of a writing project can strongly influence what you produce in your final paper. Therefore, one of your major concerns as a student writer will be *getting started* in an efficient and productive manner. Since every writing project starts with an actual assignment from an instructor or a textbook, your first consideration as a writer may seem obvious:

Do I understand the demands (requirements) of the writing project?

This question requires a response before any writing can begin. A paper may be strong in grammar, vocabulary, and overall paragraph development, but it is seriously weakened if the assignment has been misunderstood. To get started on the right path, it is vital that you focus on the requirements of each assignment.

UNDERSTANDING THE ASSIGNMENT

Some of the writing assignments you receive during your college career will be fairly easy to understand, such as these three:

1. Describe a memorable character from your childhood.

2. In your opinion, what is one course that should be a requirement for all high school students?

3. Do you feel that Americans place too much emphasis on staying young? Explain your point of view.

All three are relatively easy to understand for this reason: they are directed to you on a *personal* level. The first is the most personal, for its topic is your childhood, no one else's. The second and third assignments, although they present issues of interest to anyone in our society, allow you to provide your opinion—whatever it may be. In addition, assignments 2 and 3 are easy to understand because they are questions, and *questions demand answers.* Other types of assignments, however, are more complex, as is this one:

4. Television exerts some degree of influence upon everyone in our society. Select one aspect of this powerful force, and discuss it thoroughly.

In contrast to the first three, the fourth assignment is objective and is not directed to you on a personal level. Instead, you are being asked to examine a phenomenon in society (television) and to comment intelligently on it. This type of objective assignment is common in academic courses and usually has two distinctive features:

- Impersonal, objective wording

- The demand to focus the writing effort

Each of these features will influence your thought processes and your choice of words when the draft is begun.

Impersonal, Objective Wording

Examine the following pair of sentences, and choose the one which is impersonal or objective in its choice of language.

1. I think that violence in television cartoons is dangerously misleading to small children.

2. Violence in television cartoons is dangerously misleading to small children.

The second sentence is more impersonal and objective in its wording. It is written in the *third person;* its phrasing is neutral because it focuses on the idea that is the topic, rather than on the speaker or the writer. In contrast, the "I think" phrasing of sentence 1 makes it too personal to use when an assignment does not ask for personal experiences or opinions. Sentence 1 is written in the *first person,* using *I*.

The majority of your college writing topics will fall into the objective category, especially in classes such as history, political science, and sociology. Avoiding the first person, the *I* approach, may seem restrictive to you. However, remember this fact about objective writing: Even though the language you use in your writing is impersonal, it is *you*, the individual person, who chooses which aspect to write about and what information to include. In this sense, even the impersonal is personal because it provides you with the freedom of choice.

The Demand to Focus the Writing Effort

Just as a photographer can narrow a camera's focus to a smaller part of a scene, so a writer can select a smaller part of a large issue or area. In assignment 4 about television, the demand to focus the writing effort appears in the second sentence: "Select one aspect of this powerful force, and discuss it thoroughly."

In this case, focusing the writing effort involves the choice of a smaller aspect to discuss. If you were unsure of what the term *aspect* meant and if you overlooked the direction to select *one* aspect, you might not meet the demands of this part of the assignment.

What is an *aspect?* This term refers to a smaller, more specific part of some larger concept. Television, for example, is extremely complex, containing many aspects or parts. The five aspects listed below focus on a smaller area or part or component of television:

1. the effect of commercials on the buying habits of teenagers

2. how television violence affects children

3. the use of television as a teaching tool

4. whether television has replaced reading as the main source for what we know

5. the influence of television commercials on our grammar

Of course, there are many other aspects of television in addition to these five. Many of these other aspects also provide a narrower focus. Once you understand the need to select a smaller focus, you have a better chance of meeting the demands of an assignment.

Misunderstanding this need to focus the writing effort tends to produce what might be called a "smorgasbord" paper: a little of this aspect, a little of another aspect, and so on. This approach is inappropriate for two reasons:

1. The assignment has *specifically requested* a single focus.

2. College-level writing requires *development and depth* of discussion; depth is impossible if you are trying to do too much at one time.

FOR YOUR MENTAL FILE

Whether an assignment is given to you verbally or written on the board, record it *verbatim*, meaning word for word, so that no important details are omitted. Regardless of how you receive the actual assignment, read it slowly and examine each word. Skimming and speed reading are useful skills for some purposes, but they are not effective for interpreting writing assignments.

TIME AND THE WRITING PROCESS

Good writing takes time. Although *writing* is one small word, it embraces many different thought processes. In *prewriting*, for example, you not only generate ideas, you evaluate them, reject some, expand others, and present opinions. In *drafting*, you use prewriting and work your ideas into sentences and paragraphs, using all of your language skills in this process. With *editing* you use another level of evaluation and judgment to improve upon your first effort. It is no wonder that good writing takes time.

Other factors also involve time. College writing is distinguished by depth of analysis, discussion, or thought. Seeing relationships between ideas in order to write about them does indeed require time. In addition, college-level writing is expected to be relatively free of problems in spelling, grammar, and punctuation. For some, these concerns may not require much effort. However, the vast majority of us do experience some difficulties in one or more of these areas. Once again, time is needed to make corrections and revisions.

To use your time effectively to produce well-analyzed, error-free prose, experiment with the following suggestions:

1. *Start writing early.* This is especially critical if you have several days or longer to complete a paper. If you encounter major problems with a draft, you will have the time to rewrite it.

2. *Break up the process.* The main advantage to dividing the process is to keep yourself from attempting to squeeze all of the writing activities into a short period of time. If, for example, prewriting and drafting are done in a first sitting, then editing and revising may be saved for the next day when your editorial eye can be more objective. You may also have greater energy then for making whatever revisions are necessary to improve your writing.

3. *Be sure that you prewrite.* The easiest of the writing stages to skip is prewriting, but the results are rarely satisfactory. If you jump to a quick solution or hurry in choosing your topic, you may find that you produce a weak, undeveloped paper. Even for in-class essay exams, use the first several minutes to read the assignment carefully and make notes of responses that occur to you.

4. *Use your marked, graded themes as references.* Papers returned to you by your instructor can be useful in a number of ways. For instance, you can make a quick check of grammar markings to help you identify and correct your most frequent errors. Or, you can check the notations in the margins for comments on development of ideas or use of language. Allow yourself time to understand such problems and to find ways to remedy them in order to improve the quality of your next writing project.

5. *Study in a quiet environment, free from distractions.* Concentration is broken and time wasted if you are sidetracked by the phone ringing, the television or stereo playing, or people talking. In other words, you need time and quiet away from the classroom to digest the facts, ideas, and impressions that you have gathered in the classroom.

6. *Schedule additional time for outside sources.* Writing in response to an outside source, such as a book or an article, requires time to locate the work and read it thoroughly before you begin writing. In the case of a book, you will need to maintain a regular reading schedule. In this way, you will have time to absorb themes and ideas that may add to the strength of your final paper.

CLARIFYING THE WRITING PROCESS

THE LARGER PICTURE: THE DYNAMIC PROCESS

Most of us perform more confidently when we have an overall grasp of the task ahead of us. If, for example, you know the basic workings of a car engine, you can probably correct malfunctions or at least speak intelligently about them with a mechanic. This kind of comprehensive understanding adds to your sense of competence and self-confidence.

The same situation applies to writing, perhaps even more so because much of this special activity occurs in the mind. The greater your familiarity with the writing process as a whole (the larger picture), the more likely you are to attack a specific writing project with energy and efficiency. When problems arise, you are better able to recognize them and communicate the difficulty to your instructor.

Although each individual project is unique, the process underlying all of them is quite similar. Examine the following sequence of activities moving to the final copy and note the purpose of each:

Prewriting: to explore an assignment and make an intelligent writing choice.

Drafting: to turn prewriting into sentences and paragraphs.

Editing/Revising: to examine and correct the draft and to rewrite any or all of it.

Final Copy: to submit acceptable work to the instructor.

Breaking up the writing process in this manner allows you to understand it better. As you work through the sequence of activities, however, remember that writing is a *dynamic* process. The first three steps are interrelated; they blend and sometimes occur simultaneously because the human mind is capable of such multidimensional thinking. Whenever possible, allow yourself to experience and enjoy the flow of ideas as you write. However, if you do become confused or unsure about your work, refer to the previous checklist to clarify the larger picture of the writing process and to get you working once again.

COMPLETING THE PICTURE: YOUR AUDIENCE

There is one further element in the larger picture of the writing process: the *audience* or *reader*. In one sense, you are the first reader of any writing you produce.

In a larger sense though, your audience refers to a reader in general. After all, writing does not exist in a vacuum. It is a primary form of communication, so the process is complete only when the audience or reader absorbs the final product.

Suppose you wanted to write a magazine article on women's issues. You would need to know something about the magazine and its readership before you could write your article. A magazine for working women would require one kind of article, whereas a magazine for women athletes would want another. Your choice of topic and the kind and amount of detail you supply would also be determined by the readership.

As a college student and writer, you might think that your *instructor* is your audience. This, however, is only partially true. Although your instructor provides your writing assignment, you do not write directly to him or her in a personal way. If you write directly to your instructor, you may not develop a topic adequately. As you draft, for instance, you might arrive at a complex point and find yourself saying, "My instructor will know what I mean; we talked about it in class." Your instructor, however, does not know whether *you* understand the complex point unless you can explain it clearly and thoroughly in your writing. Therefore, instead of trying to write to your instructor, imagine that you are writing to a general reader. This means that what you write should be clear to anyone with reading skills, whether or not that person already knows about your topic or has taken your class.

USING PREWRITING TO GET STARTED

AN INTRODUCTION TO PREWRITING

Once you understand the assignment requirements and the overall writing process, you are ready to start working. This first phase of writing is often called *prewriting*, and it consists of all work done before a draft is written. The key to successful prewriting is the work you do *before* actually writing sentences and paragraphs. Study this sequence of prewriting activity:

1. Gathering data to explore and respond to an assignment

2. Choosing a tentative writing topic from the data gathered

3. Gathering more data, now related only to the topic chosen

4. Formulating a thesis statement only after you are satisfied that your tentative choice is suitable

When you prewrite, you give yourself time to discover what you wish to write about. In the process of this exploration, you have an opportunity to record ideas that you will use later to "flesh out" your draft. Finally, as you complete prewriting, you will narrow your focus to a writing goal, the thesis, which is the keystone of your paper.

As with any complex activity, a number of prewriting strategies are available to you. On the next few pages, the method that corresponds to the scheme given above will be presented in greater detail. In addition, two variations will be provided as possible alternatives. After experimenting with them, use the one that yields the best results.

A PREWRITING MODEL

As you study this model, keep in mind the basic prewriting goal: *the development of a thesis to guide your writing.*

Sample Assignment: Television exerts some degree of influence upon everyone in our society. Select one aspect of this powerful force and discuss it thoroughly.

Prewriting begins with a mental exploration of the influence of television on our society. The writer gathers *data* by recording related ideas such as the following:

1. *violence in cartoons—effect on very young*

2. *use of TV as a teaching tool*

   documentaries

   actual courses in college

   alphabet, numbers, etc., for children

3. *affects a person's concentration span (e.g., student?)*

4. *influence of commercials on grammar (see "fewer/less" confusion*

on popular commercials)

   Some of these ideas, such as item 2, highlight positive aspects of television's influence; some, such as items 1 and 4, concern negative aspects. All, however, relate to the assignment as *smaller aspects* of it. At this early stage of data gathering, you do not need to write whole sentences or worry about punctuation.

   This type of data gathering encourages you to generate many ideas in response to a topic, more ideas than you will actually need. Gathering data in this way can help you reach a deeper understanding of the assignment. And, if you keep these initial ideas, you will have writing alternatives ready in case your tentative choice does not work out successfully.

   After gathering data, you are in a position to choose *one* aspect of television's influence. In this way you focus your prewriting effort and respond to the demand of the assignment for *one* aspect.

   Topic: *influence of commercials on grammar*

Having made a tentative choice, you now gather more ideas and responses but only those relating to the choice.

1. *Person on commercial says a product has <u>less</u> calories! Poor*

grammar—should be <u>fewer</u> calories.

2. *Most commercials shown at prime time, esp. during sports*

telecasts—MILLIONS watch! hear same error over and over every

10–12 minutes. Sort of <u>brainwashing</u>.

Person who writes (student) often writes the error and is penalized.

Speech also affected.

3. Television—very powerful medium! Can influence/change speech/

communication patterns. Why not use it to help communic.? <u>Fewer</u>

headaches for writers/students and instructors if done with correct

grammar. Do not see this as control or censorship—just common

sense.

If you've generated enough ideas to support your choice of topic, then the process can continue. If, however, your tentative choice seems unsatisfactory, you can return to the original data gathering and experiment with another aspect.

Once you're satisfied with the choice, you can construct a *thesis statement:*

Thesis statement: *Television commercials often have a*

negative influence on a viewer's grammar in both

speech and writing.

With the construction of a thesis, you move to the next set of activities: organizing and writing the first draft of the paper.

While examining the prewriting model, you may have some questions.

What is the advantage to me of gathering more data than I need in the early part of prewriting? By gathering a wide variety of data, you can explore an assignment more fully. When you allow your mind to range freely over a topic, you can call upon direct experience as well as information from your classes, the media, and your own private reading. Another advantage is that this kind of data gathering helps you to get beneath the surface of a writing assignment.

Why did the prewriter avoid writing sentences or paragraphs while gathering information? In this first stage, you are not yet writing, but prewriting. You are still formulating ideas. Writing out full sentences while you are exploring the assignment or your topic slows down the process. Writing complete sentences may also cause you to worry about other areas, such as your spelling or grammar. Concerns such as these may interrupt your focus on the assignment and slow your momentum. The use of abbreviations, partial sentences, and symbols can help you record your ideas almost as quickly as they occur to you.

In a sense, the model was "perfect," but what if I evaluate my prewriting and find a major error or problem? When you locate problems *during* prewriting, they are relatively simple to solve. If some material is inappropriate, eliminate it. If you have not thought of enough ideas for your topic, you can add more. Probably the most distressing discovery is that there is something wrong with your chosen topic. If your topic is too large or does not respond to the demands of the assignment, then a major overhaul may be needed to correct the problem. However, it is much better to find a problem of any kind while prewriting than it is to discover the same problem while you are writing the final copy.

SOME PREWRITING ALTERNATIVES

Variation 1

Not everyone gets ideas in response to an assignment in the same manner. The model just highlighted suggests that you begin prewriting by gathering *many* related ideas or responses, more, in fact, than you would actually need. Variation 1, however, provides you with an alternative that may better suit your thinking style.

Basically, this variation allows you to respond to an assignment in a faster, more direct manner. Instead of recording 10 or 15 varied responses (some of which you automatically reject as unworkable), you can focus immediately on any idea and treat it as a tentative topic. If, for example, your first response happens to be your best or strongest, you would have then begun work on it sooner and completed prewriting faster. The following illustrates this prewriting variation:

> *Sample Assignment:* Focus on one aspect of the aging process in our culture, and discuss it thoroughly.

The first idea that occurs to this student is: older people treated unfairly. Rather than generating additional ideas on the topic of the aging process, the writer sees this thought as a tentative topic and begins to gather data about the unfair treatment of older people.

hard to get a new job when you're older

older women ignored by fashion industry

society forces people to retire too soon

too many of the frail elderly living alone

Now the student evaluates this data to see what kind of material has been generated and whether it could support a thorough response to "older people treated unfairly." Because these four responses are so *broad* and *general*, the writer does not attempt a thesis statement. Instead, the writer returns to the assignment and generates a second response to the topic of aging: assuming role of grandparent. Again, the writer gathers data for this second response:

1. *Can be extremely rewarding:*

   direct relationship to a young person/family member often can be

   more communicative than actual parent.

2. *Gp's are "once removed" and w/age comes patience, realization*

   that grandkid's problems (in school, socially) can be solved over time.

3. *Seeing the new generation in family: sense of history and*

   continuity of line.

4. *A real role of assistance to not only grandchild but to children—*

   gp's can give advice on parenting, etc.

5. *Use example of my own grandparents—how they help me and*

   my parents; their importance to me.

With this collection of more specific data, the writer can feel satisfied that the topic chosen—"assuming role of grandparent"—has real possibilities. The writer can then think ahead to a possible thesis statement:

One of the most rewarding aspects of aging is assuming the role of grandparent.

If, for any reason, this thesis and supporting material do not work out when drafting the paper, the writer can go back through variation 1 to generate and evaluate a third idea and writing choice.

Advantages of Variation 1

1. This technique gets you working on an idea faster because it treats each response as a tentative writing choice.

2. For many of us, this "think-of-it, then-work-with-it" approach is com-

fortable and natural; therefore, you may find it a more successful method of prewriting.

Variation 2

This second prewriting variation is not concerned with the way you think about an assignment. Instead, it focuses on the way you record your responses. Therefore, this variation can be used for the original prewriting model or for variation 1.

The act of thinking about and concentrating on an assignment can be complicated for some people because of the need to record ideas. In some cases, writing may be physically difficult or tiring. Or, the ideas may come so quickly that writing them down, even in abbreviated form, slows the prewriting and even interrupts the thinking process.

If you have ever had such experiences while recording data, then consider this alternative: Use a tape recorder to record all your ideas, thoughts, and responses. Eventually, you will have to write but probably not until you have explored the assignment and chosen a topic.

Advantages of Variation 2:

1. Hearing your own voice stimulates your involvement with the assignment and your ability to think of ideas. Remember, too, that speech precedes writing in our development. First we talk; later in life we learn how to write. You can use this first, primary ability to help develop your writing.

2. Using a tape recorder eases the burden of the hand playing secretary to the mind. If you get bogged down or lose your concentration, then rewind and replay the tape.

FOR YOUR MENTAL FILE

Regardless of the technique you use, you will notice an interesting feature of prewriting: its *elastic* nature. When, for example, you write a relatively personal paper, prewriting may move quite rapidly because you have first-hand knowledge of the situation. But if a project is objective and requires familiarity with outside material, prewriting may take more time and energy. Your enjoyment of a particular class and its subject matter may also make prewriting move faster.

The next sections discuss in detail each activity within prewriting—gathering data, choosing a topic, developing analytic techniques, and formulating a thesis statement. The unit ends with drafting strategies and guidelines for those of you who are using a computer in the writing process.

EFFECTIVE DATA GATHERING

Data gathering allows you to explore an assignment in depth before making any writing commitment. Whatever you do to develop this skill is beneficial because it puts you in a stronger position when you are ready to choose your topic. The questions below can help you generate ideas. No matter where your ideas and information come from, keep track of your sources so that you can identify them in your final paper.

1. *Do I have any direct experience with the subject of the assignment?* Direct or first-hand experience can provide you with powerful writing material. For instance, if you were asked to discuss one reason why people have trouble communicating, you could use a direct experience in your response. Whenever you gather data about such experiences, make notes of what the situation was and when, where, and why it occurred.

2. *Can I gather information from other people?* Perhaps your family, an instructor, or someone else you know has had experiences or has information that would help focus your prewriting. If so, interview this person, and take notes on this material.

3. *Can I use information from the media (television, radio, magazines, or newspapers)?* Staying informed about the day's events can be very helpful to your writing. For example, a particular news program or documentary related to the assignment may provide you with useful data. Record the relevant facts or issues that you remember.

4. *Can any of my classes or textbooks be of use?* Your courses were designed to provide you with both facts and ideas, so pause a bit to think back to your other classes. Perhaps facts, ideas, or issues raised in another class might figure into your paper.

Exercise 1.1   EFFECTIVE DATA GATHERING

Assignment: There are many reasons why parents and children have difficulty communicating. Focus on one reason, and discuss it thoroughly.

Gather data in response to the above assignment. Use the various suggestions presented earlier to help you record as many ideas as possible. Try to generate 10–14 responses. Be sure, however, that they all relate to difficulty in communication. Note that the wording of the assignment indicates parents and children *in general*, not just your own communication problems with parents or children.

Special Note: Most of the exercises in this book can be done on a word processor. See the section ''If You Are Using a Word Processor'' at the end of each unit for helpful comments on using a word processor. In this unit see pp. 33–36.

Exercise 1.2   EFFECTIVE DATA GATHERING

Assignment: Focus on one specific aspect of being a celebrity. You may consider any field—sports, entertainment, politics, religion, and so on.

Record 15–20 responses that relate to celebrity status. To produce a variety of ideas, you might wish to reflect on both positive and negative aspects in addition to any other responses that occur to you.

CHOOSING YOUR TOPIC

After beginning prewriting and gathering data, your prewriting efforts begin to narrow to a specific purpose. As a general rule, the shorter the writing assignment, the more restricted your choice of writing topic will need to be. In the sample below, the writer was asked to write a short paper on one aspect of the general topic of pets. After gathering data on pets, the writer made this choice: pet dogs.

Unfortunately, this choice needs more work. Even though the topic of pet dogs *seems* more focused than pets in general, it is still too broad for a short paper. Rather than give up the topic altogether, there is a way for the writer to salvage it.

By gathering data again on the writing choice, it is possible to narrow the writing focus even further. For instance, the topic *pet dogs* could be broken down into:

importance of training

expense of feeding

not good for a busy person

great companion for children

source of home protection/security

Now, a new, more focused aspect of the topic can be chosen. By narrowing and limiting the choice, the writer increased the likelihood of developing an in-depth discussion rather than a superficial one.

Choosing a topic that is specific will always be a major concern for you as a writer. Study the following comparison of writing topics in the following table. Those at the top are simply too broad—too general—to be workable. But as you move down to the bottom of each row, the topics get progressively more specific and more acceptable as writing choices.

General	Nutrition	Television	World War II
Less General	Minerals	Comedies	U.S. civilian effort
Smaller	Calcium	Use of stereo-types in comedies	Role of women in wartime economy
Smallest	Need for calcium in menopausal women	The dumb athlete in comedies	Rosie the Riveter—grandmother of Women's Liberation?

As you read through the table, you can see that general ideas such as nutrition are large and include many smaller aspects. By concentrating on a broad area, you can work your way down to a more specific aspect within it, one that will be more suitable as a topic.

You might wonder when you should stop reducing a general concept to smaller and smaller aspects. The length of a finished paper will determine how far you need to reduce the concept. For example, if you were writing a fairly long paper on an aspect of the general topic of stereotypes, you might consider "negative images of athletes in television comedies." In a long paper you could discuss several negative images and several programs, thus fully developing the topic. But if you were writing only one paragraph of slightly less than a single page, you would need to refine and specify the topic even further. A possible tactic would be to confine yourself to *one* specific character in *one* particular television program.

Your best teachers in this area of choosing a topic will be your own experiences and your English instructor. However, these guidelines can help you:

1. When choosing a topic, make the choice *your own*. If you write what you think the instructor wants to hear or what a friend has casually suggested, you may have trouble working with the choice and end up wasting valuable time.

2. Avoid choosing topics or using wording that speaks to too large an audience. If you tried to write a paper about "crime in America," yours would truly be an impossible mission! You would require several lifetimes to write about the general topic of crime, not to mention crime all over the nation.

Exercise 1.3   MAKING A WRITING CHOICE

Read the assignment below; then evaluate the seven writing choices made in response to it. Evaluate these tentative topics using the criteria for choosing a suitable topic; on a separate sheet of paper, rate each of the choices as either a, b, or c. Be prepared to discuss your ratings.

a. = The choice is too general to be considered.

b. = The choice has possibilities but needs to be specified.

c. = The topic choice is workable as written.

Assignment: Write a short paper about some issue or aspect related to the automobile.

1. has killed many Americans

2. spoiled me for walking short distances

3. an expensive necessity in many ways

4. major cause of pollution in our nation and world

5. standard transmission in a car has advantages over automatic

6. influences our lives in many ways

7. car chase—a major part of television programs

GATHERING DATA FOR YOUR TOPIC

Regardless of which prewriting method you use to choose a topic, the next activity involves focusing that choice and gathering only information that relates to it. This work is tremendously important, for it can form the basis of a better first draft later in the writing process.

Keep the following suggestions in mind as you gather data:

Describe the choice, including the particulars: *when, where, why,* and *how* it is or occurred (if these are relevant).

Draw from first-hand experience for an example or use information from books, classes, or the media to provide details.

Speculate, if possible, on any negative or positive aspects of your choice or on possible consequences.

Philosophize a bit. This means backing up from your own immediate concerns to see if there is any larger value, meaning, or danger to others or to society in general.

An example of this type of data gathering follows.

Sample Assignment: Write about one way that you use music in your life.

Topic: *use music to help me exercise*

The writer begins gathering data by describing the choice and giving particulars, drawn from personal experience:

1. *Put on a long-play cassette so I won't have to stop to change music.*

2. *Generally pick rock or fast jazz to keep me moving.*

3. *Exercise daily for ½ hour instead of running, etc. On weekdays, it's after school (4PM) but on weekends, it's at 7AM to start off fresh.*

4. *W/music, the time goes quickly; don't feel like quitting.*

5. *Began this a year ago—lost 10 lbs—improved health and conditioning. Get compliments (ego boost) and feel much better/ energetic.*

The writer can also speculate on the effects of the choice and add a philosophical dimension:

6. *Without music, would probably not exercise on regular basis/would then gain weight—get out of condition. The music seems to be the reason I can stay with regimen.*

7. *Perhaps the key for many human problems is to find vehicle/way to make good things occur. Health/conditioning = a goal; Music w/ exercise allows me to reach the goal/because I like music. Importance of pleasure in what we do may influence outcome/success.*

Describing your choice and providing particulars are effective ways to gather data. In trying to speculate or provide some philosophical outlook, you add an enriching dimension to your work.

Exercise 1.4   GATHERING DATA FOR YOUR TOPIC

> *Sample Assignment:* We hear many reports on the various forms of pollution in our society. Focus on one aspect of pollution, and present a thorough discussion. Assume this writing choice was made:

> Topic: *noise pollution, especially in larger cities*

Use the earlier suggestions to gather data related to the topic. Include in your responses any direct experience with noise pollution. Consider whatever information you have gathered from reading, television, and any classes. Also, try to speculate on the effects of this situation. Record your responses on a separate sheet of paper.

DEVELOPING ANALYTIC TECHNIQUES

If you are satisfied that you have sufficient data for your tentative choice, you are ready to formulate a thesis statement. First, however, pause for an analysis and evaluation of your prewriting work. If left unchecked, any errors, inaccuracies, or omissions could affect not only your thesis statement but the content of your entire paper.

Use the following guidelines and related questions to focus your attention:

1. Carefully examine your topic and ask yourself:

   Is the topic related to the assignment? If not, revise your choice.

   Is the choice specific enough for the length of the assignment? If not, narrow your choice further.

2. Next, look at your remarks and notes relating to the topic:

   Do all of the notes and ideas relate to the topic?

   Are there specific details and explanations?

   Do the notes show an attempt to study the topic in more than one way? For example, besides describing it, you might also note its effects, your opinion about it, and so on.

   Are there opinions or personal impressions about the topic?

A Model for Developing Analytic Techniques

The following model illustrates the use of analysis and evaluation to locate errors, inaccuracies, and omissions *before* the thesis is constructed. Examine the following sample assignment, the chosen topic, and the data gathered on that writing choice:

Sample Assignment: Write about an aspect of the first week of college.

Topic: *being on a waiting list for a class*

Data gathered on the topic:

Didn't know until end of week if I got into class.

Waiting made me tense, frustrated.

W/out the class, I can't transfer on schedule.

Did run into an old buddy from high school.

Student on w. list needs to be persistent.

The following analysis and evaluation questions are used to check the work:

1. Do all of the notes and ideas relate to the topic?

   One response is not related to the writing choice: "did run into an old buddy from high school." This notation would be eliminated.

2. Are there specific details and explanations?

   Few details are present in the gathered data. Although "the class" is mentioned, there is no indication of which class it is. Noting the writer's actual position on the waiting list would add interest as well as indicate how long the student had to wait. Finally, further explanation would clarify what is meant by the need for "persistence" and what form the writer's persistence took. All of these details and explanations would help to enrich the paper.

3. Do the notes show an attempt to study the writing topic in more than one way?

   The writer has attempted to regard the topic in more than one light. For example, emotional reactions (tense, frustrated) are mentioned as is an indication of the effects or consequences of remaining on the waiting list and not being allowed to register. More descriptive details are needed, however: *which class, what position* on the list, and so on.

4. Are there opinions or personal impressions about the topic?

   An opinion emerges when the writer notes the need for persistence. The writer also could add other opinions or impressions about the overall wisdom of having a waiting list at all or whether the school could use a slightly or greatly different kind of waiting list policy.

This sort of analysis will prove very valuable to you. The time you use to check your work and correct or expand your prewriting will usually make its benefit felt in all other activities to come, especially in the creation of the thesis and drafting of the actual paper.

Exercise 1.5   DEVELOPING ANALYTIC TECHNIQUES

Examine the following sample prewriting. Analysis and evaluation questions follow. Write your answers on a separate sheet of paper.

Sample Assignment: Develop a short paper based on one aspect of the Christmas season.

Prewriting Responses:

1) *shopping*

2) *traffic congestion*

3) *family gatherings*

4) *lonely time for some*

5) *philosophical time of year*

6) *excitement everywhere*

7) *special TV programming*

8) *foods! weight gain!*

Chosen Topic: **excitement everywhere**

Data gathering on the choice:

Stores—malls have lights, special decorations often very elaborate, spectacular.

Streets—garlands across the entire road, window dressings, Santas on corners; traffic is easier to bear.

School—everyone; students and teachers get excited. Vacation and holiday on everyone's mind.

Home—getting house ready; tree and lights; little brother adds to my enjoyment—believes in Santa, planning Christmas dinner and what presents to get.

Job—boss is in a good mood! Party being planned. Bonus?? Lots of excitement!

Questions

1. Is the topic choice, "excitement everywhere," related to the assignment?

2. Is the choice specific enough for the overall length of the assignment? If no, write why.

3. Do all of the notes and ideas for "excitement everywhere" relate to the topic?

4. Are there specific details and explanations? If no, suggest additions.

5. Do the notes show an attempt to study the topic choice in more than one way? Explain your answer.

6. Are there opinions or personal impressions? Explain your answer and be specific.

GENERATING A STRONG THESIS STATEMENT

When you are ready to formulate your thesis statement, you are at a critical moment. In one sense, all of your prewriting leads to this one point. Teachers in all subject areas will look for the thesis in a writer's paper because it represents the overall intent or design of the paper. This statement may also be called the *main idea*, the *controlling idea*, or, in a paragraph, the *topic sentence*. Regardless of its name, this particular sentence gives meaning to all of the others in the paper. Because of the importance given to the thesis statement, you will need to develop your *thesis sense*. Begin by examining these three general characteristics of thesis statements in essays (or of topic sentences in paragraphs):

1. A thesis is a complete sentence.

Basically, a thesis must be a complete grammatical unit, not a fragment of a sentence. (If you are uncertain about what makes a complete sentence, review the section about the complete sentence and the fragment in Unit V.) Some students also confuse the title of their paper with their thesis statement.

Title: One More Time

Thesis: Summer reruns on television give me an opportunity to catch up on programs missed during the school year.

The title of your paper would appear on the very top line and would be centered, whereas the thesis would appear as part of the introductory paragraph.

2. A thesis contains a topic.

This topic or writing choice is specific enough to be developed in detail. The degree to which you specify your topic will depend on the length of the assignment.

As a general rule, the shorter the assignment, the more specific your thesis topic and its focus. For example, if you chose "Congress" as a topic for a relatively short paper, you would be unable to present a thorough discussion, for the topic is too large. Instead, you would need to restrict your topic to a smaller aspect of Congress, such as the role of the seniority system in one of the two branches or the function of a particular committee.

3. A thesis provides some direction, angle, or point of view.

It is impossible for any one human being to write everything about a single topic; therefore, a writer has to angle a topic in a particular direction. The term *point of view* is often used to describe this characteristic of a thesis because an angle can also represent the writer's opinion or perspective.

Watch what happens when point of view or perspective is added to the topic of "the seniority system in Congress":

The seniority system in Congress *tends to place undue power in the hands of Old Timers.*

or

The seniority system in Congress *provides for and encourages experienced leadership on key committees.*

Each thesis is usable. The first suggests a negative appraisal; the second points to a positive effect of the system. Each would result in a different paper because of the differing angles chosen by the writer.

Of the three characteristics outlined above, the most complex is the third: the need to angle a topic and give it some direction. One of the best ways to heighten your awareness of this important aspect is to study sentences that *lack* direction or perspective.

Last semester, I took Botany 101 with Professor Vernon.

Although this sentence is specific, it provides no direction or angle. The reader is told only the name of the course, when it was taken, and who the instructor was. Even if a sentence is factual and grammatically complete, it is *not thesis material if there is no suggestion of what the writer intends to say.*

The flat, factual statement above can be turned into a thesis statement by the inclusion of a point of view or direction. Compare the basic statement to the three potential thesis statements that follow it:

Last semester I took Botany 101 with Professor Vernon.

Angle 1: Last semester I took Botany 101 with Professor Vernon and *really learned the value of taking good lecture notes.*

By adding this angle, the writer has a direction. Now the paper can center on a discussion of how the lecture notes figured in the class and whether or not the writer improved in the general ability to take good class notes.

Angle 2: Professor Vernon's Botany 101 class last semester was the *most challenging and difficult course I have had in college.*

The angle chosen by this writer would require an explanation of how and why the course was challenging and difficult—perhaps it was the reading material, lab work, or memorization of scientific terms. The writer might also contrast this class with one or two others that were easier.

Angle 3: Professor Vernon's lectures in Botany 101 last semester were *unbelievably tedious and dull.*

With this angle or direction, the writer would explain why the lectures were so unbearable. Did the professor speak in a monotone? Did the professor lack good speaking skills (eye contact, emphasis, visual aids)? Part of the paper could also be devoted to the effect of the lectures on the writer and on the other students in the class.

FOR YOUR MENTAL FILE

The key to the creation of an effective thesis is actually quite simple: *Know what you wish to say* about a specific assignment. If you have given sufficient time to prewriting, you will have a better grasp of what you want to say, and you will be more likely to produce a thesis that is clear, organized, and fully developed.

The Vague Thesis

In constructing your thesis statement, you may find that your thesis has a topic and a point of view but is weak and vague. As a result, its meaning (and your writing goal) is unclear. A vague thesis can come about in many ways, especially if the demands of the assignment are not understood, the choice of writing topic is too large, or the point of view is unclear. Consider the following situation: A student has been given the assignment below and finished prewriting by generating a thesis.

Sample Assignment: Write a well-developed essay which comments on or further analyzes any one of the ideas or opinions presented in our guest lecturer's discussion of the need for censorship in the movie industry.

Thesis: *I found Mr. Amato's lecture on movie censorship*

very interesting.

In theory, this writer has the basics of a thesis. This sentence states a topic: "Mr. Amato's lecture on censorship in the movie industry," and a point of view, "very interesting." However, the statement is vague because even after reading it, you do not know what direction the paper intends to follow. More specifically, the topic does not respond to the assignment, which asked for a discussion of *one* of the points made in the lecture. By not responding to the demands of the assignment, the scope of the paper is too large.

The second specific difficulty lies with the point of view—"very interesting." Although many people would use *interesting* in a positive sense, indicating something worthy of attention or notice, it is possible that some might use the word negatively. As a point of view, therefore, the word is not precise and only adds to the overall vagueness of the thesis.

What should this student do? The best tactic would be to reread the notes taken during Mr. Amato's lecture and any existing prewriting material. Then the demand of the assignment to focus on one specific area could be met. Here are two possible theses, each with a specific focus and writing goal.

> Mr. Amato's basic idea that one national review board could effectively censor the entire movie industry is utterly ludicrous.

> With the rise of violence in today's society, Mr. Amato's proposal to remove certain forms of violence from films is admirable.

Either one of these thesis statements has a clear picture of the writing goal. Each focuses on one aspect of the lecture on censorship, and each presents a point of view that leaves no doubt about the writer's position.

Avoiding the Tendency to Herald in a Thesis

In addition to vagueness, a thesis sentence can also suffer from the effects of heralding or announcing what you intend to say in your paper. This tendency may actually lead you away from making a specific declaration of your topic or point of view. To get a feel for what heralding actually means, suppose a student is asked to write about her opinion on an issue such as solar power. She produces the following topic sentence:

> In this paper I am going to provide my opinion of the need to develop solar power as an energy source.

The "I am going to" wording of this sentence is an example of heralding in a thesis. A sentence like this would not be considered a college-level writing response. The writer has not expressed an opinion; she has merely said she plans to. A personal stand should be reflected in the thesis.

A revision might produce this sentence:

> In this paper, I am going to provide my opinion of why the United States must develop solar power as an energy source.

This rewrite now responds to the assignment, but it is still heralding.

This final version removes the heralding altogether:

> In my opinion, the United States must continue to develop solar power as an energy source.

Saying what you want to say instead of announcing what you intend to say is the key to avoiding this type of thesis problem.

Exercise 1.6   GENERATING A STRONG THESIS STATEMENT

Learning to locate both topic and point of view can help you to develop your thesis sense. All of the sentences below contain both these features. Study the example. Read each sentence and write down its topic and point of view on a separate sheet of paper.

Example: The view from my balcony is breathtaking!

Topic: *view from my balcony*

Point of View: *breathtaking*

1. The English language can be confusing to those whose first language is not English.

2. My wife was overjoyed at the news of the football strike.

3. Self-discipline is vital to a college student's success.

4. Making up the guest list for a wedding can provoke heated debate among all concerned.

5. My political science teacher is a gifted and articulate speaker.

Exercise 1.7   GENERATING A STRONG THESIS STATEMENT

Examine each of the items below to determine whether each has the necessary characteristics of a thesis: complete sentence, specific topic, and a direction or point of view.

Using the criteria above, on a separate sheet of paper rate each sentence as either acceptable or faulty. Give a faulty rating if any of the three elements is missing; then briefly explain the problem.

Example: Crime in America is getting out of hand.
Faulty

Reason: The topic (''crime in America'') and point of view (''getting out of hand'') are too general.

1. Tenacity is an essential quality for any student.

2. Viewing a production of *Hamlet.*

3. Good conversational techniques can be of great help to a person working in sales.

4. Sports are important to good health in anyone's life.

5. My first job interview was an utter disaster!

 Exercise 1.8   GENERATING A STRONG THESIS STATEMENT

Human beings quite naturally make generalizations about the people, objects, and events around them. Sometimes a generalization may be accurate: ''A good study plan is useful for any class.'' At other times a statement may be too sweeping to be accurate: ''There's no life after 40!''

If your topic sentences generalize too much, you may have problems in constructing your paper or in developing it adequately. Rewrite each generalized thesis statement below into two statements that are specific and directed. Use a separate sheet of paper.

Example: Inflation affects everyone in America. (Too general)

   a. The average person often feels inflation first in the local supermarket. (More specific)

   b. I learned the meaning of inflation when I bought my textbooks for this semester. (More specific)

1. Weather affects everyone's life in some way.

2. Without the necessary skills, students experience difficulty succeeding in their classes.

3. In my opinion, television insults people's intelligence.

4. The automobile has ruined our nation's cities.

5. Politics are very complicated.

 Exercise 1.9   GENERATING A STRONG THESIS STATEMENT

Your first objective in this exercise is to determine the writer's point of view or direction based on the prewriting evidence. After determining the point of view, write a topic sentence that expresses what this writer wants to say. Use your own paper.

Assignment: Discuss one memorable aspect of the first week of classes this term.

The writer gathers data.

1) *parking* _____   4) *cafeteria food* _____

2) *meeting old friends* _____   5) *long registration lines* _____

3) *cost of textbooks* _____   6) *crowded classrooms* _____

Topic: *parking* _____

Additional data is gathered on the topic choice.

Came to school half hour early to get a parking place before 8 AM

class.

Terrible traffic jam for blocks around campus.

All the good spots were taken: had to drive around the neighborhood

farther and farther away from campus.

Ended up seven blocks away—left my car at 7:50—had to run to

class.

Dashed into the room 20 minutes late—sweaty, panting—missed the

taking of roll and had to stay after class to be sure I wouldn't be

counted absent.

Affected my whole day.

1. Based on your reading of this prewriting, state the writer's point of view on parking.

2. Generate a thesis sentence. Be sure to write out a complete sentence with a capital letter at its start and a period at the end.

Exercise 1.10   GENERATING A STRONG THESIS STATEMENT

Each of the following sentences is a potential thesis statement but is marred by vagueness or heralding. Using your imagination or direct knowledge, rewrite these sentences as thesis statements. Each sentence should be a college-level, specific statement. (You may have to add material to some, take out material in others, or do both.) Check your revised sentences to be sure that they have the necessary characteristics of thesis statements. Use your own paper.

1. In my paper, I am going to discuss one reason why gifted children have problems in school.

2. I thought that the lecture on space-age careers was very interesting.

3. My recent trip to the logging area of Washington was quite eventful.

4. The topic of this paper is the need to train security officers effectively and thoroughly.

5. Daylight savings time affects all of us in some way.

6. I will attempt to explain my thoughts on the lottery.

PREPARING FOR THE ROUGH DRAFT

SUGGESTIONS FOR DRAFTING

When your prewriting efforts yield a thesis statement, you have already begun the work toward drafting a *first* edition of your final paper. This drafting effort is quite special. When drafting, you turn prewriting responses into full sentences and at the same time organize various ideas into paragraphs or parts of a paragraph.

No simple formula exists for writing the rough draft. The process is as varied and complicated as the writers themselves and their purposes for writing. However, the following guidelines can help you in your drafting work:

1. *Focus on and review your prewriting data.* Before you begin to draft sentences, review all related notes and ideas. In a sense, this kind of refocusing helps you to get your bearings and to begin a smooth transition to actual writing or drafting.

2. *Organize your data so that related ideas are grouped together.* Prewriting notes do not necessarily appear in any particular order and, in fact, may be jumbled. When you made your prewriting choice and gathered related data, you probably made many different notations, all mixed together on the same page. It is normal for this mixing to occur; expecting to reorganize notes when you draft will allow you to produce a well-organized paper.

3. *Give yourself reasonable drafting goals.* If, for example, you are working on the first draft of an essay, set a writing goal that is constructive: "My first goal is to write an introductory paragraph." If you do the opposite— "Now I have to write an entire essay"—you may overwhelm yourself. Take one step at a time.

4. *Don't worry about proper grammar, spelling, and punctuation during the drafting stage.* This situation is comparable to overloading a circuit and blowing out the entire system. Remember that you will have time to polish your grammar and correct the mechanics after you have completed your draft and begin editing. The important goal to accomplish now is to get your ideas on paper in draft form.

A MODEL FOR GROUPING IDEAS

Study the following model as it may prove useful to you when you begin to draft your own papers.

A student has been asked to write a short paper about one difficult aspect of the first month on a new job. After exploring the assignment, the writer makes a choice, gathers data related to it, and constructs a thesis statement. Here is the work thus far:

Chosen Topic: *Lack of self-confidence*

Data gathering on the choice:

1. *Happened to me on my first job! Took more than month to get everything straight/ lots of personnel.*

2. *Stems from "not knowing the ropes"—who has power? who gives good advice? how much freedom do I have?*

3. *Seems to be unavoidable—no matter what the job or who has it takes time to get used to the situation. Pres. of the USA probably had this problem at first.*

4. *My first job also put me in situation with lots of rules and regs. to absorb in short time.*

5. *Would seem natural that everyone has problem with self-confidence at the beginning.*

6. *Had to keep reminding myself that things would improve—can be hard to do if someone is nervous or very conscientious.*

7. *Does get better in time/as experience increases.*

Thesis Statement: *A natural but difficult aspect of any new job is the lack of self-confidence that comes when*

someone is unfamiliar with the routine.

To begin planning a rough draft, this writer would first focus on the data gathered about the writing choice. After reading through the various responses related to ''lack of self-confidence,'' the writer would then decide which ideas belong together. Because prewriting is usually jumbled and mixed up, the writer needs to put related ideas together.

The prewriting below illustrates the process a writer goes through in deciding which responses are related to the topic and how best to begin drafting.

Chosen Topic: *Lack of self confidence*

Data gathering on the choice

Happened to me on my first job! Took more than month to get everything straight/lot of personnel

Stems from "not knowing the ropes"—who has power? who gives good advice? how much freedom do I have?

Seems to be unavoidable—no matter what the job or who has it takes time to get used to the situation. Pres. of the USA probably had this problem at first.

My first job also put me in situation with lots of rules and regs. to absorb in short time.

Would seem natural that everyone has problem with self-confidence at the beginning.

Had to keep reminding myself that things would improve—can be hard to do if someone is nervous or very conscientious.

all relate to how/why problem occurs

all relate to actual job

Does get better in time/as experience increases.→ For conclusion?

Three prewriting notes concern the writer's personal experience. Notice, though, that these ideas do not appear together but are mixed in with other remarks. Three other notes relate to a description or explanation of how or why the problem arises. The writer also has identified the final response as a potential conclusion.

Marking such groupings on your prewriting or jotting such notes on a separate sheet of paper will allow you to begin drafting with a better grasp of what you want to say or, at least, what responses should be discussed together. As you look over your notes and ideas to see which points are related, add comments, draw connecting lines or arrows, number points in order, recopy notes to make a list for each related group, or use your own organizing system. Feel free to add new ideas if you recognize a gap or to drop points that seem isolated or less important for your point of view. Identify introductory or concluding points as well as related ideas. Once your prewriting is organized, you are ready to begin the physical process of writing out sentences to suit the overall length and type of assignment. The next two units explain and illustrate how to draft a paragraph and an essay.

FOR YOUR MENTAL FILE

As you actually write your draft, you might experiment with skipping lines or triple-spacing if you type. In this way, you'll have room to make any additions, comments, or corrections when you are editing. Alternating lines will use more paper, but it can be a time saver later in the process.

🕏 *If You Are Using a Word Processor*

Getting Started

One of the farthest reaching technological developments of our century may be the computer with its incredible capacity to process information at high speed. When a computer is used for word processing, it can indeed serve as a tool to facilitate the writing process. Although the computer cannot think for you, it can store your ideas, place them on a screen for visual evaluation, rearrange them to suit your desires, and print out as many revisions as you need—all with the touch of a few buttons! If you have access to a machine, then these and other word-processing sections appearing at the end of each unit will provide guidelines for its use as you work through the text.

If you are a beginner at word processing or are thinking of learning this skill, visit your school's writing laboratory or learning resource center to learn if classes are given. Many campuses provide word processors for student use and schedule classes throughout the day. Learning to use the machine is a process in which mastery may seem to come in small steps; don't be discouraged if at the beginning you are not learning as quickly as you think you should. You will find that the more you learn, the more you *can* learn.

Before you begin work on any writing project, be sure to familiarize yourself with the machine and the word-processing system it uses. Different brands of computers use different word-processing systems, and every individual user has a favorite.

Familiarize yourself, too, with the language of word processing. For instance, to a nonuser, a file is something in which you store papers. But in computer talk, a file is the text on which you are working, and it always has a name so that you can find it when you want to work on it again or print it. As is the case with any language, the more of it you understand, the more comfortable you are with its use.

Use the following suggestions as you get started in the writing process:

1. Do the best you can to give *clearly understandable* names to your files. Sometimes file titles are so abbreviated and cryptic that you waste time looking at the contents of each file before finding the one you want.

2. *Avoid* making *long files.* Although disk errors and power failures are rare, either one can erase your work. It is less painful to lose one or two pages than to lose a ten-page file.

3. Use your *save* command often. Sometimes the machine gets turned off, either by human hand or power failure, before your work is saved. If you save your work after each page or so, there is less chance of your losing a great deal of work.

4. Use the *best quality diskettes* you can. A diskette with an imperfect area (called a bad sector) can destroy a file.

5. *Take your diskettes with you* when you finish your work. Leaving your work in the computer center opens up the possibility of loss or accidental erasure of your material. If you are working at home, get in the habit of keeping your working diskettes for this class separate from others so you can easily find your material.

6. Finally, *consider the quality of your printer.* Most learning centers provide dot-matrix printers for student use. Although some instructors welcome papers produced on a word processor and are not too concerned with print quality, others will not accept papers produced by a dot-matrix printer. Talk with your teacher about this before submitting your first paper. You might also talk to the person who is in charge of supplies and encourage him or her to keep fresh ribbons in the printer to ensure the highest possible visual quality.

In Unit 1, you will be able to use the word processor to practice prewriting and to do the unit exercises. In addition to prewriting and doing the exercises, consider keeping a general file on the unit, where you make notes about what you've learned in class, questions you may have, and so on. The following comments suggest how to adapt the exercises in this unit to the word processor.

Exercise 1.1–1.2   EFFECTIVE DATA GATHERING (SEE PP. 14–15)

The word processor is ideal for the process of gathering data. You can record your ideas almost as quickly as they come into your mind. Concentrate on typing your ideas in rough form without stopping and interrupting your thinking. At this point, disregard any typing errors as long as you can understand what you've written.

After reading the assignment, begin gathering data. You can fill the page with responses and then delete any that are unrelated to the topic. Be sure you generate the number of responses requested in each exercise.

If you are comfortable reading and making changes directly on the screen, you can do all your work at one time. Otherwise, print out your work, read through it for any changes you want to make, and then go back into the file to edit and print again.

Exercise 1.3   MAKING A WRITING CHOICE (SEE P. 16)

You will record the answers for this exercise on a separate sheet of paper in class. If the exercise is assigned as homework, however, you can use the word processor to help you evaluate the seven writing choices. You can type out the choices and then, using your understanding of the criteria for choosing a topic, comment on how well each meets the criteria. This will help you decide on a rating. Or you can just type the number of each choice, comment, and then decide on the rating. By typing out your responses, based on the criteria, you will get a better picture of how suitable each choice is.

Exercise 1.4   GATHERING DATA FOR YOUR TOPIC (SEE P.19)

For this exercise, type the names of various categories such as direct experience, reading, television, and classes. Then gather data on each. When you have generated as much data as you can, go over your responses and delete those that do not seem to relate to the topic. Make a final selection, and then print your work.

Exercise 1.5   DEVELOPING ANALYTIC TECHNIQUES (SEE P. 21)

If these questions are done in class, you will use regular lined paper. If, however, they are assigned as homework, the word processor can help you prepare clean, error-free answers.

Exercises 1.6–1.7 GENERATING A STRONG THESIS STATEMENT (SEE P. 26)

If these exercises are done in class, use regular lined paper. If, however, they are assigned as homework, the word processor can help you prepare a clean, error-free text.

Exercise 1.8   GENERATING A STRONG THESIS STATEMENT (SEE P. 27)

In this exercise, you will rewrite one very general thesis statement into two more specific and directed statements. Type in the original thesis statement, and then begin generating smaller ones. You can generate as many as you want and then go back and choose the best two for each of the sentences. When you have completed the work, go over the sentences to be certain that each has a topic and a point of view, is specific and a complete sentence. Change single words, parts of the sentence, or even the entire sentence if you need to. If your sentence does not seem specific enough, focus on replacing a general topic with one that is more specific. You can do this as many times as necessary until you are satisfied with the final sentence.

Exercise 1.9   GENERATING A STRONG THESIS STATEMENT (SEE P. 27)

For this exercise, keep the prewriting text in front of you as you work. If it is easier for you, type in the data you gathered on the topic so you can have it right in front of you as you work. Make as many choices of the point of view as you need. Then isolate each one on the screen, and see if it seems to reflect the point of view of the data. When you've made your choice, delete all the others so they won't distract you. Generate a number of thesis statements before deciding on your final version. Be sure that your final version states a topic, has a point of view, is as specific as you can make it, and is a complete sentence with a capital at the beginning and a period at the end. Before you write your sentence in the text, do one last analysis of it by typing out on a separate line or otherwise highlighting the words that state the topic and those that indicate the point of view.

Exercise 1.10   GENERATING A STRONG THESIS SENTENCE (SEE P. 28)

As you work on this exercise, use the techniques of underlining or isolating words to be certain you have included all the elements of a thesis sentence in your work and that you have eliminated vagueness.

UNIT II

Writing the Paragraph

- **ANALYZING THE PARAGRAPH**
- **EVALUATING THE PARAGRAPH**
- **WRITING A PARAGRAPH**
- **PARAGRAPH SUMMARY**

OVERVIEW

Analyzing the Paragraph *examines paragraph structure, paragraph content, and topic sentence placement.*

Evaluating the Paragraph *outlines four criteria for judging paragraphs.*

Writing a Paragraph *follows the development of one student's paragraph from prewriting to final copy.*

Paragraph Summary *reviews the main features and types of paragraphs presented in this unit.*

Introduction

The single paragraph is one of the most widely used written forms in the academic and business worlds. In college, the paragraph is the desired form for many types of examinations when an instructor wishes a detailed yet direct response to a specific question. In the business world, memos in paragraph form often serve as the primary means of communication between employees at all levels of an organization. If you remember the maxim that "Time is money," you can see how a short and accurate piece of writing becomes a necessity.

To begin work with this useful form, a definition is in order.

> A *paragraph* is a group of sentences working together toward a common purpose. Regardless of its length or type, a single paragraph is held together by a three-part form consisting of sentences that introduce, develop, and conclude discussion of a topic sentence.

As you study this definition, keep in mind the dual function of the paragraph. This unit focuses on the single paragraph. Here the term *paragraph* refers to one unit of writing with a topic sentence and the other characteristics given above. The topic sentence, like the thesis introduced in Unit I, is a complete sentence that specifies the topic and the point of view that control the paragraph.

But when you are introduced to essays in Unit III, you will see that the paragraph also refers to a more specialized unit that works with other paragraphs to form an essay. In that case each separate paragraph with its topic sentence follows from the thesis statement that guides the development of the entire essay. The next sections analyze paragraphs—discussing their structure, content, and topic sentence placement.

ANALYZING THE PARAGRAPH

PARAGRAPH STRUCTURE

There are many types of paragraphs just as there are many types of communication, but a well-constructed paragraph usually has a three-part structure. To the eye, the paragraph takes on a characteristic block shape with its upper left corner set in (indented) from the left side (margin). Examine the following diagram which includes the three basic parts:

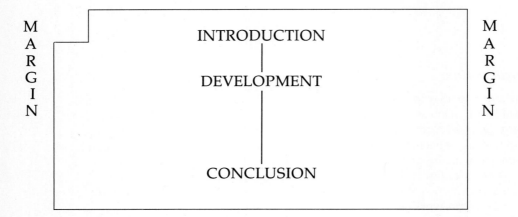

The largest portion of any single paragraph tends to be the middle, for it is here that support or explanation of the topic sentence occurs. The typewritten paragraph below discusses the various parts of the paragraph in greater detail.

INTRODUCTION (consists of one sentence: topic sentence)

Three key parts mark the well-written paragraph. The introduction usually consists of the topic sentence, which is often the first line. Like the thesis statement in an essay, the topic sentence in a paragraph serves as a guideline for both writer and

DEVELOPMENT
(consists of <u>10</u>
sentences)

reader. The next and largest part of the paragraph is the <u>development</u>. In this area, the writer must explain and support the topic sentence in a specific manner. Without development, the reader would be unable to understand the reasoning behind even the most forceful topic sentence. If there is some development but it is unclear or poorly explained, then misunderstanding may result. Although there is no set rule for the number of developmental sentences, most paragraphs need about six to ten. Lastly is the <u>conclusion</u>, which depends heavily on the kind of topic sentence and development generated. Some conclusions are philosophical; some are humorous; others restate the thesis in new language. Whatever its type, the conclusion officially closes the communication supplied by the paragraph. When a paragraph contains these three elements, its construction is sound.

CONCLUSION
(consists of one
sentence: the last)

From this explanation of paragraph structure, you can see and understand how the three parts work together because this discussion is itself in paragraph form. To recap, all single paragraphs display these structural elements:

an introduction: to provide a main idea (with a topic sentence comparable to a thesis statement)

development: to explain, describe, or discuss that main idea

a conclusion: to end the discussion of the main idea

PARAGRAPH CONTENT

Although all paragraphs look alike, with their block shapes and indented first lines, their contents can differ depending on the type of information they contain. The next three paragraphs provide examples of *narrative, descriptive,* and *analytical* writing. Notice, however, that in all of them, you can locate the three-part structure that allows each one to function as an integrated whole.

When a writer wants to relate an incident, the *narrative* type of paragraph naturally emerges:

I met my husband for the first time on the telephone. My best friend had suggested that we get together, but we decided to begin our acquaintance over the phone. For two people who had never met, we managed to chat for nearly three hours, talking about everything from where we had traveled, gone to school, and lived to the kind of food and music we both enjoyed. I can remember thinking how easy it was to talk to him. He must have thought so, too, because soon after that we met in person, and the rest is history--marital history.

Paragraphs of this sort present a *sequence:* first this happened, then that. Holding this particular narrative writing together is the topic sentence—the first sentence. A bit more introduction is provided in the second sentence, which tells who was responsible for bringing the narrator and her husband together. Next come details that develop various aspects of the phone conversation. Finally the conclusion wraps up the entire package—the fact that the two were married.

At other times, the content of a paragraph may be *descriptive* as in this example:

Modern high-rise offices can become unbearable when the air-conditioning system fails at the height of summer. The windows in this type of office are sealed, so there is no possibility of opening a window and getting some cross ventilation. Even the hardiest workers will begin to feel ill when offices become ovens that register 100 degrees or more. Concentration and attention to detail are impossible even though a well-placed fan may be in operation. The

```
only realistic way to cope with this problem is to leave the office

until the system is repaired.
```

In this paragraph, the topic sentence also appears first and is immediately followed by details that support the idea of an *unbearable* situation. Further explanation provides more detail, and the last sentence concludes by suggesting a solution.

The *analytical* paragraph emerges, especially at the college level, as a way of responding to the demands of most assignments. It is used when ideas, problems, and situations must be examined, analyzed, or explored from an intellectual or probing slant:

```
Because medical technology now has the capability of sustaining

life through the use of sophisticated machinery, many questions

arise. What are the ethics of keeping a terminally ill person alive

with a machine? This question becomes even more critical when the

patient is of an advanced age--80 or 90 years old--and may be

unconscious or in extreme pain and discomfort. Considering the value

placed on individual freedom in our society, does a terminally ill

patient have the right to request that he or she be taken off the

machine, even if death will result? Questions such as these are being

raised and debated by medical ethics committees all over the world.

Concerned citizens, too, perceive the complexity of the issue.
```

Once again, we can see how this paragraph differs in content from the previous two. The topic sentence, the first one, presents the idea that questions arise when life can be sustained by technology. The development highlights two or three of these questions; the conclusion suggests that the debate goes on.

Paragraphs can also be blends of various types of writing. Regardless of the type of writing produced, however, the three-part structure underlies all of them.

TOPIC SENTENCE PLACEMENT

In the process of reading the three previous sample paragraphs, you might have noticed that the topic sentences appeared first in each. Although paragraphs are often organized this way, the topic sentence does not necessarily have to be the first sentence. A popular reversal (called a *climactic ordering*) places the thesis last where it pulls together the preceding material in a coherent and often dramatic manner. Examine the following paragraph, and pay particular attention to the building of the scene.

> The students begin arriving early, and the streets jam with vehicles as early as 7:00 AM. Everyone seems to be trying to get into the same parking spot, and it is miraculous that so very few accidents occur in the melee. Lines at the bookstore stretch out the door. Some are for students waiting to enter, but the largest one is for those laden with books and supplies, restlessly waiting to pay. Everywhere there is noise and confusion--people talking, doors slamming, and feet clattering. For all these reasons, I genuinely detest the first few days of a new semester.

You can see the dramatic effect as the paragraph builds to its conclusion—the topic sentence, which expresses the writer's point of view while clarifying the material preceding it. Although you may wish to experiment with this type of climactic paragraph in creative writing classes, in most of your college writing, you will structure *single paragraphs* (as opposed to essays) with the topic sentence first. There are a number of advantages for you as a writer when you place the topic sentence first.

1. *You have your key sentence in front of you as a writing guideline,* and you are ready to develop it. Sometimes students who decide to be a little different in their writing will work along and never actually pin down a topic sentence. An omission of this sort can be a major problem, adversely affecting the entire paragraph.

2. *A thesis-first order corresponds to the harmonious idea of a beginning, middle, and an end*—a structure that most of us enjoy and appreciate. If you have ever sat through an entire film, watched the closing credits appear, but still had no idea what happened or what to make of the movie, you have some idea of the need for a structure that makes sense. Some filmmakers like to experiment with the traditional idea of a three-part form. And although some of these films have been quite creative, all too often the filmmaker is the only one who can make sense of the experiment. If you

try to be similarly experimental with your writing and your reader does not understand the communication, then a serious problem has occurred.

3. *In most of your classes, there is little time for much creative playfulness.* If your teacher has asked a specific question such as "What was the South's major weakness in the Civil War?", you are expected to answer (topic sentence) and follow up that answer with explanation (development) that supports your response, and then conclude.

The following exercises related to both structure and content will give you a chance to analyze paragraphs and further your understanding of this form.

Exercise 2.1   ANALYZING THE PARAGRAPH

Read the following paragraph several times; then answer the questions beneath it on a separate sheet of paper.

Wisteria

One of the most stunning plants in my yard is my wisteria bush. All winter long, it appears to be dead because it is bare of all leaves and flowers. But in the spring, changes take place. By June, leaf buds appear and soon open, revealing thousands of slender green leaves on long, dangling stems. Soon, pale lavender blossoms open. Although the individual flowers are tiny, there are so many of them that the stems hang and droop from their weight. When I look from my bedroom window at the wisteria in bloom, my imagination turns it into a six-foot-tall bridal bouquet that has somehow landed in my yard. As you might expect, I spend a great deal of my time in the backyard when this graceful, eye-catching plant is in flower.

1. What is the title?
2. Which sentence is the topic sentence?
3. In sentences 2–7, what are some of the specific details provided to develop the topic?
4. Which sentence serves as the conclusion?

✎**Exercise 2.2   ANALYZING THE PARAGRAPH**

Read the following analytical paragraph, and answer the questions following it on a separate piece of paper.

Balance of Power

One of the major causes of marital discord in modern society is an imbalance of power between a husband and a wife. By tradition, men have had greater power in marriage, largely by virtue of earning the family income. However, with the increase in education of women and their employment outside the home, the traditional role is no longer acceptable to many women, who now wish to have an equal share in major domestic decisions. A prime area of concern is power over money. If only one marriage partner controls the spending or investing in a two-paycheck family while the other merely watches, the less powerful partner is likely to resent the situation. If a couple's social activities are dominated by the needs and desires of one party only, friction can result because the accommodator will eventually feel misused. Continued over a long period, such an imbalance of power serves to alienate partners, who may bicker, argue, or simply withdraw and cease to communicate at all. Divorce is a common result when one person in the marriage is seriously deprived of power. Although few couples achieve a 50-50 balance all of the time, it is crucial for the health of the modern marriage that couples share in major decision making. If this sharing can occur, harmony is far more likely to exist.

1. What is the topic sentence?

2. Which is the first *developmental* sentence?

3. Which sentence announces the beginning cf the conclusion?

EVALUATING THE PARAGRAPH

When you evaluate a paragraph, you apply standards common to all such writing—your own included. To arrive at a fair and accurate judgment, ask yourself the questions below. Each is derived from the structural requirements for an introduction, development, and conclusion and will provide you with a standard or criterion for judgment.

1. Is there a topic sentence that states a specific topic and some angle, direction, or point of view?

2. Has the writer been faithful throughout the paragraph to the topic and the point of view expressed in the topic sentence?

3. Has the writer provided necessary explanation and detailed discussion to explain the meaning of the topic sentence?

4. Is there a conclusion which relates to the topic sentence and to the development?

If your answer to all four of these questions is yes, then the structure and content of the paragraph are acceptable. If your answer to any of the four questions is no, then the paragraph is faulty and would require some revision to remedy the problem.

 Exercise 2.3   EVALUATING THE PARAGRAPH

All of the following paragraphs have problems, making them faulty pieces of writing. After reading each carefully, give one or more specific reasons why the work is faulty. (Be sure to keep the four criteria in mind.) For easy identification, the sentence intended as a thesis is underlined. Use your own paper for your answers.

PARAGRAPH A

My work as a pediatric nurse brings me a great deal of pleasure and satisfaction. Helping to ease the pain and suffering of a helpless, frightened child is so gratifying. Sometimes, though, a child will keep crying long after there is any reason to, and this can be irritating. I find that I am especially irritable if I have been working too many hours. Most of the nurses I work with complain of the long working day we all have. I think the nurses' union should put some pressure on the hospital administration to decrease the heavy work load we all carry.

Why is this paragraph faulty?

PARAGRAPH B

<u>Last Monday was the first day of the new semester</u>. My first class was located across campus from my second, so I had to sprint to reach it on time. There were so many confused students that it was like running an obstacle course. Later, I met an old friend from high school, and we sat around talking about old memories. The bookstore was a shock! The line went out the door, and everyone in it, including me, had a long, grueling wait either to buy or exchange books. I was really glad to get home by the end of the day.

Why is this paragraph faulty?

PARAGRAPH C

<u>One of my greatest pleasures is watching the birds that come to my backyard</u>. Every morning crowds of birds land on the feeder. There are many different kinds of birds, some brightly colored and some plain. I really enjoy scattering seed for the birds and watching them eat it.

Why is this paragraph faulty?

PARAGRAPH D

<u>Getting enough exercise is important to my health</u>. In summer, I swim in the ocean three times a week and then play volleyball for at

least an hour. As the days get colder, I change my routine. I play tennis three times a week and run two miles on the track every day. I used to play golf, but the game wasn't vigorous enough for me. Although I am often very tired from all the exercise I get, I do know that I have worked on maintaining my health.

Why is this paragraph faulty?

WRITING A PARAGRAPH

Writing a paragraph will allow you to experience the writing process firsthand. To help you reach this end, we've given you a detailed paragraph writing model. Before studying the model, however, keep in mind the writing process as a whole:

Prewriting: exploring the assignment, choosing a topic, and formulating a topic sentence.

Drafting: transforming prewriting material into sentences and a first edition or rough draft of the paragraph.

Editing/Revising: locating trouble spots and correcting them, thereby strengthening the work.

Final Copy: producing, in this case, a *paragraph.*

If you have any difficulties getting started writing your paragraph, you may wish to review the beginning of Unit I and the section on prewriting (see pp. 8–36).

A PREWRITING MODEL

Assume that a student has been given the following assignment.

Sample Assignment: Develop a paragraph that explains one type of situation that is psychologically uncomfortable for you.

Once the demands of the assignment are clear, prewriting begins with data gathering.

Data Gathering

1. *fancy or formal parties*
2. *funerals*
3. *being with new people*
4. *a first date*
5. *going to the doctor*

6. *1st day of school term*
7. *a job interview*
8. *giving an oral report*
9. *a French menu*
10. *asking for a raise*

Choosing a Topic

After reviewing the 10 options, the writer chooses the following single situation as requested in the assignment:

Topic: *applying for a job*

Gathering Data Relating to the Topic

Concentrating on the topic, the writer gathers more data but only that relating to "applying for a job."

Fearful of rejection.

Want to appear relaxed, calm.

Afraid of being late—get there early.

Symptoms: upset stomach, sweaty hands, racing heart.

Also very uncomfortable position to be in.

Need for self-confidence.

I often rehearse for the interview, plan what to say.

Spend time in front of the mirror—study my appearance, manner.

Am careful about what I wear/ good impression.

Using Analytic Techniques

The writer analyzes prewriting and concludes that the work is on target. The point of view of the topic sentence comes from the assignment itself: "psychologically uncomfortable."

Generating a Topic Sentence

The writer generates the following topic sentence:

Topic Sentence: *Interviewing for a job is an experience that makes me very uncomfortable.*

A ROUGH DRAFT MODEL

Grouping Ideas

To begin writing actual sentences, the writer must refocus attention on the pre-writing notes. Notice how the material is organized before writing starts:

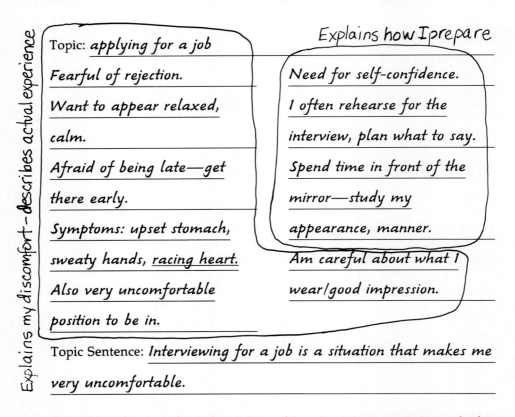

Explains how I prepare

Topic: *applying for a job*

Fearful of rejection.

Want to appear relaxed, calm.

Afraid of being late—get there early.

Symptoms: upset stomach, sweaty hands, racing heart.

Also very uncomfortable position to be in.

Need for self-confidence.

I often rehearse for the interview, plan what to say.

Spend time in front of the mirror—study my appearance, manner.

Am careful about what I wear/good impression.

Explains my discomfort—describes actual experience

Topic Sentence: *Interviewing for a job is a situation that makes me very uncomfortable.*

By making these marks and notations, this writer tries to organize and relate prewriting ideas. For example, some of the remarks relate to how or why the writer feels uncomfortable, whereas the block at the right concerns what is done to prepare for an interview.

Writing a Rough Draft

At this point, the writer could begin with the topic sentence as the first sentence of the paragraph. Then the writer could add the other blocks of material in the typical three-part paragraph order—introduction, development, and conclusion. Watch what happens. (Don't forget that first drafts are indeed rough and imperfect.)

```
        Interviewing for a job is a situation that makes me very

uncomfortable. I want to appear confidente, but in reality my face

gets read, and sometimes my voice cracts. what makes the situation so

awful is my fear of being rejected. To get reddy for the interview, I

stand in front of a mirror and rehearse hwat i'm going to say. After

studying jmy expressions and gestures, I'm a little more self-

confident. I may still be nervous, but at least I've otten the

courage to go thru with it. When the day arrives I pick what I will

wear so that I made good impression and make sure I'm early. I don't

know if this sort of situation could ever be comfortable, but prepare

for it does make it easier to deal with.
```

In this first draft, the writer presented the prewriting material in this basic order:

Thesis	First sentence
Development	{ Explanation/description of discomfort Preparation/rehearsal to help get ready What is done on actual day of interview
Conclusion	Last sentence

A three-part order is emerging that will help to organize this piece of writing. Once this rough version is created, the writer continues with the writing process.

AN EDITING MODEL

When the drafting of a paragraph is complete, a new sequence begins—namely the editing and revision so vital to the success of the final written product. In the most basic sense, you edit to locate any trouble spots in your work. Once these are found, then revisions can be made to improve the quality of the writing.

A valid question to raise at this point is this one:

What is the best way to go about editing so that a strong revision is possible?

Of course, we all recognize the need to read the draft, but for most people, this means a silent reading only. Your editing will be more successful, however, if you read your work aloud or *voice* it. Voicing allows you to use not only your eyes and mind but your voice in a careful, oral reading. You will always want to read silently as well, but voicing allows you to hear problems that might otherwise be overlooked. The problems you miss with silent reading, you probably will find with voicing; both together are extremely effective!

The main reason for using your eyes, mind, and voice is that if you are careful to *speak* exactly what you have drafted on paper, you are more likely to become aware of problems such as choppy, repetitious sentences. Awareness is the key here. Voicing is discussed further in Unit IV, which treats editing for content in greater depth.

When the model rough draft provided earlier is read both silently and aloud, editing and revision can begin. Before you examine the edited model, study these two general categories of trouble spots:

Content Deficiencies: These are problems with *what* is written—the ideas presented in the three-part form, the language used to express these ideas, and the sentences constructed to state the ideas. Many times you can note editorial remarks in the margin as you will see in the editing model.

Mechanical Errors: These are problems with *how* ideas are written including spelling, grammar, punctuation, missing material, and physical considerations such as indentations and margins. You can often correct mechanical errors as soon as you locate them, especially if they are relatively simple.

As you edit your paper, get into the habit of making editorial remarks on your rough draft to remind yourself what changes you need to make for your final copy. In the margins and in the spaces between lines, indicate content deficiencies such as the need for development and mechanical errors such as spelling corrections.

Editing a Rough Draft

Interviewing for a job is a situation that makes me ~~very~~ *terribly*
uncomfortable. I want to appear confident, but in reality my ~~face~~ *When? Explain*
gets ~~read~~ *red*, and sometimes my voice cracks. ~~what~~ *k cap* makes the situation
so ~~awful~~ *miserable* is my fear of being rejected. *Develop "rejected" sp* To get ~~reddy~~ for the *how long* *develop!*
interview, I stand in front of a mirror and rehearse ~~hwat~~ ~~i~~'m going
to say. After studying ~~my~~ expressions and gestures, I'm a little *too many I's"*
more self-confident. I may still be nervous, but at least I've
~~gotten~~ the courage ~~to go thru with it.~~ *weak wording* When the day arrives I ~~pick~~
what I will wear so that I ~~made~~ *a* good impression and make sure I'm *on whom?*

← *why?*

early. I don't know if this sort of situation could ever be
                    ing ← *repeats* ×   *weak* ×
comfortable, but prepare for (it) does make (it) easier to (deal with.)

Content deficiencies in the preceding paragraph include the need for developing what "rejected" means and adding specifics such as how long the person studies in the mirror. Mechanical errors include not putting a capital letter at the start of a sentence, omitting a letter such as the *g* in *gotten*, or writing *read* for *red*. When producing a second draft, the writer needs to keep a close eye on the various editorial remarks, especially those relating to the need for more information.

Writing a Second Draft

Interviewing for a new job is a situation that makes me

terribly uncomfortable. I want to appear confident, but in reality

my face gets red, and sometimes my voice cracks when I am in the

presence of the boss. What makes the situation so miserable is my

fear of being rejected. What will I do if the answer is no or

"Sorry, we don't have anything for you"? By nature, I am usually

optimistic, but such responses would dampen my spirits. Before the

interview, I stand in front of a mirror and rehearse what (I'm) going

to say. After half an hour of studying my expressions and gestures,

(I'm) a little more confident. I may still be nervous, but at least
                                                    still too many
(I've) gotten the courage to go to the interview. When the day *contractions*
                                                    with "I" — too
arrives, I select my clothes carefully so that I make a good *casual*

impression on the interviewer. In addition, I arrive early so that

there is time to collect my thoughts. It is unlikely that this sort

of situation could ever be comfortable for me, but preparing ahead

does help me cope with the experience.

This second effort is much stronger than the first, mainly because it is better developed. There are still some problems, but they can be corrected in the process of moving to the last phase of writing—*the final copy.*

THE FINAL COPY

Most of us breathe a sigh of relief as we near the end of the writing process because we are almost finished. In the excitement of that final typing or writing of the acceptable draft, it is possible to make new mistakes or to get sloppy. Keep the following general guidelines in mind *before* you start this last activity.

Remember what you are producing and how it should look. Allow margins at the sides and the bottom, space between the title and first line of the text, and indent your first sentence. Make any final corrections as neatly as possible. If a paper has visible smudges, scratch outs, or typeovers, start on a new sheet of paper. If your instructor has distributed a style sheet, get it out and study it so that your *final copy meets the standards set forth*. Following the style guidelines in the *MLA Handbook for Writers of Research Papers*, Second edition, the model writer's final draft would look like this:

```
Carol Jackson

Professor Marks

Composition 1

7 March 1988


               Interviewing for a Job



     Interviewing for a new job is a situation that makes

me terribly uncomfortable. I want to appear confident,

but in reality my face gets red, and sometimes my voice

cracks when I am in the presence of the boss. What makes

the situation so miserable is my fear of being rejected.

What will I do if the answer is no or "Sorry, we don't have

anything for you?" By nature, I am usually optimistic,

but such responses would dampen my spirits. Before the

interview, I stand in front of a mirror and rehearse what

to say. After half an hour of studying my expressions and

gestures, I am a little more confident. I may still be
```

```
nervous, but at least I have the courage to apply for the

job. When the day arrives, I select my clothes carefully

so that I make a good impression on the interviewer. In

addition, I arrive early so that there is time to collect

my thoughts. It is unlikely that this sort of situation

could ever be comfortable for me, but preparing ahead

does help me cope with the experience.
```

With content deficiencies and mechanical errors corrected, this paragraph is ready to be submitted.

Exercise 2.4   PARAGRAPH WRITING

Assignment: All of us have eaten at a restaurant at one time or another, whether the place was fancy, plain, or somewhere in between. Based on your experiences, write a paragraph that focuses on one aspect of dining out. Be specific as you discuss it. Write a paragraph that is between three-quarters and one page long.

Guidelines for Writing Your Paper

This assignment does allow you to get personal, for it says "based on *your* experiences." This means literally *what you know firsthand,* not what you've read or others have told you. Note that the assignment provides no point of view. You will be the one to decide what aspect (positive, negative, neutral) to cover.

In prewriting, make sure that you look at dining out from many angles. Be specific as you gather data related to your choice. If you select, for example, *poor service,* then be sure to jot down what this means specifically and how this affected your experience. When constructing your topic sentence, be sure to express your point of view and respond to the assignment.

Weak: I really enjoy eating exotic foods.
   (The statement does not respond to the assignment, despite the point of view, because it gives no indication of *where* the experience took place. The assignment specifies eating at a restaurant.)

Improved: Dining out gives me a wonderful opportunity to sample exotic foods.
   ("Dining out" indicates a restaurant and is more responsive to the assignment.) Keep your notes in front of you as you draft; voice your paper when you edit to help locate trouble spots.

Exercise 2.5   WRITING A PARAGRAPH

> *Assignment:* In daily life, you have duties and obligations in your various roles as student, family member, worker, and citizen. What is one duty you must perform but that you consider especially *unpleasant?* Describe the duty and explain why it is unpleasant in a single paragraph that is between three-quarters and one page long.

Guidelines for Writing Your Paper

In this assignment you are free to write about your personal experiences, but you are given a point of view—"unpleasant." When you gather data, keep this point of view in mind and concentrate on those obligations you *dislike.* For your prewriting, explore the many obligations you have in various areas of your life: those as a student, parent, sibling, employee, and citizen.

After you have made a writing choice, gather specific and detailed data so that your draft is not too thin. If your instructor has returned any writing with comments or corrections, use these as guidelines when you draft and revise this current project.

**Exercise 2.6   WRITING A PARAGRAPH**

> *Assignment:* Focus on a memorable character from *one* of the following: a television program, movie, or book. To provide a sharper focus, isolate one aspect of this character to discuss in your paragraph (between three-quarters and one page long).

Guidelines for Writing Your Paper

With this assignment you are being asked to deal with firsthand knowledge, whether from reading or viewing of a memorable character. "Memorable" as a general point of view means that the character you choose to write about is worth remembering either for positive or negative qualities. When you are prewriting, jot down some characters you find memorable from *all* of the categories listed in the assignment.

After you have chosen the character, write out what aspect stands out the most and gather data on it. When you construct a topic sentence, be sure that it incorporates not only your choice of memorable character but the character's outstanding quality as well.

> *Weak:* Lois Lane is a television character whom I remember well.
> (There is no mention of why the character is memorable.)

> *Better:* Lois Lane is a television character whom I remember well because of her aggressiveness.

Finally, if your topic sentence does not include the title of the series, book, or movie in which the character appeared, be sure to mention this fact as part of your introductory work.

Exercise 2.7   WRITING A PARAGRAPH

> *Assignment:* In a well-developed paragraph between three-quarters and one page long, discuss one benefit a person derives from being alone.

Guidelines for Writing Your Paper

This assignment is the least personal of these four paragraph exercises. In fact, it is objective, for it directs you to consider the benefits of solitude to "a person"—not to you only. When writing in the objective or third-person form, avoid using *I, me,* or *my* altogether. Compare these examples:

> *Personal:* Solitude gives *me* a chance to solve *my* problems.

> *Objective:* Solitude gives *a person* the chance to resolve problems.

When prewriting, try to think of a number of benefits of being alone. After you have made your writing choice, gather enough data related to it. This means that you need to explain, specify, and give details of what is beneficial and why.

Be sure to use all your editing expertise as you read and voice your work. Study any earlier writing marked by your teacher to provide insight into what sorts of problems might be present. Specifically, watch and listen for a three-part paragraph structure and for sentences with objective wording.

PARAGRAPH SUMMARY

A paragraph is a group of sentences working together toward a common purpose. When a paragraph exists as a single piece of writing (not as part of an essay), then it is organized around a three-part form: introduction, development, and conclusion. Visually, the paragraph appears as a block with its first sentence indented from the left-hand margin.

> *The Daily Journal*
>
> Keeping a daily journal can prove a tremendously rewarding experience. At first, the idea of writing everyday seems to be a strain, but as the days pass, this time spent in reflection becomes special even enjoyable in its own unique

SOME TERMS FOR YOU TO REVIEW

Topic sentence: This sentence, often the first in a single paragraph, is the keystone that identifies the overall content of the paragraph. It is a complete sentence, and it specifies the writing choice or topic and the point of view that will guide the paragraph. The topic sentence is part of the *introduction.*

Introduction: In a single paragraph, the introduction is the part (often the first two or three sentences) that introduces the main idea and provides any necessary background information. It usually includes the topic sentence.

Development: Directly related to the material introduced by the topic sentence, the developmental sentences explain, illustrate, discuss, and speculate so that the reader understands the writer's meaning.

Conclusion: The official ending of a paragraph, the conclusion satisfies the reader and writer with the sense of completion of the main idea.

Climactic Ordering: When the three-part structure of a paragraph is reversed so that the topic sentence or main idea appears at the end of the paragraph, a paragraph is said to be ordered climactically. This technique can be very effective, especially in fictional writing.

Narrative: This type of writing presents events in *sequential* order (first this, then that).

Descriptive: This type of writing features many powerful details or images to create a picture for the reader.

Analytical: This type of writing is intellectual in nature. Probing and questioning, analytical writing makes us think: What is actually happening here? Why is it happening? How did the problem or situation arise? What are the consequences? What can be done to alleviate the problem?

Organization: Organization is one of the major qualities of effective writing of any length. In a single paragraph, this term refers to the way material is ordered and placed within the paragraph. A well-organized paragraph has a clear introduction, development, and conclusion, and details within each of the parts are properly placed. Organization is essential, for it enhances our ability to understand what someone else is trying to communicate.

First-Person Writing: First-person writing has wording that is personal, featuring the use of the words *I, me, my,* and *mine.*

Third-Person Writing: Third-person writing has impersonal wording (*he, she, it,* and *they* instead of *I, me, my,* and *mine*). As a result, it is far more objective in tone than first-person writing. Many college assignments, especially those concerning cultural or intellectual topics, require third-person writing.

⚡ *If You Are Using a Word Processor*

Exercises 2.1–2.3   PARAGRAPH ANALYSIS AND EVALUATION (SEE PP. 45–47)

The first three exercises ask you to make decisions about the structural elements of a paragraph. If you do these exercises on the word processor, it will simply be a matter of typing your answers.

Exercises 2.4–2.7   PARAGRAPH WRITING (SEE PP. 57–59)

Use the following guidelines for writing each of the exercises:

Prewriting

Type the assignment so you can refer to it as you work. As you prewrite, record any ideas that come into your mind without thinking about them or judging them beforehand. You can prewrite extensively when working on the word processor because the work goes so quickly and because you can easily delete unwanted ideas. Next, formulate your topic sentence. Write it a number of ways, and then choose the version that seems to meet the demands of the assignment most directly. As you will need to refer to the prewriting, print out the prewriting sheet.

Writing the Paragraph

As it is not practical to make notes in the margins, number the sentences of your paragraph as you are writing them. In that way, you can edit by making notes to yourself on the screen, referring to specific sentences by number. After you have rewritten your sentences, delete the numbers. Or, type your paragraph triple-spaced, and make your comments in the extra space. Then go back and reform the paragraph into a double-spaced one as you apply your comments during revision. If you are not comfortable editing on-screen, print out your first draft, edit it by hand, and then go back into the file to make your changes.

After you have made all your editing changes and the paragraph is the way you want it, print your final copy. Read the final copy closely to be sure no more changes need to be made.

UNIT III

Writing the Essay

- **THE BASIC ESSAY**
- **EXPANDING THE BASIC ESSAY**
- **THE EFFECTIVE INTRODUCTORY PARAGRAPH**

OVERVIEW

Analyzing the Essay *introduces the structure and content of the basic essay.*

Evaluating the Essay *presents criteria for judging whether an essay has a sound structure.*

Writing a Basic Essay *presents a discussion, model, and guided practice in this fundamental three-paragraph form.*

Expanding the Basic Essay *explains the development of longer papers, specifically the four- and five-paragraph essays.*

Writing in Five Special Situations *features the observation, evaluation, compare–contrast, and pro–con essays as well as the summary, the commentary, and the evaluation or critique of expository writing.*

Maintaining Essay Control *focuses upon the role of the introductory paragraph in controlling the content of an essay.*

Introduction

The essay is the dominant writing form in many college courses, for it provides for a longer, more detailed discussion of a topic than a single paragraph can. Regardless of this difference in length, the essay and the paragraph share a common structural bond in the three-part form.

This unit begins with the shortest essay possible, the basic form consisting of three paragraphs: introduction, development, and conclusion. From the three-paragraph form, the text moves to four- and five-paragraph essays. Strategies are presented to help you generate this additional material comfortably and effectively. Next is a special section concerned with five writing situations common to college courses. The five include observation, evaluation, comparison and contrast, and pro–con papers, in addition to writing produced in response to outside sources.

Sometimes when studying writing, it is the numbers we tend to remember—the three- or five-paragraph essay—as if these figures had magical properties. However, the length of an essay relates directly to a number of factors: the kind of course, the type of assignment, the complexity of your topic, and the time alloted for completing the paper. One other element determines the length of an essay: *your desire* to do a thorough and penetrating job.

ANALYZING THE ESSAY

INTRODUCTION

If you are asked to write a single paragraph in response to an exam question, a certain image may come to mind—that of a single block of sentences devoted to answering the question thoroughly. However, when you are asked to write an *essay*, the task is more formidable because the essay is a longer, more complex form, consisting of several blocks or paragraphs.

The following definition describes the features of all essays regardless of length or type:

> *An essay* is a group of paragraphs united by a common purpose. Regardless of its length or type, the essay moves in a pattern: a main idea or thesis is introduced, that thesis is developed by further discussion, and the entire effort is then concluded. From its origins in the French verb *essayer*, meaning "to try" or "to attempt," the essay is humanistic in nature and represents our written attempts to discuss matters of personal interest or cultural concern.

The humanistic part of the definition is worthy of some extra attention. Unlike a research paper, which emphasizes extensive documentation, or a front-page newspaper article devoted to the who, what, where, when, and why of an issue, the essay allows a different freedom of expression.

Essays allow us to propose theories or solutions or to make observations or comparisons, all of which help us to grow as thoughtful individuals. If this sounds like part of the reason you are in college, then you can understand how the essay fits into a pattern of individual growth and development of communication skills.

Just as with paragraphs, essays can feature different types of content such as narration, description, or persuasion. In addition, a number of elements commonly are mixed in a single essay. For example, a writer may describe a particular situation in one developmental paragraph and then explain the origin of the problem in a second. The same essay may also persuade, especially if the writer believes that a solution to the problem is worthy of the reader's attention. Before launching into work on the basic essay, review these general characteristics of all essays:

1. Essays consist of at least three paragraphs.

2. Regardless of length, essays feature a pattern of introduction, development, and conclusion.

3. Essays permit a high degree of individual expression and a definite point of view.

4. Essays may be of a certain type (narrative, descriptive, explanatory, persuasive, or argumentative), or they may mix any or all of these elements.

FOR YOUR MENTAL FILE

In thinking about the nature of the essay, keep in mind its relationship with other areas of our culture. In television or film, for example, it is most common to introduce characters or a story line, develop these elements with action such as suspense or comedy, and then bring the show to some sort of conclusion. When dining, especially in better restaurants, the menu displays the three-part form: appetizers to start the meal and introduce the dining experience; entrées or main dishes to provide the major portion of the dinner; dessert and a beverage to bring the meal to a pleasant and unhurried conclusion. As these examples suggest, we are accustomed in many situations to expect a three-part pattern.

ESSAY STRUCTURE

The basic essay contains three separate paragraphs. Study the following diagrams and note the contrast between the structure of the single paragraph and that of the three-paragraph essay.

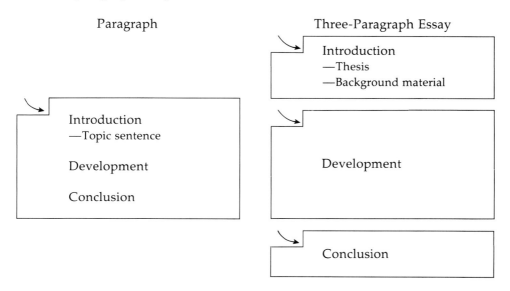

The most noticeable differences between the two are the number of writing units and the overall length. In the longer, more complex essay, you may also notice that the developmental paragraph is longer than the other two paragraphs, for it is in this section that the thesis statement is explained, clearly and thoroughly.

The most basic essay has a *three-paragraph structure unified by a common writing purpose.* Each paragraph here, however, is not a single, simple one-block form with three parts. Instead, each paragraph in the essay is separated, given special treatment, and assigned a particular function. Once separated in this manner, each paragraph gets a special label: the first becomes the introduction; the second, the development; and the third, the conclusion.

The introductory paragraph contains the all-important thesis statement, which may be placed anywhere within it. Besides stating the thesis, the other goal of a good introduction is to provide whatever background material is necessary to prepare a reader for the details to be developed in the second paragraph. When successful, a developmental paragraph makes the essay bulge in the middle. This is the largest section, and it presents the supporting material for the thesis statement. Thorough prewriting helps to develop this paragraph by supplying a wealth of thoughts from which to draw. The final part of the essay, the conclusion, completes the essay as a whole and provides the reader with the sense of an ending appropriate to the thesis statement. The conclusion generally returns to the thesis but should not repeat it word for word.

When these three elements do their various jobs, the essay produced is well organized and effective. If, however, there are faults in one or more of the three, the entire effort is affected. Although correct spelling, proper grammar, punctuation, and neatness are important, they do not override the necessity for these three essay parts to exist in harmony.

ESSAY CONTENT

The next two pieces will help you appreciate some of the differences between the single paragraph and the basic essay. Assume that both were written by a student in response to this assignment: *In a short paper, discuss one aspect of married life.* The first response to the assignment is a paragraph. Its topic sentence appears in italics. Major parts of the paragraph are highlighted in the left margin.

INTRODUCTION
Topic sentence
Definition of <u>rituals</u>

Psychologists and marriage counselors emphasize the need for newly married couples to establish rituals early in their marriages. Essentially, these rituals consist of long-term behavior patterns that bring a couple closer together emotionally and allow communication to flourish. For

DEVELOPMENT
Three examples of
rituals

> some, a special night out in a romantic
>
> restaurant might be desirable. For others,
>
> the ritual might mean lingering at the dinner
>
> table instead of dashing to the television
>
> set. Sometimes, just setting aside several
>
> evenings a week as "off-limits" for anything
>
> else is enough to give a couple a chance to

CONCLUSION
Reemphasizes why
rituals are vital

> focus exclusively on each other. In the midst
>
> of pressures from work or from other family
>
> members, newlyweds need time to grow in mutual
>
> understanding and affection. Those couples
>
> who establish and maintain such rituals seem
>
> to form longer lasting, happier unions.

With two sentences for introduction, three for development of the thesis, and two sentences for conclusion, there are seven sentences working toward a common purpose.

If, however, this writer were to use the same thesis statement but develop a basic essay, then the following product might emerge. The essay structure and the additions to enhance meaning are highlighted in the margin.

INTRODUCTION
Thesis

Definition of <u>rituals</u>

Background
information on
society

Reemphasis of thesis
before paragraph
ends

> Psychologists and marriage counselors
>
> emphasize the need for newly married couples
>
> to establish rituals early in their
>
> marriages. Essentially, these rituals
>
> consist of long-term behavior patterns that
>
> bring a couple closer together emotionally
>
> and allow communication to flourish. The need
>
> for regular contact becomes all the greater
>
> considering that both men and women may now
>
> work outside the home; consequently, they

tend to have less time and energy for each other. If couples establish and preserve some rituals, whatever they are, the two are more likely to bond as a couple.

DEVELOPMENT
A new lead sentence to prepare reader for 3 examples

3 examples with extra sentence to develop one of the three

4 additional sentences to explain rituals and their benefits

There are no set rules for marital rituals. For some, a special night out at a romantic restaurant might be desirable. With no outside pressures, a couple can relax, savor a special meal, and concentrate on each other. For others, the ritual might mean lingering over the dinner table at home to talk instead of dashing to the television set. Sometimes, just setting aside several evenings a week as "off-limits" for anything else is enough. The key to these and any other sort of rituals lies with the activity. Cleaning the house or watching television is not a suitable ritual because the focus is not on the couple, but on externals. Newlyweds must instead focus on each other so that communication can begin. Joy, laughter, disappointment, and sorrow are deepened when shared.

CONCLUSION
Reemphasizes why rituals are vital

In the midst of pressures from work or from other family members, newlyweds need time to grow in mutual understanding and affection. Those couples who establish and maintain such patterns seem to form longer

More benefits of
rituals

Mentions 'bonded' to
link this paragraph
to the introduction

lasting and happier unions. Even when major changes occur in their lives such as the arrival of children or changes in employment or residence, the emotionally bonded couple seems better able to handle them.

All of the material of the original single paragraph remains, but because the essay is a longer form, more information is added to expand meaning in all three paragraphs. With four sentences for the introduction, nine for the development, and three for the conclusion, there are sixteen sentences working together toward a common purpose.

FOR YOUR MENTAL FILE

In studying the sample essay on the need for rituals, you may have noticed a phenomenon characteristic of effective writing—links or relationships that connect one part of an essay to the other parts. Sometimes this linking is achieved through the repetition of a key word or some related form of the word; other times linking occurs when a point made earlier in the essay is reemphasized. Not only does linking produce an organized piece of writing, it enables all three essay parts (introduction, development, conclusion) to work together toward a common purpose.

 Exercise 3.1   ESSAY STRUCTURE

To increase your mastery of basic essay structure, read the following essays and, on a separate piece of paper, answer the questions that follow.

Typing

In my opinion, one of the most important skills a student can possess is the ability to type. I took my first typing course during the summer before I started junior high school. Then I followed it with several additional typing classes in both junior and senior high. Little did I realize what a good investment this one skill would become.

One simple quality stands out about typed papers, and that is neatness. Handwriting can change direction, letters can be poorly formed, but if a person can type well, the result is clean copy that just looks better. In fact, various studies have shown that typed papers generally earn better grades than handwritten ones. If a teacher were asked which is the easier paper to read and decipher, I am sure the answer would be the typed version. I tried to type just about every assignment through junior and senior high school. Not all the papers earned As, but they were neatly done and easy to read.

If I were a counselor in grade school, I would encourage every student, male and female, to take typing as soon as possible. In this way, the skill could be learned early and developed properly for success at all levels of education, especially college.

1. Which sentence in the first paragraph serves as the thesis?
2. In the developmental paragraph, what are the two basic reasons why the writer believes typing to be a valuable skill?
3. In the conclusion, the writer sets up a *hypothetical* situation (note the "if"). In other words, this person is not a counselor in real life. Imagining being a counselor, however, allows the writer to give pertinent advice related to the thesis. What is this advice?

Retreat

People who live in large cities are constantly bombarded with noise--from traffic, construction work, or even a nearby airport. Medical studies have pointed to the damage done to the body when the noise level is intense and continuous. One antidote for this problem is an occasional retreat to the desert, a marvelously soothing and unique environment.

Part of the desert's charm is that there are few people. With fewer inhabitants, the amount and volume of noise in the desert is considerably less. If the desert hideaway is relatively remote, then a vacationer from the city truly gets the full benefit of the contrast. At first, the quiet may seem unnatural, but with longer exposure, the desert dweller becomes aware of the natural sounds of crickets, coyotes, and other creatures for whom the desert is home. In addition, the wind moves freely through the less cluttered desert landscape of cacti and brush. Without the smog caused by cars and factories, the sky reveals its stars so magnificently in the night sky. Such tranquility and simple beauty give an individual a welcome sense of calm and proportion that is harder to maintain when horns are honking or the next door neighbor is partying until 3 AM. After several days of this desert life, most people tend to feel better, both mentally and physically.

Obviously, cities such as New York or Chicago are enormously attractive for their diversity, excitement, and opportunity. But when "life in the fast lane" gets too fast or the multitude of sounds drowns out a person's own inner voice, that is the time to retreat, if at all possible, to the desert.

1. In the introductory paragraph, which sentence is the thesis?
2. What sorts of specific details are provided in the developmental paragraph?
3. In what ways does the concluding paragraph relate to the introduction and the title?

EVALUATING THE ESSAY

The basic essay can be scrutinized and examined in the same manner as the paragraph for structure and content. Judging an essay accurately requires standards or criteria. As with the paragraph, these standards can be presented as questions relating to the three-part essay form.

1. *In the first or introductory paragraph, is there a thesis statement with a point of view or direction and a topic specific enough for the confines of the assignment?* Has the writer provided sufficient background or introductory data to prepare the reader for the more concentrated material to come?

2. *In the second or developmental paragraph, did the writer remain faithful to the thesis?* Does this portion contain specific information and enough explanation to support the thesis statement? Has the material been organized in a reasonable way for the reader to follow the path of the discussion?

3. *Finally, in the third and concluding paragraph, has the writer completed the essay in a way that is faithful to the thesis?*

If your answer to all of the questions above is "yes," then the essay is solid from a structural point of view. If, however, you answer "no," to one or more of the questions, the structure of the essay needs to be revised.

The essays in the following exercises display a variety of problems with respect to the three-part form. As you read each essay, remember that examining a draft for its content and structural strength is vital for improving your papers.

Exercise 3.2   EVALUATING THE ESSAY

Read the following essays with care. Visually, they look good; however, each is faulty and needs revision for one basic reason. Use the three criteria questions at the end of each essay to help locate the problem. Record your answers on a separate sheet of paper.

Small Town Life

   I grew up in a small town and live in one today. Life here is very

pleasant, especially for children. In fact, I hope to raise my family in a small town rather than in a big city. It is my firm belief that life in a big city is harmful to children.

One of the enjoyable aspects of small town life is the relationship that develops between the children who live here and the people who have shops and businesses. When I was a child, I used to love to visit the lumberyard. The owner saved leftover scraps and pieces of wood for me because he knew I was building a tree house. Our local drugstore supplied free bandages for scraped knees and elbows and jelly beans to help erase the memory of the pain. In addition, children live at a slow pace in our small town. Every Saturday, for example, families gather to shop or to have lunch in the park, and if a child has trouble choosing a toy or deciding between a hot dog or a hamburger, people have the patience to wait until those important decisions are made.

Watching the children in our town, I can see how wholesome and spontaneous they are. For these reasons, small town life is the best for the growth and development of children. That is why I plan to raise my family in this healthier type of environment.

1. Does the introductory paragraph have an acceptable thesis, and does it provide enough background information?
2. Is the developmental paragraph faithful to the thesis, and does it provide specific development or explanation of the ideas presented?
3. Does the conclusion relate to the thesis?

The Drama of History

Injecting some drama into the study of history could make history courses far more interesting. In a fast-changing society, modern students often have trouble relating to the past, so anything that a history teacher could do to enliven the material would be helpful. There are a number of methods at a teacher's disposal.

One of the most effective ways of adding drama is to include visual materials such as films. Another is to invite guest speakers who have lived through a particular time or who are specialists in some area that is being studied. Even one well-chosen field trip to a museum or historical site could have a profound impact upon the student's outlook and response to the material being studied. All of these strategies would do so much to intensify a student's understanding of the subject.

Although all of the above methods would demand more of an instructor's time, they would be well worth the effort. Nothing could be more exciting for an instructor than to see students comprehend aspects of the past for the first time or to watch the growth of appreciation and interest in the efforts of our forebears.

1. Does the introductory paragraph have an acceptable thesis, and does it provide enough background information?
2. Does the developmental paragraph relate to the thesis, and does it provide sufficient explanation of the ideas presented?
3. Does the conclusion relate to the thesis?

The Ideal Gift

If you ever find yourself wondering what gift to buy someone, you might seriously consider giving a magazine subscription. The key is to match the interests of the people on your gift list to the wide range of possible magazine choices. A visit to any well-stocked bookstore or newstand will give you an idea of a specific type of magazine.

A person who enjoys travel and other cultures might appreciate a year of National Geographic, which is filled with fascinating articles and breathtaking photography. A sports fanatic, on the other hand, might enjoy Sports Illustrated, which covers many types of sports popular throughout the world. For someone who enjoys reading about ways to improve or beautify the home, there are numerous magazines such as Better Homes and Gardens, Sunset Magazine, or Architectural Digest. For the all-around person on your list, perhaps nothing is as suitable as the Reader's Digest, featuring articles on all sorts of topics, plus interesting contributions from readers.

I believe that it is very important for people, especially Americans, to read more. With all of the problems experienced by our youngsters and adults as they struggle with the printed word, we should do whatever possible to encourage reading in the home.

1. Does the introductory paragraph have an acceptable thesis and provide enough background information?

2. Is the developmental paragraph faithful to the thesis, and does it provide specific development or explanation of the ideas presented?

3. Does the conclusion relate to the thesis?

WRITING A BASIC ESSAY

A PREWRITING MODEL

A full model of a basic, three-paragraph essay is presented over the next several pages. Compared with the paragraph model in Unit II, this model includes:

- More prewriting material
- A blocking sheet

Additional prewriting work is necessary because an essay requires more material than a single paragraph. In other words, the longer the paper, the more prewriting you will need to provide vital information for the reader. In addition, a longer paper based on more prewriting can be more complicated to organize. Thus the blocking sheet is designed to help you organize prewriting ideas into potentially effective, purposeful paragraphs.

> *Sample Assignment:* Present and develop a candid opinion of your first or given name in a three-paragraph essay.

Francis—totally unacceptable!

Seems to be more of a girl's name; few guys have it. Mike, Dave, Bill, etc. are popular male names.

Was named after grandmother, Frances! Was 4th boy; brothers got the better names (Jeff, Steve, Mike)—I got the male version of Frances . . . Francis.

Worst Aspect! When growing up—Francis the Talking Mule movie popular! No end to the jokes, teasing by classmates. Tried to call self Frank but teacher in 1st grade called me Francis. Got into fights more than once to defend/protect my honor.

Would never name my own kid any kind of unusual, odd name; could

cause trouble in school or w/being accepted by peers. Children can be

just as intolerant as adults--especially if someone is different.

Now as adult—call myself Frank; no problems . . . still get chuckles if

I have to write my full name as given. Some compare me to St.

Francis!! Easier to handle as adult.

With a thesis statement and prewriting to support it, this writer may begin blocking prewriting material.

Blocking Your Prewriting Material

When working on an essay, one concern becomes vital: *How do you arrange* your prewriting ideas? If your ideas are not organized properly, a number of problems could result. First, your essay may be disorganized and actually confuse the reader. Or, you may repeat yourself from one paragraph to the next. For these reasons blocking is suggested as a simple technique to use after you construct a thesis and before you begin the first draft.

What is blocking? *Blocking* refers to the placement of ideas so that each paragraph of your essay has a clear purpose that matches its function. For instance, your introductory paragraph should include the thesis and any other prewriting material that provides necessary background information related to the thesis. If you were to place concluding statements in the introduction, your first paragraph would not be serving its function.

When blocking your prewriting ideas, try this sequence of activities:

1. *Focus on the area related to your topic.* In the model, this area would be the material appearing after "Francis—totally unacceptable." *What information seems suitable for an introductory paragraph?* (You know that the thesis will appear in the introduction, but additional information is necessary so that the first paragraph is well developed.)

2. *What information works to support or explain the thesis statement?* This information belongs in the development paragraph.

3. *What could I use to bring the paper to a formal conclusion?*

Watch how the writer marks the prewriting, using these basic questions:

Francis—totally unacceptable!

Seems to be more of a girl's name; few guys have it. Mike, reason-
Dave, Bill, etc. are popular male names. use in
#2

Was named after grandmother, Frances! Was 4th boy; For #1
brothers got the better names (Jeff, Steve, Mike)—I got as
the male version of Frances . . . Francis. background

Worst Aspect! When growing up—Francis the Talking Another
Mule movies popular! No end to the jokes, teasing by class- reason-
mates. Tried to call self Frank but teacher in 1st grade #2
called me Francis. Got into fights more than once to
defend/protect my honor.

Would never name my own kid any kind of unusual, odd
name; could cause trouble in school or w/being accepted by
peers. Children can be just as intolerant as adults—espe-
cially if someone is different.

Now as adult—call myself Frank; no problems . . . still get for
chuckles if I have to write my full name as given. Some conclusion
compare me to St. Francis! Easier to handle as adult.

A Blocking Model

Now examine the model blocking sheet. Notice that most of the entries are written
in the form of commands. Using the command form is helpful because it is one
way to *tell yourself* what to write when you actually begin drafting.

BLOCKING SHEET

Introduction

$\left\{ \begin{array}{l} \end{array} \right.$

Use my thesis sentence.

Give background (grandmother).

Say there are two reasons to dislike

my name.

Development

$\left\{ \begin{array}{l} \end{array} \right.$

Discuss the reasons:

1. It's like a girl's name.

2. Francis the Mule/teasing by

schoolmates.

Include material about children being

intolerant.

Conclusion

$\left\{ \begin{array}{l} \end{array} \right.$

Move to my current adult status.

Current name (Frank) is not so bad.

Include that my children will not be

given odd or unusual names.

This blocking sheet is an informal sketch of the prewriting material otherwise known as an *outline*. Why is it informal? An outline that is too rigid might not allow for changes or additions in the drafting stage. The lack of any outline, however, would leave you with no guideline. This type of blocking is a balance between the two extremes. It will prove particularly helpful with the longer essay forms presented later in the unit.

Before moving on to the model draft, study these facts about blocking:

1. *A blocking sheet is not a draft but a plan for a draft.* In the model blocking of the essay about the name Francis, the writer literally gave commands about what to write when the drafting stage begins. This is similar to what some of you might do when you make a list planning the day's activities, deciding what to do first, second, and last: "go to the bank; then pick up groceries," and so on.

2. *Blocking helps you see any writing problems.* As you transfer your prewriting ideas to the blocking sheet, you may notice that you do not have enough material to fill three paragraphs and complete the blocking sheet. If this happens, you can do more prewriting to gather more information.

3. *Blocking may also stimulate you to think of new details or ideas.* Not every idea you have for an essay comes in prewriting. Because you are further along in your thinking by the time blocking begins, it is quite likely that details or related ideas will occur to you and can be used.

4. *Blocking makes you more aware of the structure of the essay and the important fact that every paragraph in an essay serves a purpose.* A common complaint in all academic fields is that many student papers are disorganized and repetitive. The problem in such papers may lie in individual paragraphs that do not have a clear purpose with respect to development of the thesis. When you take the time to block paragraphs, you recognize that each paragraph needs a reason to exist; hence, the writing becomes better organized and easier to understand.

FOR YOUR MENTAL FILE

Blocking does not require special paper or great quantities of it. Remember that Abraham Lincoln is said to have jotted down notes for his Gettysburg Address on the back of an envelope. In a sense, he was both recording and blocking ideas that occurred to him as he prepared to speak. Blocking works well as an intermediate step between thoughts and their formation into a final product, whether for writing or for public speaking.

A BASIC ESSAY ROUGH DRAFT

Using both prewriting and blocking sheets for guidance, the writer produces a first draft of the paper on the name Francis.

Everyone has a given name, but the problem is that someone else chooses it. I was name after my grandmother Frances. She was upset that none of my other brothers had been given a name from her side of the family. That is how I--a male--got the name Francis. My first name Francis is totally unacceptable to me for a number of reasons.

My name is too much like a girl's name. Instead of a masculine sounding Jim or Doug, Francis sounds soft and feminine by comparison. The worst aspect to have this name comes from the old movie character Francis the Talking Mule. I was in the first grade at this time, and that was when the problem started. This kind of trouble is hard on a kid. Interestingly, other kids can be very unkind to other children when one of them is different in some way.

As an adult, I now use the shorter, more masculine name Frank. About the only time I might still het ribbed by friends or assoicates is when I have to use my official first name. Even though I don't have any permanent scars with my name, I do not intend to pass it on to my son or daughter.

This writer has been faithful to the guidelines given on the blocking sheet, drafting a beginning, middle, and end. Even though there is a good essay skeleton here, you have probably noticed a number of trouble spots (just as there were trouble spots in the model draft for the paragraph discussed in Unit II). These trouble spots again fall into two main areas: content (*what* was written in the way of ideas and language) and mechanics (*how* the ideas were written). These problems can be corrected in the next sequence of editing and revision.

An Edited Rough Draft

With the first draft completed, the writer improves his work through the use of editing. Examine this writer's remarks and corrections carefully.

Everyone has a given name, but the problem is that someone *echoes* else chooses it. I was name after my grandmother Frances. *Give names/ explain more* She was upset that none of my other brothers had been given a name from her side of the family. That is how I--a *Repeats/ reword* male--got the name Francis. My first name Francis is *specify* totally unacceptable to me for a number of reasons. *say this is the 1st reason*

My name is too much like a girl's name. Instead of a *the* masculine sounding Jim or Doug, Francis sounds soft and *why?* feminine by comparison. The worst aspect to have this *add details here* name comes from the old movie character Francis the Talking Mule. I was in the first grade at this time, and *what problem?* that was when the problem started. This kind of trouble is *Explain* hard on a kid. Interestingly, other kids can be very *too casual* unkind to other children when one of them is different in some way.

As an adult, I now use the shorter, more masculine name Frank. About the only time I might still get ribbed *where? what occasion?* by friends or associates is when I have to use my official first name. Even though I don't have any permanent scars with my name, I do not intend to pass it on to my son or *Why?* daughter.

Content deficiencies are marked in the right-hand margin or at the end of the paragraph. Mechanical errors include misspellings and the fact that the first paragraph was not indented. (The symbol ¶ stands for paragraph.)

A Second Draft

Because the first draft was skimpy, especially in its developmental paragraph, this writer works on a second effort. See how well the new version deals with the trouble spots in the original. Problems in this second draft are not as numerous as in the rough draft, but the writer again has marked them.

Everyone has a given name, but the problem is that someone else chooses it. I was named after my grandmother Frances, who was upset that none of my other brothers (Jeff, Steve, and Mike) had been given names from her side of the family. With a little pressure on my folks, she got *←reword* them to name me Francis, the male version of her name. For *reword* two basic reasons, I find my first name totally *(too many in ¶)* unacceptable.

First of all, my name is too much like a girl's. *←change* Instead of a masculine sounding Jim or Doug, Francis sounds soft and feminine by comparison. Perhaps it is because Fran-cis has two syllable and many men's names *)develop* are strong and short--Kirk, Grant, Clark. Shortening my name only leaves Fran, which is not too good either. However, the worst aspect of my name had to do with an old movie character named Francis the Talking Mule, who became popular in a number of comedies. When the first Francis movie came out, I was in the first grade, and that was when the joking and teasing began. Many times I came home with bruises after defending my honor and manhood. This sort of problem is difficult for a child because a name is permanent. Children can be just as unkind as adults and will ridicule someone who is different in some *)) Explain: different how?*

way. Since I was the only Francis in my peer group and my

(teachers) called me by this name, I got the full force of

the teasing. *specify 1ˢᵀ grade teacher*

As an adult, I now use the shorter, more masculine

name Frank. About the only time I might still get (ribbed) *poor direction*

by friends and associates is when I have to use my

official name on a document or an application. Even

though I (don't) have permanent scars as a result of my name *reword*

and that mule, I (do not) intend to pass it on to my son or

daughter. Hopefully, I can think of a name that will not

cause him or her any needless embarrassment.

Although this second draft still has some problems (see the notes in the right margin), it is far better than the first one. Repetitive sentences such as the two that echoed one another in the introduction (sentences 2 and 3) have been revised and combined. The thesis itself has undergone some change so that it does not repeat the word *Francis* and is actually more specific about the number of reasons to be discussed. Furthermore, the second paragraph in particular is developed to a much greater extent by the addition of pertinent information.

With this better second draft and the remarks designed to improve it, the writer can set about producing the final copy.

THE FINAL COPY

Here is the final version of this paper. Errors remaining in the second draft have been corrected, and the author has decided upon a title.

Frank McMahon

Professor Klinger

English 201

15 January 1988

What's in a Name?

    Everyone has a given name, but the problem is that someone else chooses it. I was named after my grandmother Frances, who was upset that none of my older brothers (Jeff, Steve, and Mike) had been given names from her side of the family. Using a little pressure, she persuaded my folks to call me Francis, the male version of her name. For two basic reasons, I find my first name totally unacceptable.

    First of all, my name is too much like a woman's. Instead of a masculine-sounding Jim or Doug, Francis sounds soft and feminine by comparison. Perhaps it is because Fran-cis has two syllables and ends with a whispery s sound while many men's names are short and end in strong, hard-sounding letters--Kirk, Grant, Clark. Shortening my name only leaves Fran, which is not too good either. However, the worst aspect of my name had to do with an old movie character named Francis the Talking Mule, who became popular in a number of comedies. When the first Francis movie came out, I was in the first grade, and that was when the joking and teasing began. Many times I came home with bruises after defending my honor and manhood. This sort of problem is difficult for a child because a name is permanent. In fact, I learned that children can be just as unkind as adults and will ridicule other children who are different in some way whether in name, behavior, or attire. Since I was the only Francis in my peer group and my first grade teacher always called me by that name, I got the full force of the teasing.

As an adult, I now use the shorter, more masculine name Frank. About the only time I might still get teased by friends or associates is when I have to use my official name on a document or an application. Even though I have no permanent scars as a result of my name, I do not intend to pass it on to my son or daughter. I will make every effort to think of a name that will not cause him or her any needless embarrassment.

This neat, well-organized paper is ready to be submitted. The structure and content of this essay are acceptable for these reasons:

1. The paragraphs are well-developed, not skimpy, and the paragraph sizes compare well, with the middle one the largest of the three. There are no one-sentence paragraphs.

2. Throughout the essay, the writer has developed the thesis statement, which, in turn, directly responds to the assignment.

3. The writer used specific information in all three paragraphs so that his meaning is clear. In the developmental paragraph in particular, the information explaining the two reasons is presented in an organized manner. The less important reason is discussed first, and the second, more important reason occupies the remainder of the paragraph.

4. The essay has a definite sense of a beginning, a middle, and an end.

To develop your skill in producing the basic essay, try the four writing activities that follow. Consult Unit IV for more detailed discussion of content evaluation and presentation of material to achieve greater organization.

Exercise 3.3   WRITING A BASIC ESSAY

Assignment: If you were offered a free two-week vacation anywhere in the world, where would you choose to go and why? Present and discuss your choice in a three-paragraph essay

Understanding the Assignment

This assignment is relatively straightforward, but there are still a number of considerations as you begin work. If you find yourself thinking of a country such as France or Brazil, do your best to narrow your choice further to a specific city or region. After all, you only have a two-week vacation according to the assignment.

Guidelines for Writing Your Paper

When you gather data about your chosen vacation spot, be sure to provide many kinds of responses:

1. Jot down *why* you selected your specific place or city.

2. Include what you want to see. Once again, note why you want to see that site or do whatever it is you want to do. Some people, for instance, want to visit museums or other historical buildings; others simply wish to relax on a beach or go fishing. Because people travel for different purposes, your reasons need to be clear.

3. Write whether you have been to this place before. If so, when and for how long? If you have never visited the place, then write how you know of it—from friends, television, travel posters, reading, art or history class, and so on.

Once you have gathered data and grouped related ideas, prepare your blocking sheet. Be sure to consider what information you wish to include as introduction, development, and conclusion.

Review the sample blocking sheet as you begin to organize your prewriting material. For this first paper, allow yourself at least 10–15 minutes to block your ideas. It is a good idea to set aside a separate sheet of paper just for the purpose of blocking.

When editing your rough draft, evaluate your language. If your draft contains words such as *nice, great, pretty,* and *fun,* then your diction is not very powerful. You need to be specific to express your fascination with a place. Use a thesaurus to help add new, fresher language.

Weak: Hawaii has *a lot of nice* beaches.

Better: Hawaii's many spectacular beaches attract any visitor.

Exercise 3.4   WRITING A BASIC ESSAY

> *Assignment:* All of us spend money differently, depending on our needs, values, and desires. What is one area where a change of spending habits would be beneficial for you? Write a three-paragraph essay that addresses this question.

Understanding the Assignment

First of all, note that the assignment is directed to you personally with the words ''would be beneficial to you,'' so you are at liberty to draw from your own experiences. However, the phrase ''a change of spending habits'' is critical in that it can mean both the need to cut back or to spend more, so keep this in mind as you begin gathering data. Finally, explain your points thoroughly even though the assignment does not come right out and say to explain or discuss your ideas.

Guidelines for Writing Your Paper

When prewriting, take special care to think about how you spend your money. As you jot down spending areas, note whether you overspend or underspend.

After you choose a spending area and state whether you need to spend more or less, then gather data. First, describe the current spending behavior. Be specific about *what* is being spent and use actual figures: avoid writing ''I spend a lot;'' write instead *how much*. Then write down what you should be spending and how to go about realizing the changes. You could also jot down how making some changes would be helpful to you. If you were to cut your social expenses by $50 per month, for instance, where would this money be used and why?

Make your thesis respond to the assignment.

Weak: I am spending too much money on clothes.

Better: I would be wise to change my spending habits by buying less clothing.

Exercise 3.5   WRITING A BASIC ESSAY

> *Assignment:* In a three-paragraph essay, discuss one specific skill all college students should master.

Understanding the Assignment

To be successful with this assignment, you should be clear about the meaning of *skill,* as opposed to personal quality or talent. In general, skills can be learned and usually require a person to master a process such as shorthand or to use some type of equipment such as a typewriter or calculator. Note also that the assignment does not ask for the *most important* skill. Finally, the wording of the assignment is objective, so you should avoid using *I* or other personal words.

Guidelines for Writing Your Paper

When you are gathering data, be sure to give enough thought to various skills used either by you or by other students whom you have observed. If you have trouble getting started, mentally walk yourself through an average class day and see if any ideas start coming. Watching other students in class, at the library, or elsewhere on campus may also suggest some useful ideas.

When you choose one particular skill, be sure that it is fairly specific so that you are able to write about it in some detail. For example, writing is a skill; but because it combines so many other skills such as organizing ideas or spelling, you would have a problem developing the topic in three paragraphs. You would do better to select just organizing ideas *or* spelling, for each is more specific.

When you gather data on your skill, be sure to examine it from many perspectives:

1. Describe the skill and note specifically how it is helpful for *all* college students. Is it useful for all courses or just certain ones?

2. Is this skill difficult to master? Does it require any unusual expense, practice, or equipment?

3. What happens to the college student who lacks the skill? Be specific about the kinds of problems the student will experience without the skill.

4. Comment on whether the skill is traditional (such as notetaking or test taking) or relatively recent (such as the ability to use a personal computer).

Exercise 3.6   **WRITING A BASIC ESSAY**

> *Assignment:* Develop a three-paragraph essay that focuses on one advantage of living in a small family.

Understanding the Assignment

This project has a positive focus in the sense that it asks for an *advantage* to life in a small family. Note also the phrase ''living in a small family,'' for it is fairly wide in scope. In other words, you could develop a paper on an advantage experienced by a child who grows up in a small family. Or, you could focus on an advantage for the mother or father who is part of a smaller unit. If you have had no experience or firsthand knowledge of the topic, formulate an opinion based on your own observations. Be sure, however, to word your draft objectively.

Guidelines for Writing Your Paper

When gathering data, be sure to think of as many advantages as possible. If you currently live in a small family, think about the advantages that this lifestyle has brought. Reflect on the experiences of any of your friends who may live in small families. Also, think about courses you may have taken in psychology, child development, or sociology. Don't forget to include information you have absorbed from the news media.

When you have made your writing choice by picking a specific advantage, gather data on it as fully as possible. If, for instance, you choose ''greater privacy'' as the advantage, then be specific. Explain what you mean by privacy. Explain how and why this type of privacy is beneficial to an individual.

Take care in framing your thesis.

Acceptable: One advantage of living in a small family is a greater degree of privacy. (This thesis directly responds to the assignment but does not focus on any particular family member.)

Better: A teenager who lives in a small family has the advantage of a greater degree of privacy. (This version is more specific, for it mentions a particular family member. This narrower focus helps the writer develop a stronger paper.)

Before editing, assemble any of your essays that have been graded and returned. Watch for recurring errors, and edit your draft with such problems in mind.

BASIC ESSAY SUMMARY

The basic essay consists of three paragraphs, each with its own function:

Introduction: presents the thesis statement and provides any necessary background material.

Development: explains and discusses the thesis statement.

Conclusion: brings the essay to an official close.

With the presence of three separate paragraphs comes the addition of an intermediate step in the writing process—blocking. Examine this fuller version of the various stages in the writing process.

Prewriting: gathering data and generating a thesis statement.

Blocking: grouping prewriting ideas into paragraphs and setting up the order of events.

Rough Draft: writing the first version of the paper, using the blocking sheet and prewriting as guides.

Editing/Revising: locating, marking, and correcting problems in content and mechanics; rewriting whatever needs revision.

Final Copy: preparing the final copy for your instructor.

EXPANDING THE BASIC ESSAY

A three-paragraph essay may often be too small to meet the demands of an assignment. Because college courses stress in-depth analysis of social problems, issues, or physical phenomena, you will need to write essays that adequately and fully develop a given topic. In this section we feature a four-paragraph essay and then continue with the five-paragraph form (sometimes called the basic college essay).

As you begin your work with these longer essays, keep the following general guidelines in mind:

1. Make time your ally, for it is even more critical when essay assignments are longer and more complicated. Be sure to give yourself the time needed to begin with prewriting and then to work through all of the various stages of the writing process.

2. The practice and technique of blocking (grouping prewriting ideas into paragraphs) will become even more critical, particularly in the developmental paragraphs.

THE FOUR-PARAGRAPH ESSAY

Compare the three-paragraph essay outline with the four-paragraph form on page 94. Pay particular attention to the plan for the two developmental paragraphs.

The developmental paragraphs in a longer essay present various aspects of the thesis statement. In other words, a longer essay explores its thesis in *greater depth.* This additional development allows you to communicate far more to your reader. Your ability to develop a thesis in greater depth lies not only with your personal commitment to a writing project but also with your efforts in prewriting and blocking.

A Prewriting Model for the Four-Paragraph Essay

The following writing model for a four-paragraph essay illustrates the development of a thesis in greater detail. The major emphasis here is on prewriting and blocking because these are critical to achieving length and organization in a longer paper.

Sample Assignment: Focus on one way in which travel has enriched your life. (Travel does not only mean visiting a foreign country; any point in the U.S. would suffice.) Develop a four-paragraph essay that discusses your choice.

The Three-Paragraph Essay   The Four-Paragraph Essay

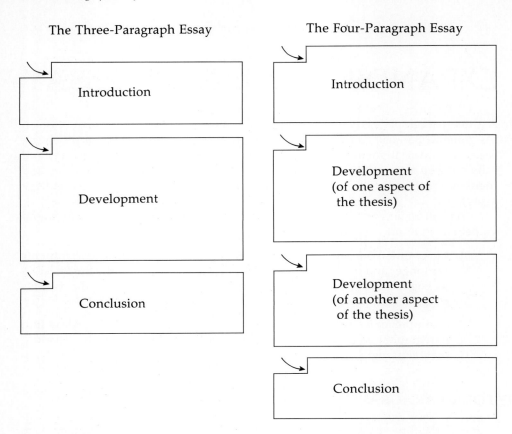

     Once the writer understands that the assignment is asking for one way that travel has enriched life, then prewriting begins. To explore the area before making a decision, the writer assembles the following list:

1. *Met new friends.*

2. *Saw historical buildings and sites; sometimes awe-inspiring (Taj Mahal, the cathedral of Notre Dame in Paris).*

3. *Appreciate conveniences of my own country.*

4. *Makes me aware of different lifestyles (Amish/reeval. my own).*

5. *Opportunity for "first-hand" education, not reading about—but seeing and doing.*

With this collection of possible choices, the writer can evaluate them and select one:

Chosen Topic: *Makes me aware of different lifestyles (Amish).*

Having chosen a topic, the writer next gathers material on that topic:

Visited Pennsylvania—Lancaster County this year; beautiful rural area, numerous Amish settlements.

Did not meet any Amish but could see by their attire, means of transportation, and homes that their lifestyles were very diff.!

Attire—simple, old-fashioned dresses for women, bonnets. men wore hats; many men had beards cut a cert. way. No frills, loud colors, jewelry, mini-skirts, etc.

Transp—saw horse and buggy rigs on regular streets; mules w/plows occasionally. My home city is dependent on car—not the trad. Amish.

Homes—farms were common. Many w/no TV antennas, no electricity!! Beautiful crops, fields well-tended; did not see pools, motor homes, boats, etc.—all common for city-dwellers.

Whole experience made me question my own lifestyle or at least what I'm used to—

Too materialistic? Too much emphasis on looks/dress—not on substance, work, contrib. to community?? Not enough courage to be different (as Amish are)?

Not an expensive trip or as exciting as going to Europe but personally very valuable—thought provoking.

With this prewriting material, the writer can construct a thesis statement:

Thesis Statement: *Seeing different lifestyles is one particularly enriching aspect of travel, at least for me.*

So far, so good! Now, however, the writer needs to consider the best way to use this prewriting material to construct paragraphs with a clear purpose in the development of the thesis. This is where blocking enters the picture.

Blocking a Four-Paragraph Essay

The writer can use the following four questions to make decisions about *where* to place prewriting information:

1. What material (other than the thesis sentence) is introductory in nature and would help my reader understand the important background facts?

2. What information would best begin the development of the first aspect of the thesis in paragraph 2?

3. What second aspect of the topic could add depth to the thesis or extend what I have discussed in paragraph 2?

4. How best could I finish the paper? Should I add a note of humor, use a philosophical conclusion, or reemphasize the thesis?

Examine how this writer responded to these four questions as you study this blocking sheet:

Introduction	*Use my thesis.*
	Mention backgrnd.—Pennsyl. + AMISH
	Emphasize that lifestyles are different.
1st Development	*DESCRIBE—how Amish differ in attire, home, transport.*
	Try getting specific details.

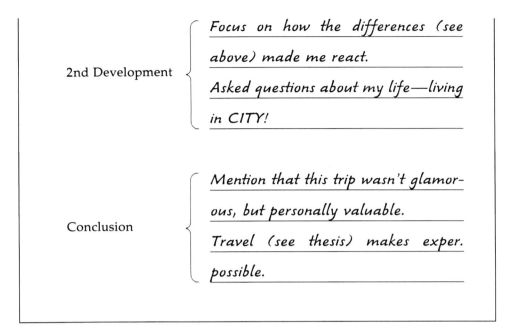

2nd Development

> Focus on how the differences (see above) made me react.
>
> Asked questions about my life—living in CITY!

Conclusion

> Mention that this trip wasn't glamorous, but personally valuable.
>
> Travel (see thesis) makes exper. possible.

Review the blocking model as you consider the following questions and answers:

1. *Why set up paragraph 2—the first developmental paragraph—this way?* This writer has chosen to use paragraph 2 to *describe* what was seen in the Amish area. These sights are probably fresh to the writer, and it is possible that the reader has never visited this area to see firsthand the Amish lifestyle. In most papers, in fact, this choice to describe (a culture, problem, or situation) is extremely effective, for it allows a reader to see *through words* what the writer has chosen to discuss. Without some details about the Amish way of life, a reader would have difficulty understanding the effect this trip had on the writer.

2. *How does the material in paragraph 3—the second developmental paragraph—help the development of the thesis?* Once the reader has been given a description of the Amish lifestyle, then the writer can move smoothly into a critical part of the essay: an explanation of how the experience of seeing the Amish enriched the writer's life. This paragraph is vital, for it directly relates to the assignment and explains the writer's responses. Both the first developmental paragraph describing the Amish and the second analyzing the writer's response present different but related aspects of the thesis.

3. *What is the value of reworking travel (in general) into paragraph 4, the conclusion?* Remember that the overall assignment began with a focus on travel as a means of enrichment. By making reference to general travel

after having discussed a specific trip to the Amish country, the writer has helped to unify the paper and to relate the last paragraph to the first.

The following sample four-paragraph essay shows the importance of this early blocking strategy. As you read, keep in mind the outline that holds together and adds depth to the writing picture:

1. an *introduction* that specifies the writing choice, states the thesis, and presents sufficient background material

2. *one developmental paragraph* to describe what was seen on the trip

3. a *second developmental paragraph* to respond to the assignment and explain how this trip caused reflection and questioning

4. a *conclusion* that closes the essay in a nonrepetitive and unified manner

Matthew Crispin

Professor Montoya

English 72

22 October 1988

Looking at Life Differently

Seeing different lifestyles is one particularly enriching aspect of travel, at least for me. Just last summer, my family and I visited Lancaster County in Pennsylvania, where many Amish people live. In our era of "high tech" and fast living, it came as quite a surprise to see firsthand this unique sect following traditional ways set forth generations earlier. Not only was I made aware of the enormous differences in lifestyle, but I was forced to question some of my own beliefs and social patterns.

Although I did not actually meet any Amish people, I was able to see how very different their way of living is. My first awareness was of the rural landscape. Instead of parking lots surrounding skyscrapers, well-kept fields of corn, alfalfa, and tobacco were spread between attractive farmhouses--farmhouses with roofs unadorned by television antennas or electrical wiring. I took my first photograph in the area when I spied a horse and buggy moving along a side road. The Amish vehicles directly contrast with the motor vehicles that have dominated my home city for decades and that represent the American passion for freedom of movement. When I got closer views of some of the people, I could see the utter simplicity of their clothing. Whether dresses or suits, all outfits were simple and what many would call old-fashioned. No particular frills, exotic colors or patterns, and no jewelry or fashion fads were to be seen (except on the tourists). Once again, I could not help but compare the simplicity of the Amish lifestyle with many of the extravagances of my own area.

Visiting the Amish communities had the general effect of making me question my own lifestyle and that of mainstream America. By comparison, we non-Amish are far more materialistic. Instead of being content with what we have, we seem to want whatever is newer, faster, and shinier. Our ties to the land, too, are not as strong because others such as the Amish do our farming for us. Given the less materialistic Amish society and the connection with the land, I wondered how many Amish visit psychiatrists for identity crises or the other problems that are so prevalent in other parts of this nation. Although such questioning about our society can become depressing, in general it makes me more aware of what direction my life is taking and how important it is for me to keep in mind what is most enduring--home, family, community, friendships, and a good day's work.

I have taken trips to places that were far more glamorous and exciting than the Amish countryside, but these places did not give me such food for thought and reflection. In fact, the one "luxury" I would always allow myself, no matter how simple my life became in other ways, would be the luxury of travel. Watching a travel documentary is one way to see new places, but it does not equal the experience of being there and seeing firsthand how other people live and how their lives compare with my own.

You can see in this final version how the blocking outline provided an order for presenting the prewriting ideas in an organized fashion.

Exercise 3.7   THE FOUR-PARAGRAPH ESSAY

Assignment: What is one job or career that would be totally unsuitable for you? In a well-developed four-paragraph essay, provide at least two reasons why the job is undesirable.

Understanding the Assignment

Make a special note of the limitation that at least two reasons are required. The presence of the pronoun, *you,* directs your attention to the personal level. In making your choice of an unsuitable career, avoid focusing on jobs that are too obvious in their lack of desirability. Include consideration of careers that may be high-paying and prestigious but are still unsuitable.

Guidelines for Writing Your Paper

In prewriting, use these questions to help generate material:

How do I know that the job is unsuitable for me?

What are the two strongest reasons for disliking the job?

When you decide on two reasons, leave space beneath each reason so that you can explain it.

Block your material so that your paragraphs each have a clear purpose. You have a possible blocking tactic provided by the assignment itself—"provide at least two reasons." Your blocking may follow this pattern:

Introduction	*Thesis—Mention of the two reasons*
1st Developmental Paragraph	*Discussion of the first reason*
2nd Developmental Paragraph	*Discussion of the second reason*
Conclusion	*Whatever tone or approach will best close the essay*

When your first draft is completed, pay special attention to content, especially to how well you explained the two reasons for not wanting the particular type of career. Suppose you felt that law enforcement, for example, was not a suitable career for you because it is too dangerous. You would need to make sure you had specified what *dangerous* means or what a hypothetically dangerous situation might be in this line of work.

Exercise 3.8   THE FOUR-PARAGRAPH ESSAY

Assignment: Think back on all of the various classes (academic, athletic, or vocational) you have taken. Select one course that was special or outstanding for you. For example, you might have learned a new skill, gained new knowledge about an area or about yourself, or simply enjoyed the information or the activity. In a four-paragraph essay, describe the course and tell why it was so memorable.

Understanding the Assignment

Here you are able to draw upon your direct experiences in the class of your choice. The assignment contains two vital clues to what your paper should include: a *description* of the course and the *reason* it was such a positive experience.

Guidelines for Writing Your Paper

In prewriting, make your selection of the course; then give your full attention to gathering data. Ask yourself these questions:

What was the course like?

How would I describe it?

Why was this course so special to me? (Was it the instructor's interest or style? The kind of information you were given? The fact that it changed your way of thinking or way of life? Explain.)

Would I recommend this class or one like it to others—why, or why not?

Complete your prewriting and block your work. *Hint:* a logical purpose for your second paragraph (the first developmental paragraph) would be a *description* of the course to help your reader understand what the class was about.

Exercise 3.9   THE FOUR-PARAGRAPH ESSAY

Assignment: Modern technology has accounted for many inventions that have made life in American society much easier and more pleasant. For this essay, focus on one appliance or invention you use regularly; discuss how it fits into your lifestyle and the value it has for you. (Don't choose the automobile.)

Understanding the Assignment

This assignment focuses on *one* useful invention or appliance, so be selective. In addition, be sure to choose one with which you are indeed familiar, no matter how common it may seem. The word *value* also has implications. Value can refer to more than the cost of an item; in fact, something of value may not be costly at all. It may have value for you for other reasons such as saving time or energy.

Guidelines for Writing Your Paper

In prewriting, begin by thinking of the many items you use. To get you started, think of the following areas of your life and the appliances that may be a part of these areas:

Food related: microwave oven, blender

Entertainment: videocassette, cassette tape player

Communication: home computer, telephone answering machine

Personal grooming: hair dryer

Landscape: power lawnmower

Cleanliness: vacuum cleaner, dishwasher

These examples should help bring your own ideas to mind. When you make a choice of one appliance, be sure to consider it thoroughly. How does it fit into your lifestyle? When and how do you use it? And why is it valuable to you?

To block the prewriting, be sure that each paragraph has a purpose, especially the two developmental paragraphs.

Before editing the first draft, you might assemble any of your returned and marked essays to check for problems. Then be on the alert for any similar trouble spots in this current draft.

THE FIVE-PARAGRAPH ESSAY

By expanding the basic essay even further, you can create the five-paragraph essay, sometimes referred to as the *basic college essay*. As the following diagram on page 104 shows, the additional paragraph serves to develop the thesis statement at even greater length.

To accommodate the expanded size, you will need to allow more time, especially for prewriting. Although there are no exact limits, a five-paragraph essay would tend to fill three to five handwritten pages or two to three typed pages. Therefore, you need additional time to generate enough information. You probably will need to spend at least three separate work sessions on a longer essay also. If you plan ahead, you will not be pressured to complete the entire writing process in one short sitting.

On the next few pages, you will see an extensive model of the writing process as it is used to generate a five-paragraph essay. In addition, there is a brief and specific presentation on time management for the model assignment.

As you read through the model, be aware of some important changes. First of all, prewriting has been dramatically increased to generate the additional material necessary for a five-paragraph essay assignment. You will also notice that the prewriting entries tend to be longer and closer to sentence form in length. Finally, the blocking sheet has been expanded to allow for the blocking of five essay sections.

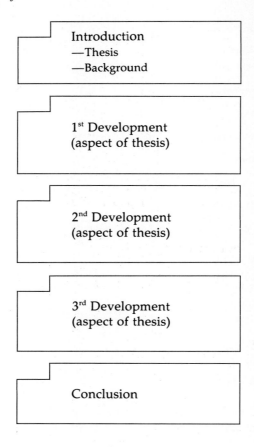

Managing Writing Time

A student has been given the following assignment in class on Monday morning; the paper is due on Friday of the same week.

> *Sample Assignment:* In terms of your own community or neighborhood, discuss one situation or condition that, in your opinion, could use improvement. Form your response into a five-paragraph essay.

Here is a possible schedule to help this student manage time effectively:

Monday	*Wednesday*	*Thursday*
In Class: Ask any questions you may have about the assignment; listen to those raised by other students.	*In Class:* Listen to any discussion of the pending assignment; ask any further questions you may have.	*Allow 2–4 hours:* Review your last draft, and revise as needed. Then, neatly hand write or type the final copy.

Monday	Wednesday	Thursday
Afternoon/evening: Allow a block of time (2–4 hours) to begin prewriting; if at all possible, work to form a thesis.	*Afternoon/evening:* Allow 2–4 hours to finish any prewriting; then block your work and begin the rough draft. Edit! If a 2nd draft is needed, do the revision now.	Proofread and correct errors in type or script in a professional manner.

If the writer uses the maximum time suggested by this scheme, then 12 hours would have been invested in the paper during the week. If this seems excessive, remember that a good paper does take time in addition to a great deal of effort. Starting early and allowing enough time will also prove valuable if you need to do a second or third draft.

A Prewriting Model for the Five-Paragraph Essay

The writer begins prewriting in response to the assignment.

1. *Better lighting in wooded areas*

2. *More parks/or neighborhood parks for kids or people just to sit— fountain?*

3. *Neighborhood coffees/teas to get acquainted*

4. *Getting businesses to fix up their buildings: often run down or dirty*

5. *Major recreational facility: gym, baseball field, track, swimming pool?*

6. *Fines imposed upon pet owners who let dogs soil areas without cleaning up afterwards.*

7. *Neighborhood Watch—to organize homeowners vs. crime.*

8. *Crossing guards for all elementary school areas*

9. *Resurfacing of pavements/streets—tree root damage and rain damage make poor surface to walk or drive on*

10.   *Major local campaign vs. litter*

 After evaluating the list of ideas, the writer can focus on one specific problem to discuss.

 Chosen Topic: *Crossing guards for all elementary school areas*

 The other nine ideas are now set aside, and the writer gathers material only on this topic.

1st reason

 Safety of kids. Kids are often least aware of traffic rules—tendency to walk or run without looking. Just don't have exposure to regulations as have adults, especially kids in grades K through 6. Heartbreaking tragedy to lose child or injure one because someone isn't watching intersections.

2nd reason

 Good activity for semi-retired person or person who does not want indoor, high-demand job. Guard looks after kids, earns modest salary, gets fresh air, attention of kids, and sense of accomplishment and protection for young ones. Could be person from the neighborhood—this would mean no battling traffic to get to work.

Overall belief/value

 Obligation of society to care for its young, even if a kid is not my own.

 Drove past Wilson Elementary School in my neighborhood for over a year as I went to work. Great system of guarding—knew kids, greeted them personally. Friendly and responsive to one another. Felt good seeing this and I'm not even a parent! Wrote letter of commendation to principal of the school.

Need something like this set up for <u>all</u> schools in my community; definitely a worthwhile cost for school district or the local taxpayer.

Because the prewriting done so far has worked out well, the student is able to generate a thesis statement:

Thesis Statement: *In my opinion, every elementary school in my community should have crossing guards at all intersections used by children.*

A Blocking Model for the Five-Paragraph Essay

Using the prewriting, specifically the material related to the writing choice, the writer blocks or outlines the ideas by writing command sentences. You can already see the element of control emerging, for each paragraph has a particular function.

Introduction	*Topic Sentence + explain why I am interested/how I became aware of situation; mention there are several reasons why.*
1st Development	*Give 1st reason why: kids' safety and explain reasoning for my point of view in this issue.*

2nd Development	*2nd reason why: see good employment for semiretired/explain how the job is particularly good.*
3rd Development	*Use the Wilson Elementary School as specific example of a good guard set-up/describe.*
Conclusion	*Emphasize obligation/necessity of all members of society to care for the young—new generation, etc.*

With a purpose for each paragraph and a guideline for drafting, this writer is ready to continue working.

A Drafting Model for the Five-Paragraph Essay

Using the prewriting and blocking sheets, the writer can begin the rough draft. As you examine this first drafting effort, see how well the writer follows the directions on the blocking sheet. Pay particular attention to paragraph length.

When I look around my comunity, there are a # of conditions shch could us some imrovement. But I think that care for the younger generation is most important. This is why I believe that every elementary school should have crossing guards at all intersections used by the children.

Having a Xing guard program would ensure the safety of the kids. It is a tragedy to the entire comm if harm or death comes to a child at the hands of a careless drive or a disturbed person.

Another benefit if for the guards themselves. Not everyone

wants a full-time job so the job would be perfect because the hours
would match the times that the students go to school. Working out of
doors is also desirable to many people who don't want to be stuck at a
desk.

Wilson Elementary School near my home has a great system of
crossing guards. After seeing the program at work, I even sent them a
note of congratulations on their fine performance.

Even though I don't have children, I believe that care of the
young is everybody's job.

As is the case with rough drafts of paragraphs and basic essays, the problems here
tend to fall into one of two major categories: content deficiencies and mechanical
errors. In this draft, the content of the paragraphs is a major concern as this draft
is very thin with only a few sentences in each paragraph.

An Edited Rough Draft

At this point, the writer assumes the role of critic in order to evaluate the work
generated in the drafting stage. The remarks in the margins are especially important for these comments relate to content deficiencies. Most corrections made
directly in the text are designed to correct mechanical errors.

When I look around my community, there are a (#) of   *sp mention some conditions*

which

conditions (shch) could us some imrovement. But I think

that care for the younger generation is most important.

This is why I believe that every elementary school should

have crossing guards at all intersections used by the

children.

Having a Xing guard program would ensure the safety)   *Explain how or why*

weak

of the (kids.) It is a tragedy to the entire (comm) if harm or   *Make clear how guards would help*

death comes to a child at the hands of a careless drive, or

a disturbed person.

Another benefit it [if] for the guards themselves. Not *who would? specify*

everyone wants a full-time [job] so the [job] would be perfect *repeats*

because the hours would match the times that the students

go to school. Working out of doors is also desirable to

many people who don't want [to be stuck at a desk.] *poor language*

    Wilson Elementary School near my home has a great *Rewrite: seems too abrupt;*

system of crossing guards. ⊗ After seeing the program at *needs transition*

work, I even sent [them] a note of congratulations on their *Who?* *Describe it!*

fine performance. *too casual*

    Even though I [don't] have children, I believe that *Why? Explain/refer to thesis*

care of the young is everybody's job.

With so many problems in both categories, rewriting will be necessary to ensure a well-developed final paper.

A Second Draft   Because the first draft of a model was so very thin, the writer revised and made additions in a second draft. Examine this second version to see how it incorporates the corrections and suggestions noted on the edited rough draft.

    When I look around my community, there are a number of

conditions that could use some improvement such as the poor

lightning in some of our wooded areas or the methods for control of

neighborhood prevent crime. But I think that care for the younger

generation is most important. This is why I believe that every

elementary school in my community should have crossing guard at all

intersections used by the school children.

    First of all, having a crossing guard program would ensure the

safety of the youngsters. Little ones are often unaware of the

dangers of cars and rules of the road, so they becomes in a sense

perfect victims. All of us have heard of children who were taken

while walking to school. Having guards could helpt to lessen the
likelihood of some accident or criminal act.

Antoher benefit is for the guards themselves. There are many in
our community who would enjoy an opportunity to work outdoors in a
physically undemanding job. Retired people who don't want to stop
working would make fine guards. Not everyone wants a full time job,
so the position of guard would be perfect.

One of the reasons why I am supportive of this guard program is
because I have seen it work beautifully at Wilson Elementary School.
Each morning, I used to pass the school on my way to work. Guards were
located at each important intersection, and they got along well with
the children. I remember being so impressed that I sent a note to
Wilson's principal praising this policy.

A reader may think that my concern in this area comes from being
a parent, but I have no children. I simply believe that care of the
young is everyone's obligation and should be a priority in any
shschool of city budget.

This second version is far superior to the first draft; however, it too must be
edited before the final copy can be made. The same two concerns will be evident
in the second round of editing: content deficiencies and mechanical errors.

An Edited Second Draft　Again notice the errors corrected and the content ideas
or suggestions marked on this draft. In this evaluation, the writer has repeated the
editing process used with the rough draft. Each editing improves the paper as it
moves toward a final version.

use better words

When I (look around) my community, there are a number

of conditions that could use some improvement such as the

poor lightning in some of our wooded areas or the methods *use*

sense ?　　　　　　　　　　　　　　　　　　*neighborhood*

for control of neighborhood prevent crime. But I think) *watch/rewrite* that care for the younger generation is most important.

This is why I believe that every elementary school in my

community should have crossing guards at all   *Add a sentence to*

intersections used by the school children. ⊗   *introduce ideas in ¶2 & ¶3*

    First of all, having a crossing guard program would

ensure the safety of the youngsters. Little ones are

often unaware of the danger of cars and the rules of the

road, so they becomes in a sense perfect victims. All of   *better word needed*

us know of children who were (taken) while walking to

⊗   *comment here*

school. Having guards could helpt to lessen the   *Add: say how or why*

likelihood of some accident or criminal act.

    Another benefit is for the guards themselves. There   *of what?/rewrite start*

are many in our community who would enjoy an opportunity

to work outdoors in a physically undemanding job. Retired

people who don't want to stop working would make fine   *⊗ Anyone else?*

guards. Not everyone wants a full time job, so the

position of guard would be perfect.   *Why?*

    Another

~~One of the~~ reasons why I am supportive of this guard   *say where school is*

program is because I have seen it work beautifully at

Wilson Elementary School. Each morning, I used to pass   *how long?*

the school on my way to work. Guards were located at each   *what does this mean?*

important intersection, and they got along well with the   *give examples*

children. I remember being so impressed that I sent a note

to Wilson's principal praising this policy.   *Comment?*

    A reader may (think) that my concern in this area (comes) *reword*

from being a parent, but I have no children. I simply

believe that care of the young is everyone's obligation   *Comment—*

and should be a priority in any ~~sh~~ school (of) city budget.   *say why*

The Final Copy

Compare the final copy below with the drafts appearing earlier. Pay particular attention to the three developmental paragraphs. Each has been further developed in line with the editing remarks made in the earlier drafts. The writer has also added a title.

Kimiko Nakamura

Professor Grummetz

English Composition 1

10 March 1988

A Community Need

When I observe my community, there are a number of conditions that could use some improvement. It would be valuable to have a Neighborhood Watch on our block to prevent crime or to get better lighting near some of the wooded areas. But I think that the need to care for our younger generation is most important. This is why I believe that every elementary school in my community should have crossing guards at all intersections used by the school children. There are two excellent reasons for such an action.

First of all, a full crossing guard program would ensure the safety of the youngsters. Little ones are often unaware of the dangers of cars and the rules of the road, so they become, in a sense, perfect victims. All of us have read of children who were hit by cars or abducted while walking to school. It is a tragedy not only to the family but to the entire community if a child is injured or killed by a careless driver or a disturbed individual. Guards positioned at key areas can help to lessen the likelihood of some accident or criminal act. In fact, the sight of crossing guards is often enough to cause many drivers to be more cautious or to discourage a potential abductor.

A full crossing guard system is beneficial not only to the children but to the guards themselves. There are many in our community who would enjoy an opportunity to work outdoors in a physically undemanding job. Retired people who do not want to stop working would make fine guards. A woman or man whose children are grown may wish to care for the school children to fulfill a need to nurture and to protect. Not everyone wants a full-time job, so the position of a guard would be perfect because the hours are limited to those times when students go to and from school.

Another reason why I am supportive of this guard program is because I have seen such a program work beautifully at Wilson Elementary School, just six blocks from my home. Each morning for two years, I passed the school on my way to work. Guards were located at each intersection. Not only did they watch the children, but they obviously enjoyed the youngsters, just as the youngsters enjoyed the guards. Most guards knew the children by name and made enough of a fuss over them to get their days started on a pleasant note. Believe it or not, my spirits were improved as a result of watching their interaction. I remember being so impressed that I sent a note to Wilson's principal praising this policy. I only wish that the same system could be set up at the other elementary schools in our community.

A reader may conclude that my interest in this program stems from being a parent, but I have no children. I simply believe that care of the young is everyone's obligation and should be a priority in any school or city budget. A well-staffed crossing guard program is one way we can help the children who will, after all, be the new generation of citizens.

Exercise 3.10   WRITING THE FIVE-PARAGRAPH ESSAY

Assignment: Your school is the starting point for this assignment. Reflect on your direct experiences and observations while on campus; then write a five-paragraph essay on one area that could be improved.

Understanding the Assignment

The key wording in this assignment is the phrase ``one area.'' *Area* could refer to any aspect of the school—its course offerings, the condition of the buildings, registration procedures, parking, student services, employees, and so on. Be sure, however, that you focus on only *one* area.

Guidelines for Writing Your Paper

Once you have selected an area needing improvement, thoroughly gather data on it, making sure that you *describe* the problem. Explain why it is troublesome for you and other students, and suggest how the situation could be remedied and why it should. Can you recall any firsthand experiences you have had in regard to the problem?

Block your essay with an eye to the purpose behind each of the paragraphs, especially the developmental ones. A good choice of content for paragraph 2 would be a description of the problem area to enable your reader to understand the nature of the difficulty. If you do have a firsthand experience, you may wish to dramatize it in the second developmental paragraph.

Before you begin editing this paper, assemble and review all of your previous writing that has been returned to you by your instructor. Make a point of watching for recurring errors or problems marked on these papers.

Exercise 3.11   WRITING THE FIVE-PARAGRAPH ESSAY

Assignment: Stereotypes occur in every society. Although some of them can be amusing, the vast majority are insulting to individuals or groups because the stereotype generalizes and does not allow for individual differences. Consider, for example, the meddling mother-in-law, the corrupt politician, the dumb blonde, the large but not too bright athlete, and the superwoman who does it all—keeps house, raises her children, satisfies her man, and holds down a full-time job—superbly. Because stereotypes erase individual differences and qualities and often focus on negative images, they are generally harmful. For this paper, choose *one* stereotype, and develop a five-paragraph essay that discusses it and the harm it causes.

Understanding the Assignment

This is the first of the more objective essay assignments in this part of the text; therefore, your wording should be third person or objective. If you have personally suffered from the stereotyping you are discussing, you may use your experience to generate ideas, but the choice of language should still be impersonal (*he, she, it,* or *they,* but not *I, me,* or *my*).

Guidelines for Writing Your Paper

To help generate ideas, think about the stereotypes to which you have been exposed. Magazine and television advertisements tend to perpetuate stereotyping as do many television programs. (Think of the stereotypes portrayed in many soap operas or situation comedies.)

When you have chosen your stereotype, respond to the following directions or questions, for they will help you to generate paragraphs when you draft:

1. Describe the stereotype you chose. How does it portray people—and which people?

2. Analyze the stereotype's effects. How does it cause problems or do damage to the individuals it labels and to the people who believe the stereotype?

3. Approach the topic philosophically and *enrich* your paper. (For more discussion about the concept of enrichment, consult pages 182–186 in Unit IV.) Why do you think that people believe in this stereotype? What is there about human nature that would allow the idea to be perpetuated? What, if anything, can be done to rid our culture of this stereotype?

When blocking your prewriting, remember the need for each paragraph to have a clear purpose. *Hint:* Your first developmental paragraph should describe the stereotype because the reader may not be completely familiar with it.

Exercise 3.12   WRITING THE FIVE-PARAGRAPH ESSAY

> *Assignment:* In a sense, everything produced by a culture ''says something'' or reflects on some aspect of that culture—from a simple pen to a sophisticated computer. For this assignment, purchase a greeting card for an occasion of your choice (birthday, funeral, wedding, anniversary, friendship, holiday, and so on); then examine it in light of this question: How does the card you chose reflect our culture, and what does it indicate about us as a group? Submit the card with your five-paragraph essay.

Understanding the Assignment

Because you are required to purchase and study a specific card, you must allow time for two priorities: choosing the card and analyzing it as a cultural reflector. In addition, be sure that your paper is worded objectively.

Guidelines for Writing Your Paper

Begin prewriting by gathering data on the contents of the card and on what these contents imply. You could, for example, divide your notepaper in half. On one side write what is actually on the card, and on the other side write what these components indicate about our culture.

Some areas for you to consider as you work:

1. Examine the card carefully, studying its color, overall design, special artistic flourishes, written messages, symbols or images (such as flowers, guns, and so on), and any other aspects you notice.

2. Consider the relationship between the occasion celebrated and the tone of the card: humorous, romantic, overtly sexual, formal, or restrained.

3. Then examine the larger implication behind the card. If you choose a humorous birthday card that suggests the recipient celebrate by first getting very drunk and then acting out all fantasies, what does this say about our culture? What about a card that features drunken (but very cute) little animals inviting you to a cocktail party? What about the birthday card that pokes fun at a person's advanced age and implies that ''all the good times are gone''?

As you evaluate this data, try to reach a decision about what this card is saying with respect to our society. Is it an unhealthy reflection of some aspect of our culture, a healthy reflection, or possibly a mixed message? Whatever your decision, it must be expressed in the thesis in the introductory paragraph.

Do your blocking, drafting, and editing as carefully as possible. Concentrate especially on correcting any recurring problems in your writing.

Some Tips on Choosing a Card

Whatever type of card you choose, be sure you feel a strong response to it, whether your response is favorable or unfavorable. If you can afford to buy two or three cards, do so. In case one does not work out, you can move to one of the others.

Exercise 3.13   WRITING THE FIVE-PARAGRAPH ESSAY

> *Assignment:* Look through a magazine and select an advertisement. After analyzing it carefully, write a five-paragraph essay in answer to this question: In what ways does the advertisement attempt to manipulate its viewer? Limit the discussion to two major ways. Attach the advertisement to your final paper.

Understanding the Assignment

This type of project also requires more time because of the necessity to search for and choose an appropriate advertisement. Once that is accomplished, you need to examine it thoroughly. If you are unsure of the meaning of *manipulate,* look it up in the dictionary. An understanding of this term is necessary for your overall grasp of the assignment. Write your paper in the objective style without using personal forms of *I, me,* and *my.*

Guidelines for Writing Your Paper

Once you have selected an advertisement, your prewriting effort should be directed to a detailed examination and analysis of it. Use any of the following questions to help you get beneath the surface of the visual effect. Record *all* of your responses:

1. *What colors are used?* What symbolism or suggestive value does each have? (White, for example, symbolizes purity, cleanliness, and innocence. What is its effect in a cigarette ad?)

2. *What is the location or scene of the ad?* How does the scene contribute to the selling of the product? Is there anything ironic about the scene and the product? (For example, is there a scene of unspoiled mountain wilderness in a cigarette ad?)

3. *How is the lettering or wording used, and where is it located?* You should read not only what is written but notice the location and its effect on the viewer's eyes. What kind of writing is used? Is it factual or humorous?

4. *What age group and sex is the ad designed to attract?* Answer and explain how you are able to reach this conclusion.

5. *What kinds of images do the persons in your ad suggest?* Would this image have anything to do with manipulating the viewer? If there are both male and female models in the ad, be sure to see what roles they are playing. For example, are they traditional (husband and wife) or more modern (young business people)? Is there anything about the way men or women are presented that indicates stereotyping?

6. *Does your advertisement play upon any fears, guilt, insecurities, or romantic or sexual fantasies a person might have?* If so, what are they, and how does the ad work to manipulate the viewer's feelings? *Hint:* consider how many deodorant or cleaning product ads use guilt or embarrassment to appeal to a viewer's insecurities.

From your notes in this examination phase, you should focus on the two most prominent aspects of manipulation and gather any further information related to them.

Block your material, keeping in mind the necessity of making two strong points about the advertisement. Try to include one paragraph that reaches for a higher philosophical plane than mere description. You might think about the long-term effect that ads such as yours might have on the general public. Are there any negative possibilities or dangers? Is there any effort to mislead the public?

Some Tips on Choosing an Advertisement

Certain ads, by the nature of the products they advertise, are highly manipulative. Some of the more manipulative ads include those for cigarettes; liquor; luxury goods such as expensive cars, furs, and jewelry; and beauty products.

WRITING IN FIVE SPECIAL SITUATIONS

The next seven writing exercises feature types of writing projects commonly assigned to college students. While you are in school, you will probably write these types of papers either for in-class examinations or for take-home compositions. The five categories include papers that ask for the following types of writing:

1. Observation

2. Evaluation

3. Compare–Contrast

4. Pro–Con

5. Writing about *Other* Writing: the Summary, the Commentary, and the Evaluation or Critique

THE OBSERVATION PAPER

Introduction

Many classes in school, as well as many jobs or professions, require that a person be a good observer. A fine way to develop this valuable skill is by writing observation papers. In general, such papers fall into two groups:

1. *The scientific observation paper, emphasizing what is actually observed by the senses.* The observer/writer must be thorough and neutral and must cite specific evidence or observations: "Students in the cafeteria threw cigarette butts and paper napkins on the floor." *Not* "The students in the cafeteria were too messy." "Messy" is a personal interpretation or judgment, not an objective, scientific statement about behavior. Instead of using a formal topic sentence, the introduction section of this kind of paper would most likely provide the basics: the place, the date, and time, and the overall reason or motive for the observation. The development would then describe the scene thoroughly.

2. *The combination observation paper, blending objective scientific observation—what was actually seen—with subjective or individual commentary, interpretation, and opinions—how you react or what it means.* This kind of

observation does allow a writer the latitude and freedom of a point of view, but the opinions and comments must still be firmly based in accurate observation of the scene. The more specific the writer/observer is, the more acceptable the point of view.

In either type of observation, data gathering is extremely important. Observing marine life in a specific area or the behavior patterns of a classroom of preschool children may require several pages of data gathering, instead of only part of one page. The major change in the model prewriting sheet reflects the fact that data gathering must be expanded.

A Prewriting Model for the Observation Paper

Sample Assignment: Choose a small area of your campus, community, or home to observe for at least 30 minutes. The area should be small enough that you can stay in one spot to watch and write without strain. The library, the cafeteria, a shopping area, a park, and your backyard are all possible sites. Develop a five-paragraph essay that combines what you observed with your commentary and interpretation of the scene.

Prewriting has been modified to allow for the gathering of more visual and other sensory data and to comment on the data recorded. Study the student's sample entries carefully.

After getting situated, the writer notes what is actually seen (left column) and the impressions that emerge (area at right).

PREWRITING

Observation Site: *Midtown Airport Cut-Rate Airlines Gate #5*

Date: *May 15, 1987* Time Begun: *1 pm* Time Ended: *1:30 pm*

Observations	Comments/Remarks
Large, well-lighted room w/ glass walls all around.	*Made room very pleasant + cheerful.*
Plenty of bright green plastic chairs—so no one had to stand.	

Observations	Comments/Remarks
Ash trays—3 waste cans. No plants. 3 small counters w/no personnel.	*Seemed to be an off-time/ no planes coming or going.*
Small groups of people— approx. 45–55 of all types. 5 of the men conserv. dressed w/ briefcases; same for 3 women.	*Business people?*
5–6 kids under 10 yrs. running around; noses to glass watching planes or playing "planes." others watching them.	*People seemed to enjoy watching them.*
Open spaces plus carpeting very good for running + falling—no injuries. Mothers/fathers seemed calm.	*Kids appear to have best time—fascin. by planes + each other!*

At the end of 30 minutes or so, check over the data in both columns. Watch for what seems to be emerging as your overall point of view of the observation. If you have made no comments after 30 minutes, this would be the time to add them.

Construct a thesis statement that includes the observation site and your most accurate point of view. The following is a possible thesis:

Possible Thesis: *Waiting for a plane at the Cut-Rate Airlines Terminal is quite pleasant, especially for children.*

The writer is now in a position to block the material with the help of the blocking sheet. Although this assignment may differ from earlier ones, the principles of the essay remain: the thesis statement, in addition to other introductory remarks, is placed in the first paragraph; the developmental paragraphs contain the various details to develop the writer's thesis. And the conclusion brings the observation to an official end, possibly by restating the main idea.

The next assignment will allow you to try your hand and your eye at an observation. Be sure that you have enough paper to last for the length of the observation.

 Exercise 3.14   THE OBSERVATION PAPER

Assignment: Choose a small area of your campus, community, or home to observe for at least 30 minutes. The area should be small enough so that you can stay in one spot to watch and write without strain. Develop a five-paragraph essay that combines *what* you have observed with your commentary and interpretation of the scene.

Understanding the Assignment

As you begin work on this project, be sure that you understand the distinction between factual observation (what you can see) and interpretation (what you think or conclude about what you saw).

Guidelines for Writing Your Paper

For your prewriting, follow the model presented on the previous pages.

The construction of your thesis is important in this paper because a point of view is not given to you in the assignment.

Weak: I visited the school gymnasium to observe what was going on.
(This sentence is not even a thesis because it has no angle or point of view.)

Better: On a Tuesday morning, the school gymnasium is bursting with activity.
(This sentence specifies the observation site as well as giving an interpretation. If properly developed, a paper with this thesis would focus upon ``bursting with activity.'')

Block your material and write your draft. By now, your instructor has probably returned several papers to you. Be sure to keep track of which errors you are making, whether errors of grammar or form, so that you can work on the problem areas in this paper and correct them.

THE EVALUATION PAPER

Introduction

Evaluation assignments or projects are required in all types of courses and in business and professional situations. The key to any evaluation paper is *judgment.*

Sitting in judgment on *anything* or *anyone,* however, carries responsibilities. As a writer, you need to take the time during prewriting to study whatever the assignment indicates in a careful and thorough manner just as a judge reviews a case being presented in court. The more careful the study, the more accurate the final judgment.

During your academic life, you may be asked to review many things and evaluate them: magazine articles or books, a film, or a television program. You might also be asked to judge areas of your own life or experience: how well you have performed as a student in a particular course or throughout the entire school term. A quick look at the newspaper or television will show how popular news media evaluation has become. Films and programs are rated by professional commentators as are politicians, social movements, restaurants, and so on. In the working world, as well, evaluation is extremely important, whether it concerns the productivity of a group of workers or the talents of the competition.

Because evaluation papers feature judgment, it is critical that you give enough time to prewriting. In this way, your eventual decision will be both accurate and reasonable. The next section includes a model of an evaluation assignment with its more extensive prewriting.

A Prewriting Model for the Evaluation Paper

Sample Assignment: Most people try to use their time productively in order to feel a sense of accomplishment and satisfaction. How would you evaluate your current use of time? Do you feel satisfied that in the major areas of your life you are using your time in a productive manner?

Unless a writer gathers extensive data on *how* her time is actually used, her judgment might not be accurate or convincing. When prewriting, then, the data gathering should expand to include a great deal of information about how you spend your time. Making a chart of an average week's schedule allows a more specific and dramatic evaluation of time usage.

The chart following is an example of such a weekly schedule.

	M	T	W	Th	F	Sat	Sun
6 AM	Up	Up	Up	Up	Up		
7						Up	
8	English	Work	English	Work	English	Chores–	Up
9	History	↓	History	↓	History	Domestic	
10	Math		Math		Math		Church
11	in library	↓	in library	↓	in library		
noon	Lunch	Lunch	Lunch	Lunch	Lunch	↓	with
1 PM	TV	TV	TV	TV	TV	↓	Family
2	↓	↓	↓	↓	↓	Lunch	↓
3	↓	↓	↓	↓	↓		
4	Work out	Work out	Work out	Work out	Work out	(open)	
5	↓	↓	↓	↓	↓		↓
6	Dinner	Dinner	Dinner	Dinner	Go out		Dinner
7	TV	Homework	TV	Homework	Social	Social	
8	↓	↓	↓	↓			Homework
9							↓
10	↓	↓	↓	↓			↓
11	Bed	Bed	Bed	Bed			Bed
midnight							
1					↓	↓	

To evaluate the material on the time schedule, add the hours in each major area so that you have a specific idea of just *how much* time is spent in each.

Fill in the total number of hours in each major category:

Education: __23__ hrs/week (includes __14__ Homework __9__ Classes)

Work: __8__ hrs/week

Social: __20__ hrs/week

Domestic: <u>6</u> hrs/week

Television: <u>23</u> hrs/week

Other: <u>10</u> hrs/week <u>*Work-out: run & exercise*</u>

(Write in what "Other" represents.)

Other refers to any other area such as transportation time if you drive a great deal, sports or exercise, meetings, family responsibilities, which account for a regular portion of your time. Include as many of these categories as you need.

To focus upon the demands of the assignment, the writer answers these questions:

1. What are the most important areas in your current schedule?

   a. <u>*education*</u>   b. <u>*work*</u>

2. Do you feel that you are productive in the above areas?

   Area 1 <u>*education*</u>:

   No! Grades are weak in history and algebra. I should devote afternoon or evening TV time to homework. Maybe less social life, too?

   Area 2 <u>*work*</u>:

   Yes! Schedule allows me to split time. I make extra money for books, supplies. Would be too tired to study if I worked more.

Before moving on to a thesis statement, some checking and analysis is in order. You could review the time chart to be sure that your entries are accurate. Then, check your addition so that your totals and the conclusions you reach are also correct.

Looking for point of view is still important, and for this assignment, it revolves around the idea of productivity. As you consider your answers to the two previous questions, be sure you have stated your case correctly. In this model, the person prewriting has a "split" point of view. In the area of education, the writer is not pleased with the productivity because time is being wasted. However, with respect to work, the situation is satisfactory. The writer's thesis statement will have to reflect this split type of decision.

Create a thesis statement that responds to the assignment. You must declare your final evaluation of the major areas of your schedule:

When I evaluate my current use of time, I see that I am doing well in one area but not in another.

With this as the thesis statement, the writer can then begin blocking prewriting ideas.

After studying this sample of prewriting for an evaluation paper, begin the next exercise. There you will evaluate *your own* productivity.

Exercise 3.15   THE EVALUATION PAPER

Assignment: How would you evaluate your current use of time? Do you feel satisfied that in the major areas of your life, you are using your time in a productive manner? Develop a five-paragraph essay in response to this topic.

Guidelines for Writing Your Paper:

Using the chart on page 125 as a guide, construct a schedule of how you spend your time. This will give you a solid, factual basis for your writing efforts. Follow the model in making your chart, adding up your hours, picking your main areas, and evaluating your productivity in those areas. Be sure that your thesis reflects an opinion about your productivity.

As you block your prewriting, be sure that each paragraph has a clear purpose. For example, the introductory paragraph should contain the thesis, mention the areas involved (if they are not already in the thesis), and supply any other background information. Developmental paragraphs may focus on individual areas.

When drafting, it is not advisable to write a paper that starts on Monday morning and works through Sunday night. Your sentences will get monotonous ("I do this; then I do that," and so on), and on days of similar activities you will sound repetitious. Remember, the writing goal is a discussion of your *productivity*, not of all your activities in an average week.

THE COMPARE-CONTRAST PAPER

Introduction

The compare–contrast paper is found in all areas of the curriculum because the technique of comparing and contrasting ideas, events, and people is very helpful in the process of learning. It is also a very common human activity. Although we may not always observe as closely as we should or take a side on a controversial issue, we nearly always compare and contrast ourselves with other people: how we dress, speak, think, drive, and raise children, just to name a few examples. And if we visit a new area or a foreign country, we probably spend considerable time comparing and contrasting elements of the lifestyle we see.

The compare–contrast method is also a natural learning tool because it forces a person to examine a topic in terms of relationships. For example, in a history or political science class, you might be asked to compare and contrast the political philosophies of Thomas Jefferson and Alexander Hamilton, two important shapers of policy in our nation. In an art history course, you could be asked to compare and contrast the styles of the French Impressionists Édouard Manet and Claude Monet. By the time you have finished discussing how Manet and Monet are alike (compare) and unlike (contrast), you will also better understand Impressionism as a form of artistic expression.

For a compare–contrast paper to be successful, the prewriting sheet should be modified to allow you to explore whatever is being compared and contrasted. In this way, you can begin to see the points or features held in common (the compare part) and the points or features that are different (the contrast part). The following modified prewriting sheet on eating styles allows you to do this.

A Prewriting Model for the Compare-Contrast Paper

Sample Assignment: Develop a five-paragraph essay that compares and contrasts your style of eating a meal with the style of another person.

Start with one diner or the other so that material on each side of the data-gathering chart shows a comparison.

Writer's style of eating:	*Other person's eating style:*
I enjoy salad or soup 1st—	*My friend Harry wants salad*
then main dish 2nd, and	*w/main dish—everything*
so on to dessert. Why?	*together for variety. Very*
don't like going from 1	*boring for him to eat 1*

type of temperature of
food to another or mixing
food on a plate. Very
unappetizing!

thing for 10–15 minutes

Try to time it so that 3
courses take 1–1½ hrs. I
like to savor food. I love it
and people should take
time to apprec. it, no
matter how busy.

Eats fast! Likes everything
but goes through it
quicker. Full dinner maybe
20 min! Says he's too
busy w/more important
matters than to stay at
the table.

Food is a special pleasure in
life.

Feels people tend to overdo
meal. They get carried
away with types of food.
There are too many better
activities to be pursued.

At this point, you can see three areas emerging from the data gathering:

1. The order in which a meal is consumed
2. The time allowed or speed at which food is eaten
3. An overall attitude toward food

In all three areas, the writer's style differs from—contrasts with—his friend Harry's style. About the only point in common is the fact that both need to eat to survive.

Aware of these points of contrast, this writer would create a thesis statement that reflects the situation:

Thesis Statement: *Being human, my friend Harry and I both have to eat, but our eating styles have very little in common.*

This writer would now be ready to block the material and begin work on the rough draft. In writing the opening paragraph, the writer would present the thesis statement and would also indicate that there are three basic areas in which the two contrast sharply. Here is a possible blocking scheme:

Introduction	*Thesis and mention of 3 areas of contrast. Also, identify Harry.*
1st Development	*Contrast how we consume meals— order. 1st do me, then H.*
2nd Development	*Contrast—speed element. 1st my pace, then H.*
3rd Development	*Contrast—overall philosophy of food/ dining. Me 1st, then H.*
Conclusion	*Maybe philosoph.—our differences in dining is one way we learn from each other and test each other's patience.*

Exercise 3.16   THE COMPARE–CONTRAST PAPER

> *Assignment:* Compare–contrast your style in *one* of the following areas—shopping, driv-
> ing, dressing, or studying—with the style of someone else whom you know.
> Develop a five-paragraph essay.

Understanding the Assignment

This project allows you to return to a more personal style, for you will be comparing your own
behaviors with those of another person. Although you may use the subjective *I,* avoid overusing
it or letting it dominate your sentences.

Guidelines for Writing Your Paper

Model your prewriting efforts after the sample just presented. This method helps you keep the
different characteristics you are examining in order. You will then be able to see how you differ
or match.

The construction of the thesis sentence is important, for you do not want to do any
heralding.

> *Weak:* In this paper, I will compare shopping styles between my best friend Millicent and
> me.

This sentence not only heralds but is dull and unimaginative with little indication of the angle to
be developed.

> *Better:* Although we are the best of friends, Millicent and I have absolutely nothing in
> common as shoppers.

With this effort, the writer states that although the two are close friends, they are entirely different as shoppers. The reader will be interested to find out how they differ and why.

After completing prewriting, begin blocking. If there is only one area of contrast between
the two of you, you could use the following blocking plan for your essay:

Introduction	*State the thesis and mention yourself, the other person, and the one area of difference between you.*

1st Development	*Describe the other person's behavior in this area and be as specific as possible.*
2nd Development	*Now, describe your behavior and the way in which it differs.*
3rd Development	*Discuss how this difference has affected your relationship.*
Conclusion	*Provide some sort of philosophical conclusion on the differences in human nature and behavior as shown by your example.*

If there are several areas in which you compare or contrast, follow this scheme:

Introduction	*State the thesis and mention three areas of comparison and contrast. Identify the other person.*
1st Development	*First area of comparison/contrast. First you, then other person.*
2nd Development	*Second area of comparison/contrast. First you, then other person.*

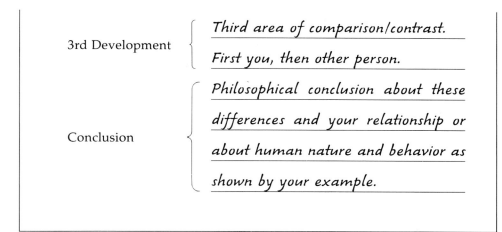

3rd Development	{	*Third area of comparison/contrast.*
		First you, then other person.
Conclusion	{	*Philosophical conclusion about these differences and your relationship or about human nature and behavior as shown by your example.*

Notice that the three developmental paragraphs all discuss you first and then the other person. This order could be reversed in each paragraph (the other, then you), but your organization will be clearer if the same order is used in *all* three paragraphs.

Proceed with your rough draft once you have a thesis and a blocking scheme. When you write, use transitional phrases like the following that naturally connect the ideas in compare–contrast papers: *by contrast, however, on the other hand, similarly.* (You may wish to review the material on transitional phrasing in Unit IV (see pp. 193–200).

THE PRO-CON PAPER

Introduction

The editorial page of your local newspaper is a fine place to get a feel for the pro–con (for or against) type of writing. Such writing takes a stand, often a strong one, on an issue such as one of these:

care of the environment	experimentation on animals
nuclear power	prayer in public schools
capital punishment	arms control

Pro–con papers can be appealing because many of us enjoy expressing our beliefs and, in the process, trying to convince our readers that we are right. However, a paper of this kind has a danger. What you as a writer want to avoid is jumping to one side of the issue without first gathering enough data to *support* your opinion. When you jump too quickly without enough support, your readers will not be convinced that your opinions are right.

Prewriting will help you gather the data to support your views. If you receive an assignment and find yourself formulating an opinion, then test it by gathering data. If you are able to generate enough information to support your opinion and if your opinion is well thought out, you can proceed to writing out your thesis and to blocking. On the other hand, if you are not able to write very much or if your opinion is weak, you need to rethink your response.

To help yourself with the pro–con mode of writing, try thinking of yourself as an attorney preparing a case. The "client" is your own point of view, and your "jury" is the reader who needs to be convinced of the correctness and worthiness of your opinion. The prewriting model will help you generate an opinion and evaluate its strength.

A Prewriting Model for the Pro–Con Paper

Sample Assignment: Some critics of the various colleges (two- and four-year) say that no one who reads below a certain level should be admitted. Would you be in favor of setting up such a limitation to college admission? Whether you argue pro or con, explain your opinion.

The writer reads the assignment to grasp its guidelines and reaches a tentative decision:

Tentative Topic: *No restrictions on college admission*

Now comes some data gathering to see if this line of thinking can be supported:

Colleges should be humane places for learning.

Don't want a lock-step type of system; compare schools where students are denied access—not very democratic.

What about adult—out of school and a little rusty? No retraining or relearning if reading is weak?

At this point it is important to evaluate the data gathering, especially the tentative opinion itself. One of the best ways to do so is by asking this type of question:

If my opinion were literally interpreted or became a law, could any trouble result?

Arguing in favor of *no* restrictions means that *no one* can be denied admittance for any reason. It would therefore be possible for a person who cannot read at all to enter college. What would the college have to do to accommodate this type of student? Obviously, many new classes would need to be offered—a big expense for the school. Who would pay for these new programs? Should they be offered at colleges—or should they be given elsewhere, such as at high school evening programs? How would a student who could not read at all function at the college level? A student with no reading skills would probably feel very uncomfortable in a college environment. As you can see, evaluating the initial opinion creates many new questions.

This writer now has to make a decision about the choice of opinion. Here are some of the options available:

1. Staying with the original opinion.

2. Changing the opinion to argue for the other side.

3. Keeping the original opinion but qualifying it to make it more workable and acceptable.

Choices 1 and 2 represent the extremes; choice 3 is a type of compromise that recognizes the complexity of the issue. The writer decides in favor of the third option and this revised opinion:

Revised Topic: *Colleges should admit people if their reading levels are at least in the high school range.*

Data gathering on the new choice:

The opinion would still be humane, especially for those needing to brush up a bit on reading skills.

The revised opinion would also be fairer to the school's budget and to the student—school could still offer higher education but without so much strain to meet everybody's needs—student needing only a little extra work would feel at home in the environment.

Good compromise: some restriction but not so much that the system is too rigid.

Would also be better for those people who might test a bit lower than their actual skill levels.

More data gathering for specific details could be done to expand each of the previous points. Remember that the success of a pro–con paper rests largely on how well thought out your opinion is. If your opinion is too simplistic, then the strength of the entire paper is affected.

In the event, however, that you select one of the extremes of an issue, you need to anticipate criticism from your opposition. (Keep in mind the attorney analogy.) With respect to the original opinion in the model, the writer would have to explain how a totally accessible college is better. Or, if the opposite position were taken, the writer would have to explain convincingly why admitting no one below a college reading level is desirable.

 Exercise 3.17   THE PRO–CON PAPER

Assignment: Write a five-paragraph essay on a social issue or problem about which you are particularly aware or concerned. Express your opinion, and explain why your ideas are valid and worthy of support.

Understanding the Assignment:

Be sure that your statement of opinion (your thesis) appears in the first paragraph so that you have sufficient space to provide support for your idea. The topic specified, "a social issue or problem," embraces virtually anything worth the consideration of a group of people in a society.

Guidelines for Writing Your Paper:

Start by making a list of social issues or problems. Use what you have learned from reading, class lectures, or the news media to supply ideas. Remember, however, that the assignment directs you to select something about which you are "particularly aware or concerned."

When you make your choice of issue, formulate your opinion. Remember that your opinion may be an extreme view or that it may be a compromise: (1) totally in favor; (2) totally opposed; (3) in favor, but with some restrictions; or (4) opposed, but with some restrictions.

Be sure to evaluate your choice of opinion. Regardless of where you stand on the issue, provide as much specific information or explanation as you can.

When you block your paper, be sure that each of the developmental paragraphs has a purpose and does not merely repeat the content of the others.

WRITING ABOUT THE WRITING OF OTHERS

Introduction

Many times during your college career, you will need to write in response to the written work of another person. These written works could include magazine or newspaper articles, special documents, or books. In one sense, the greeting card and advertisement assignments done earlier called on outside sources, but these were more visual than written. When the outside source consists strictly of printed material, your job becomes more complex.

On the one hand, you must thoroughly absorb and comprehend the source material. Imagine the consequences of misinterpreting some part of an article you were writing about. If any or all of your final paper is based on a misreading of the outside source, the credibility of your entire effort is open to question.

On the other hand, you need to keep your own identity or voice as you absorb the outside material. If it were not for our imitative talents, humans would never learn language or many other behaviors. However, this ability can prove dangerous when you read the work of other writers. You might sometimes unintentionally copy the words or even the style of the other writer. At other times, you may lose track of how that person's ideas are distinct from your own.

In this section we provide general guidelines for dealing with these writing situations and three writing projects to perfect your skills.

Using Expository Sources

Expository may be an unfamiliar word, but nearly all of the writing that is featured in textbooks, journals, newspapers, and magazines is expository in nature. Basically, exposition is factual discussion or argument in support of some thesis or controlling idea. In fact, most of the work in your courses (other than literature or creative writing) will involve outside sources that are expository. When you are asked to deal directly with an outside source of this kind, experiment with any or all of the following strategies:

1. *Plan for time to read and reread the material.* Even if your instructor talked about the article or book in class, you must read the assigned material between three and five times, especially if the work is highly technical, complex, or unfamiliar. If you are confused, it is likely to show in your paper, so read carefully and persistently!

2. *Vary your reading strategy.* First, read at your regular reading rate. *Second,* read again but slow down. Keep a dictionary at hand so that you can look up any word whose meaning is unknown or unclear. Read key passages aloud to facilitate your understanding. Mark the main points or take notes as you read. Lastly, a third, fourth, or fifth reading could be done on the following day when your mind is fresh. By this time, you should be formulating some possible responses to the assignment.

3. *Read with the requirements of your assignment in mind.* Reading in this way helps you to keep your purpose in mind. In reading complex material, you may lose sight of what you have to do for the assignment. Therefore, keep a copy of the assignment in front of you while you are reading and refer to it frequently.

4. *Be sure that you understand what kind of writing response you are expected to make.* Listed below are three kinds of writing you may be asked to produce in response to expository material.

The Summary   If your instructor wishes you to summarize an article, for example, then you must thoroughly absorb the author's thesis and supporting points. When you write your summary, you will present the main points of the article in a short piece of writing. If you are assigned to write only a one-paragraph summary, you must choose your words carefully, providing only the thesis and major supporting points. A longer summary would allow you to include additional supporting material. When you summarize, you remain neutral; only the content of the material, not your opinion of it, is included.

The Commentary   Unlike the summary, this kind of paper allows you far greater freedom of self-expression. Although you still must absorb the expository source, a commentary allows you to express a point of view in relation to any part of the material. The writer who comments is like the news commentator who discusses the story just reported. For example, if you read an article about the rapid destruction of the Amazon rain forest, you may choose to reflect on the sacrifice of so many forests or wilderness areas in your own nation to the automobile or to housing tracts. Commentaries may take negative, positive, or mixed points of view, depending on your response to the material.

The Evaluation or Critique   In a very real sense, the evaluation or critique is a type of commentary. However, the terms *evaluation* and *critique* carry with them the ideas of weak or strong and good or bad. All these approaches involve judgment in a serious way. Like many writers, you may enjoy expressing yourself in this kind of paper. Nevertheless, remember that when you call something or someone weak or poor in quality, you have a major responsibility to support your reasoning and explain specifically *why* you evaluated as you did.

5. *When you write about other writing, use your introductory paragraph to provide vital details.* Assume that you are writing a critique of a newspaper article. In a short paper, footnotes are not used, so it becomes necessary for you to acknowledge your writing source as shown below:

New York Times staff writer Joel Doe has written a misleading, one-sided account of the urban poor. His recent article (September 10, 1988, p. 34) entitled "Urban Poverty—Another Look" actually does more harm than good in attempting to explain the problem to his readers.

These two sentences, plus a few others, would appear in the opening paragraph. This opening would make sure that a reader clearly understands that the paper is about the work of another writer who is identified. In a research paper, you would list footnotes at the bottom of the page or on a special note page at the end of the paper to acknowledge important details.

6. *As you draft or edit developmental paragraphs, be sure there is no confusion between your material and that supplied by the author about whose work you are writing.* Many articles or books contain percentages or other statistics important to the overall topic. If the other author provides these statistics and you wish to use them, acknowledge the source of your figures in the wording of your sentences.

Poor: Three out of five marriages in the country end in divorce.

Better: According to the author, three out of five. . . . or, Harris states that three out of five marriages. . . .

In these two examples you would not have to use quotation marks as long as the statistics were blended into the normal flow of the sentence and not quoted or copied verbatim. Crediting the author in this way serves two purposes: It recognizes the original author's contribution. Second, it protects you in case the author was wrong.

7. *Avoiding plagiarism.* Plagiarizing is copying from another person's original material. Some people plagiarize deliberately, but it is also possible to copy *unintentionally* the tone, style, or language of the original. This can occur when you have immersed yourself in a particular article or piece of writing for some time. Then, when you write, the language and style are not your own. When drafting and editing, take a little time to look for this phenomenon, and make any necessary changes before you begin the final copy. In this way you will avoid unintentional plagiarism.

Each of the next three writing exercises presents written material as the source for your essay.

 Exercise 3.18   THE SUMMARY OF ANOTHER'S WRITING

Assignment: Summarize in one paragraph the editorial entitled ''What Are We Waiting For?'' Aim for a paragraph of one-half to three-quarters of a page in length. Guidelines for writing this paper follow the editorial.

What Are We Waiting For?

ANN WELLS

My brother-in-law opened the bottom drawer of my sister's bureau and lifted out a tissue-wrapped package.

"This," he said, "is not a slip. This is lingerie." He discarded the tissue and handed me the slip. It was exquisite; silk, handmade and trimmed with a cobweb of lace. The price tag with an astronomical figure on it was still attached.

"Jan bought this the first time we went to New York, at least eight or nine years ago. She never wore it. She was saving it for a special occasion. Well, I guess this is the occasion."

He took the slip from me and put it on the bed with the other clothes we were taking to the mortician. His hands lingered on the soft material for a moment, then he slammed the drawer shut and turned to me.

"Don't ever save anything for a special occasion. Every day you're alive is a special occasion."

I remembered those words through the funeral and the days that followed when I helped him and my niece attend to all the sad chores that follow an unexpected death. I thought about them on the plane returning to California from the Midwestern town where my sister's family lives. I thought about all the things that she hadn't seen or heard or done. I thought about the things that she had done without realizing that they were special.

I'm still thinking about his words, and they've changed my life. I'm reading more and dusting less. I'm sitting on the deck and admiring the view without fussing about the weeds in the garden. I'm spending more time with my family and friends and less time in committee meetings.

Whenever possible, life should be a pattern of experience to savor, not endure. I'm trying to recognize these moments now and cherish them.

I'm not "saving" anything; we use our good china and crystal for every special event—such as losing a pound, getting the sink unstopped, the first camellia blossom.

I wear my good blazer to the market if I feel like it. My theory is if I look prosperous, I can shell out $28.49 for one small bag of groceries without wincing.

I'm not saving my good perfume for special parties; clerks in hardware

---

Ann Wells is a columnist with Ingersoll Publications.

stores and tellers in banks have noses that function as well as my partygoing friends'.

"Someday" and "one of these days" are losing their grip on my vocabulary. If it's worth seeing or hearing or doing, I want to see and hear and do it *now.*

I'm not sure what my sister would have done had she known that she wouldn't be here for the tomorrow we all take for granted. I think she would have called family members and a few close friends. She might have called a few former friends to apologize and mend fences for past squabbles. I like to think she would have gone out for a Chinese dinner, her favorite food. I'm guessing—I'll never know.

It's those little things left undone that would make me angry if I knew that my hours were limited. Angry because I put off seeing good friends whom I was going to get in touch with—someday. Angry because I hadn't written certain letters that I intended to write—one of these days. Angry and sorry that I didn't tell my husband and daughter often enough how much I truly love them.

I'm trying very hard not to put off, hold back, or save anything that would add laughter and luster to our lives.

And every morning when I open my eyes I tell myself that it is special.

Understanding the Assignment

When you summarize the work of another author, you *restate,* in your own words, the basic content or meaning of the writing. Summaries vary in length, but in general, they mention the main idea and include some discussion of the supporting material provided by the author. The shorter the summary, the more selective you must be when deciding which supportive details are worth mentioning. You need to maintain your *neutrality* when you summarize: do not provide or include your personal opinion of the article.

Guidelines for Writing Your Paper

Read the material three to five times, making sure you have absorbed the content thoroughly. Use the dictionary if you encounter unfamiliar words, and read aloud if you reach a passage that is difficult to understand.

Before you begin prewriting, ask yourself these questions:

1. What prompted the author to write this article?

2. What was this writer trying to say? What is the thesis?

3. What kinds of support does the writer provide for the thesis—factual, emotional, or rational?

4. Is the writer directing the writing to any particular audience such as men or women or to people of a certain age or with certain interests?

Record your responses. These questions and your responses will help you to restate the article's content *in your own words* and will make it less likely that you accidentally plagiarize (copy) the writer's language or style.

In a summary, your thesis statement generally incorporates the full title of the article, the author's name, and an overall description of the content.

> *Weak:* This article is by Ann Wells and is called ''What Are We Waiting For?'' (no description)

> *Better:* Ann Well's article ''What Are We Waiting For?'' tells of the importance of _____. (description)

Decide what supporting material is important enough to include. Keep in mind that you do not have much space and must choose your words carefully. In writing your rough draft, write in the present tense. Once printed, a word *exists* and remains accessible, even if the author should die.

> *Weak:* In ''What Are We Waiting For?'' Ann Wells *wrote* of . . . (past tense)

> *Better:* In ''What Are We Waiting For?'' Ann Wells *writes* of . . . (present tense)

When your first draft is completed, read it aloud to hear how your sentences blend and whether you have done a reasonable job of explaining the main point of the original article. You may also wish to reread the article to see whether you have captured its essence in your draft.

As you edit your paper, give your attention to the following questions:

1. Have you maintained your neutrality?

2. Have you included the author's name and the title of the work, all properly spelled?

Exercise 3.19   WRITING A COMMENTARY ON ANOTHER WRITER'S WORK

> *Assignment:* The article reprinted below deals with a relatively modern phenomenon in some areas of our culture. Read the article in the manner suggested in the introduction to this section. Then write a five-paragraph essay that *comments on* one of the opinions or ideas expressed. Guidelines for this assignment follow the article.

The Kids Who Won't Leave Home

AUDREY C. FOOTE

1. Along with all the other miseries of the modern woman's middle years there is a predicament which has been a favorite motif of syndicated psychologists in the last few years. They call it the Empty Nest Syndrome. Just in case there is anyone out there who hasn't heard about it, this quaintly labeled malady is the devastating depression of the mother whose children have all grown up and left home. But current sociology is now questioning this dilemma. Delia Ephron, in *Esquire*, writes that three national surveys have exposed the Empty Nest Syndrome as a pious fiction. And Patricia Williams, in the New York *Times*, asserts, "Women whose children have grown up and gone are found to be happier than women of the same age who are still mothering on a daily basis." "The Empty Nest syndrome," she says, "is for the birds."

2. While I read these findings with interest, I am suspicious of those neat categories "children who have grown up and left home" and "mothering on a daily basis." There is a universe of nuances between those two extremes. *Whose* empty nest? I thought with only a twinge of irony as I looked up from the *Times* to see two of my children playing Mastermind at the coffee table, another slouched by the stereo replacing Vivaldi with James Taylor, and the fourth bent over his math at the dining room table. A traditional heartwarming family vignette, except for the fact that apart from the youngest, age eleven, not one will ever again celebrate his or her twenty-first birthday. And yet for a considerable portion of this past year, as in the years before, they have all been, both *de jure* and *de facto*, residents at home.

3. Like parents of the past, my husband and I assumed when our children went off to college that it was an irrevocable break. It has turned out that entry into college was not the final flight from home but merely a four-year intermission.

4. Eight years ago, when our oldest left for Harvard, I produced an elaborate dinner at which I lachrymosely observed that this might well be the last time, at least as part of the daily routine, that we six would dine together. We have had quite a number of such valedictory dinners since, but they have become mere pretexts for a party since we all now know that the youth leaving today may be back in a month and departing again the next, equally inconclusively. Had I foreseen this state of affairs, say ten years ago, I might well have

assumed that it would brand me as a Philip Wylie-style Mom, and my children as emotional and social retards. Fortunately, in the intervening years I've had the benefit of the experience of friends with slightly older children. From observing them I've learned that to have grown children living at home is not necessarily a Freudian failing or an ethnic joke but rather a new "lifestyle" of the 1970s. As we stood with bulging grocery bags on the porch of Sewards Market in Menemsha this summer, a friend observed, "In the fifties the kids went to college and got married when they graduated or else took an apartment with a pal of the same sex; in the sixties they dropped out, made leather sandals, and lived in communes. But now, why, they aren't even *living together!*"

5. The first hint of this peculiar change in youthful mores came to me a few years ago when I had tea with a friend in the library of her five-story Washington town house. Sally had always been a kind of bellwether for me as she progressed through the maternal miseries and splendors of the 1960s. She had accepted her children's idealistic but often dangerous involvements with awesome equanimity. But that day she mentioned that her oldest son had come home for an apparently indefinite stay, and remarked, "I simply don't understand it. He has a lovely girl with a nice little apartment in Georgetown who I know would be delighted to share it with him." Not long afterward I learned that they had sold their handsome mansion and moved into a chic but minuscule apartment nearby. The big house kept being broken into and robbed when they were traveling, Sally first explained. This was indeed true, but she later confessed it was also to elude all their postgraduate children who simply *would* keep coming back to camp in their old bedrooms, appearing hopefully at mealtimes and helplessly with armloads of dirty shirts.

6. Now in Sally's case this congregation of the young may well have been a deserved personal tribute, but in the following years I saw this bizarre exception become a trend and then finally a whole new alternative lifestyle. My neighbor has a twenty-eight-year-old son living at home and commuting to New York to his job in public relations; a friend of a friend in Monsey has two post-college daughters at home, one going to law school, the other a cocktail waitress. (The other innovation now is, I think, the diversity of occupations. Our children are as likely to be mechanics, carpenters, butchers, and policemen as doctors or lawyers; often there are both extremes in a family. My friend in Croton has one son who is a newspaper writer, another who is a moving man. The latter's girlfriend is a doctor and her sister is going to clown school. Their friends have produced a geologist, a magazine editor, and a short-order cook. Of my own grown children, the oldest is a postal clerk, one sister is in publishing, and the other is studying to become a costume designer. This does make life interesting, for the parents as well. Former routine inquiries at large cocktail parties concerning the offspring of acquaintances are answered no longer with prideful accounts of progress at the Chase Manhattan but often with piquant incongruities. I encountered one the other night: the older boy was already a famous rock star—*really* famous; even I had heard him on the radio—while the younger son was a nurse.) But however original and various their *metiers*, a great many of the young people we know are living in the family home.

7. We mothers quite often ask ourselves how and why this has happened. Except in classic cliché cases of flagrant Oedipal attachment or literal incompetence, the primary motive appears to be quite simple—to save money. Nothing is ever quite that simple, however. The young have always needed to save money, but in the past they would have sold themselves piece by piece—in futurity—to medical schools rather than move back home. This phenomenon must be related to another trend, the tendency to postpone marriage or even the commitment of living together. Like the costume of dirty jeans and unisex haircuts, it may be one of Nature's sneaky ways of exerting population control. But in any case, it is made feasible surely by the fact that home is an easier place to return to now that mother and father aren't so punctilious about schedules, dress codes, and table manners. The children drift in and out with often maddening insouciance.

8. I hardly ever know just how many places to lay on the table; be it breakfast or dinner, or whose socks are whirling around in the dryer. The dog starts to wag her tail and grin at no matter what hour the front door creaks open. Nor have I figured out an appropriate answer to phone calls for the children, even the 3 A.M. ones, other than to mumble, "Well, I don't know whether she's here, I suppose I might find her." A yet older generation might think this feckless, but one would feel just *silly*, I think, expressing concern for the safety or doubt about the resourcefulness of the son or daughter who has hitchhiked through Nigeria or backpacked in Nepal.

9. And as for the inconvenience, one brings that on oneself, of course, if one can't get the knack of being "laid back," or "hanging loose"; the kids don't care if they go without supper, miss phone calls and buses, have to wear the same shirt four days in a row. Other than employing the *force majeure* of "for *my* sake, then," which one needs to keep in reserve to forestall schemes like weekend parachute jumping, there is nothing a parent can say or do short of expulsion. Occasionally we sulk a little, but mostly we come to take it all in stride, with only a stumble now and then. Therefore it is obvious that the modern home offers a number of conveniences, even pleasures, and only a manageable number of "hassles." So it is after all no mystery that the children keep coming home. The real question is, Why do we let them in?

10. For the parents the situation can be a trying one. The first thing one notices is the matter of diminishing physical space. A house which once comfortably contained two adults and three to five children with rooms and furniture adequate to their size, has to accommodate five to seven big people, all adults at least in physique. These new grown-ups need large beds in place of cots, cribs, or convertibles, large closets, extra showers, and cupboards for their curling irons. Moreover, returning from their colleges and apartments, they import the funky furnishings of those temporary digs. Our basement and attic, once repositories for tools, storm windows, Christmas decorations, and old love letters, now bulge and buckle with Coca-Cola cartons filled with books and records, electric hot plates, mini-fridges, toaster ovens, fans, rolls of posters and remnant rugs, two guitars, four sets of skis, and a canoe. What a garage sale! I think wistfully; the proceeds could easily pay off the mortgage. But alas, not one

item of this vast commercial cornucopia can be sold or even given away, since the time will come when it will be shoehorned back into the weary station wagon or U-Haul and driven off many miles away to adorn yet another room.

11. Sometimes muttering "Om" and standing in that basement, which looks like a Green Stamp warehouse or backstage at a giveaway quiz show, I reflect that despite their jeans and rubber sandals, and their proudly proletarian occupations (my son was shocked when my husband once said to him, "Working in the post office isn't proletarian—it's petty bourgeois"), our children live in some ways on a more elevated economic scale than we do—at least in terms of material acquisition. Even as I type here I am tapping, gratefully, on Victoria's Smith-Corona electric with power return instead of on my $65 portable. I am wearing Valerie's Bulova Accutron, which she passed on to me when she got a watch she liked better. Beside me is our oldest's tape recorder, borrowed and not returned since he has a more elaborate model upstairs. In the next room is his Zenith color TV; our own Sears black and white portable with its wobbly rabbit ears now lives in the attic. Stereos, ten-speed bikes, Japanese cameras, calculators, hairdryers, they have them all, often in duplicate.

12. But then I remind myself that 1) many of these baubles were given by us as Christmas or birthday presents or awards for academic achievements; 2) the rest, the kids bought for themselves with money earned at jobs we would not have endured at their age; 3) the children are generous in sharing them or even giving them away, hand-me-ups, as they replace them with newer models; and 4) there is nothing much really to keep me from going out and buying at least some of these gadgets for *myself*—except for the fact that like most of my generation I did not grow up with these electronic marvels. We went off to college on *trains*—with *suitcases*. So we don't quite regard these things as necessities, and sometimes we can hardly master the intricacies of their operation. No, I begrudge the children not their possession of these tools and playthings but rather the space that they monopolize. The house swells and sags as they are moved in, is stripped and stark as they are moved out; one must be constantly making room or filling cavities.

13. After space, the major problem is transportation. Grown children living at home either still haven't learned to drive and must be chauffeured about or entrusted to their peers; *do* know how to drive but have no cars of their own and are thus invariably cruising in the parents' vehicle; do have a car/cars of their own so the driveway looks like a used-car lot and it requires the skill and recklessness of a parking attendant to get out of the garage. Actually, all these combinations have their inherent compensations. The nondrivers can be marooned at home occasionally to answer phones, welcome plumbers, or make yogurt. The carless drivers can often be bribed into collecting cat food or dry cleaning on their way to *Star Wars*. Those with multiple cars can serve as the family's private Hertz company when the station wagon—hernia'd from all that moving—is in the hospital. Our son, while not precisely forthcoming with his silver Mercedes or even his Volkswagen bug for petty chores like taking the golden retriever to the vet, carting costumes to our local amateur theater, or col-

lecting his younger brother who, the school nurse says, feels he's about to throw up, rises to the occasion when it is a question of a big mission. He is good for about one major moving job a season, and positively saintly about delivering and collecting his sisters at the airport. (Money saved roughing it at home can be diverted into holidays.) This free limousine service is no small contribution to my own leisure time and peace of mind.

14. One last problem for the mother with resident grown children is the extra housework involved, most of which invariably falls upon her *if she is at home.* Many of us have discovered that proviso and have renounced gardening and gourmet dinners for two and begun stampeding offices, boutiques, and graduate schools, which in their mercy often let us in. All statistics show that more middle-aged women are entering the work force; it has been naively assumed that a large segment are trying to escape the doldrums of an empty nest. *Au contraire!* Lots I know have abandoned housewifery to make room in that nest for all the returnees and to help pay for the extra wheat germ and long-distance phone calls. (Characteristic episode: Phone rings. Our son, age twenty-six, picks it up. Operator asks, "Is this Mr. Foote?" Short pause. Judicious answer "That depends.") But above all, the mother's flight from home is a means of decently ducking the dishes and the dusting, which somehow manage to get done by someone else in her absence but *never* in her presence. Or, if not, who notices after dark and a long day in the office?

15. In spite of the crowding, chauffeuring, and extra housework, there are rewards in having the children home again: they help with engine rattles, making rum cake, and pinning up hems, and they provide company for afternoon tea and Scrabble. What's more, one learns so much. After all those years of teaching them skills—shoelace tying, New Math, souffle baking, and parallel parking—how satisfying to learn a few from them, like putting on mascara, raising a spinnaker, and basic yoga.

16. My husband, who relishes having all the children under our roof, cherishes illusions, which periodically soar into ambitions, of making this arrangement not merely a sometime pleasure but also an economic asset like the traditional farm family. He visualizes us turning our collective talents to some sort of cottage industry. The girls have always made ingenious family gifts from various *objets trouvés*, flotsam and jetsam of the Hudson River or our neighbors' curbside offerings to Goodwill. Valerie once got a citation "Worthy" at a county fair for her apple pie; her first try, too. And as an assistant den mother I have helped make medieval castles from milk cartons, egg boxes, and beer-can tabs. So the children's father dreams of us all clustered, chortling, in a revamped corner of our dank and crowded basement, turning out boudoir wastebaskets covered with flocked wallpaper, pickled picture frames, jars of jam from our dying quince tree, velvet-covered jewel cases created from cigar boxes, scissors-holders from sequined tennis-ball cans, and decoupage umbrella stands from transmogrified plastic Clorox bottles. Our attic groans under the weight of empty but promising coffee tins, wooden cheese cartons, oatmeal boxes, and samples of tweed suit materials received in the mail. We will sell our creations in the local

boutiques or antique shops—on consignment, if necessary—or perhaps peddle them door-to-door. (Actually, our only entrepreneurial success is Andrew, who at age seven borrowed a pound of peat moss from our neighbors, put two level tablespoons in each of a stack of plastic Baggies, and sold them to the other neighbors for a quarter a shot.) Or better still, we will market them by mail order. My husband is quite prepared to leave his editorial job in the city to help Victoria, who has studied Chinese calligraphy, and Valerie, who does etchings, concoct a catalogue. When these fits come upon him, usually during snowstorms, torrential rains, or heat waves, and at breakfast just before train time, the children and I pat him fondly on the arm and hand him his briefcase. After all, he has all those mouths to feed.

Understanding the Assignment

In this commentary you are allowed great freedom to respond in virtually any way you choose as long as your response is based on a solid comprehension of what Foote actually says or suggests. Therefore, you must read the article carefully. In addition, the assignment requires that you comment on only one opinion or idea. This will give your essay a specific focus.

Guidelines for Writing Your Paper

Because this article features a high level of vocabulary in addition to some foreign phrasing, consult your dictionary as you read. To get prewriting started and to find a direction for your commentary, ask yourself the following questions and record your responses on a separate sheet of paper.

1. What is Foote's thesis? Do I agree with it?

2. What advantages do grown offspring have when they live at home? What disadvantages?

3. What advantages and disadvantages are there for parents when their grown offspring move back home?

4. Do I have experiences that parallel any of those she mentions?

5. How do I feel about the phenomenon of grown offspring staying at home once college is completed?

6. Have I read any material in history, psychology, sociology, or marriage and family classes to shed light on this area?

7. Is it healthy for an individual or society to "return to the nest" even though the person could be self-supporting?

In writing your introduction, be sure to mention the full title of the article and its author, and give a brief description of the contents of the article. Be sure that you provide a thesis that shows what your line of thought will be in the commentary.

Weak: One of the most interesting aspects of the Foote article is the author's husband's opinion of the family unit.

(This is too vague to be a thesis. What is the husband's opinion? How is it interesting?)

Better: In my estimation, Foote's husband is hopelessly old-fashioned when he visualizes the entire adult family unit working under one roof to support itself.

In the introduction, include other sentences that will help to refine and direct your thesis statement and lead to the first developmental paragraph.

When you edit, be sure to check all pertinent aspects, including your style. You want to make sure that *your* text does not intentionally copy Foote's. If you quoted the author directly, be sure to acknowledge this borrowing by using quotation marks. (See p. 331 in Unit V for a discussion of the use of quotation marks.)

Exercise 3.20   CHOOSING FROM A VARIETY OF WRITING ASSIGNMENTS

Assignment: The following passage, reprinted from a larger work by Malcolm X, is personal in nature. In it, he writes of the struggle to communicate in writing and how the dictionary, in particular, became enormously helpful in reaching his goal.

This assignment differs in that it presents several writing choices. Discussion of the assignment plus guidelines for this type of writing appear after the Malcolm X article.

After reading the article, begin work on a five-paragraph essay that responds to *one* of the following assignments:

1. Focus on one area in your own life where you had to struggle—or are still struggling—to achieve success or self-determination. Possible areas might involve learning a new language, raising children, mastering a skill such as grammar, learning to cook, or staying on a budget or a diet.

2. After he began reading, Malcolm X writes that he ''never had been so truly free.'' This may seem an astonishing statement to many who consider reading a chore. In a five-paragraph paper, concentrate on the freedoms that reading can bring. What sort of freedom have you experienced? What about Malcolm X? Explain your freedoms thoroughly.

3. In a sense, being in prison gave Malcolm X one critical commodity in abundance—time—to copy the dictionary, absorb new words, and read voraciously. For people not in prison, however, time is very limited. What program would you suggest for people who work full-time and are self-supporting but who still wish to improve their command of English? Discuss not only what you would have these people do with their precious free time but why your plans would be effective.

The Autobiography of Malcolm X

MALCOLM X WITH ALEX HALEY

I became increasingly frustrated at not being able to express what I wanted to convey in letters that I wrote, especially those to Mr. Elijah Muhammad. In the street, I had been the most articulate hustler out there—I had commanded attention when I said something. But now, trying to write simple English, I not only wasn't articulate, I wasn't even functional. How would I sound writing in slang, the way I would *say* it, something such as, "Look, daddy, let me pull your coat about a cat, Elijah Muhammad—"

Many who today hear me somewhere in person, or on television, or those who read something I've said, will think I went to school far beyond the eighth grade. This impression is due entirely to my prison studies.

It had really begun back in the Charlestown Prison, when Bimbi first made me feel envy of his stock of knowledge. Bimbi had always taken charge of any conversation he was in, and I had tried to emulate him. But every book I picked up had few sentences which didn't contain anywhere from one to nearly all of the words that might as well have been in Chinese. When I just skipped those words, of course, I really ended up with little idea of what the book said. So I had come to the Norfolk Prison Colony still going through only book-reading motions. Pretty soon, I would have quit even these motions, unless I had received the motivation that I did.

I saw that the best thing I could do was get hold of a dictionary—to study, to learn some words. I was lucky enough to reason also that I should try to improve my penmanship. It was sad. I couldn't even write in a straight line. It was both ideas together that moved me to request a dictionary along with some tablets and pencils from the Norfolk Prison Colony school.

I spent two days just riffling uncertainly through the dictionary's pages. I'd never realized so many words existed! I didn't know *which* words I needed to learn. Finally, just to start some kind of action, I began copying.

In my slow, painstaking, ragged handwriting, I copied into my tablet everything printed on that first page, down to the punctuation marks.

I believe it took me a day. Then, aloud, I read back, to myself, everything

I'd written on the tablet. Over and over, aloud, to myself, I read my own handwriting.

I woke up the next morning, thinking about those words—immensely proud to realize that not only had I written so much at one time, but I'd written words that I never knew were in the world. Moreover, with a little effort, I also could remember what many of these words meant. I reviewed the words whose meanings I didn't remember. Funny thing, from the dictionary first page right now, that "aardvark" springs to my mind. The dictionary had a picture of it, a long-tailed, long-eared, burrowing African mammal, which lives off termites caught by sticking out its tongue as an anteater does for ants.

I was so fascinated that I went on—I copied the dictionary's next page. And the same experience came when I studied that. With every succeeding page, I also learned of people and places and events from history. Actually the dictionary is like a miniature encyclopedia. Finally the dictionary's A section had filled a whole tablet—and I went on into B's. That was the way I started copying what eventually became the entire dictionary. It went a lot faster after so much practice helped me to pick up handwriting speed. Between what I wrote in my tablet, and writing letters, during the rest of my time in prison I would guess I wrote a million words.

I suppose it was inevitable that as my word-base broadened, I could for the first time pick up a book and read and now begin to understand what the book was saying. Anyone who has read a great deal can imagine the new world that opened. Let me tell you something: from then until I left that prison, in every free moment I had, if I was not reading in the library, I was reading on my bunk. You couldn't have gotten me out of books with a wedge. Between Mr. Muhammad's teachings, my correspondence, my visitors—usually Ella and Reginald—and my reading of books, months passed without my even thinking about being imprisoned. In fact, up to then, I never had been so truly free in my life.

The Norfolk Prison Colony's library was in the school building. A variety of classes was taught there by instructors who came from such places as Harvard and Boston universities. The weekly debates between inmate teams were also held in the school building. You would be astonished to know how worked up convict debaters and audiences would get over subjects like "Should Babies Be Fed Milk?"

Available on the prison library's shelves were books on just about every general subject. Much of the big private collection that Parkhurst had willed to the prison was still in crates and boxes in the back of the library—thousands of old books. Some of them looked ancient: covers faded, old-time parchment-looking binding. Parkhurst, I've mentioned, seemed to have been principally interested in history and religion. He had the money and the special interest to have a lot of books that you wouldn't have in general circulation. Any college library would have been lucky to get that collection.

As you can imagine, especially in a prison where there was heavy emphasis on rehabilitation, an inmate was smiled upon if he demonstrated an unusually intense interest in books. There was a sizable number of well-read inmates, especially the popular debaters. Some were said by many to be practically walking encyclopedias. They were almost celebrities. No university would ask any student to devour literature as I did when this new world opened to me, of being able to read and *understand.*

I read more in my room than in the library itself. An inmate who was known to read a lot could check out more than the permitted maximum number of books. I preferred reading in the total isolation of my own room.

When I had progressed to really serious reading, every night at about ten P.M. I would be outraged with the "lights out." It always seemed to catch me right in the middle of something engrossing.

Fortunately, right outside my door was a corridor light that cast a glow into my room. The glow was enough to read by, once my eyes adjusted to it. So when "lights out" came, I would sit on the floor where I could continue reading in that glow.

At one-hour intervals the night guards paced past every room. Each time I heard the approaching footsteps, I jumped into bed and feigned sleep. And as soon as the guard passed, I got back out of bed onto the floor area of that light-glow, where I would read for another fifty-eight minutes—until the guard approached again. That went on until three or four every morning. Three or four hours of sleep a night was enough for me. Often in the years in the streets I had slept less than that. . . .

Understanding the Assignment

When presented with a choice of this sort, many students feel a sense of relief because they are not restricted to just one topic. However, making a choice can, in itself, consume valuable time. To use time wisely, use the following guidelines for dealing with assignments in which you must choose among several alternatives.

Guidelines for Writing Your Paper

Start prewriting early! If you say to yourself, "I've got all week to do this paper," then you are not giving yourself very forceful directives. But by setting a deadline, you will give yourself the push needed to get started. If the instructor gave the assignment on a Monday morning, for instance, it would be excellent to set aside one hour or so *that same afternoon or evening* to explore the alternatives and to make yourself choose one of them. (Remember, that by starting early, you protect yourself if the first choice is not workable.)

Read each assignment choice, no matter how uninteresting it may seem at first. Many times in life, we prefer "going with a hunch." However, hunches can turn out to be wrong just as often as they are right. To ensure a solid evaluation of writing choices and to avoid wasting precious time, read all the topics thoroughly. As you read, jot down any ideas (in short form) that occur to you. If there is any class discussion on the topics, by all means take notes. Interestingly, what seems to be the least attractive topic may become the one with the most writing potential for you.

If at all possible, begin prewriting immediately after making the choice, setting aside a block of one to two hours to work. In this way, you will discover relatively early whether the choice is indeed a good one.

MAINTAINING ESSAY CONTROL

THE EFFECTIVE INTRODUCTORY PARAGRAPH

The single best point from which a writer controls an essay of any length is the first or introductory paragraph. Because this paragraph houses the thesis statement—the writing goal—it becomes particularly influential and can establish a powerful structure for the remainder of the essay.

A strong, well-constructed opening paragraph stimulates a positive response in both the writer and the reader. You, the writer, will feel satisfaction because you can sense the order and clarity of the information. The reader, too, will be satisfied, for an effective introductory paragraph communicates information well.

To appreciate the basic requirements of an effective introductory paragraph, review the following list of criteria and the models which follow them.

1. *The introduction must respond to the assignment.* If you are writing because an instructor has given you an assignment, then the work that you produce must respond directly to the assignment. For example, if the assignment is in the form of a question, your introductory paragraph must suggest an answer to the question rather than comment on the question or propose another question. When writing is not responsive but instead sidesteps or avoids the major issue, then first impression on the reader is a poor one. (Review Unit I for a detailed discussion of the demands of an assignment.)

2. *The introduction must include one specific sentence that acts as the thesis statement.* This one sentence identifies your topic and expresses the overall direction or angle that you wish to pursue. While you are studying composition, the thesis statement must be present in the opening paragraph. You may wonder about our insistence that the thesis appear in the first paragraph of a paper, but it is important that it be so. The longer it takes you to present your thesis, the less development you tend to have. The less development, the more superficial your treatment of the topic chosen.

3. *The introduction should contain sentences that simultaneously relate to the thesis and highlight the developmental material in a more specific manner.* Statements of this kind can be looked upon as *subthesis* sentences. If the

thesis expresses your overall response to the assignment, subthesis sentences indicate how or in what manner you will present the developmental paragraphs to support the thesis. These special sentences also serve as a bridge or transition from the introductory paragraph to the first developmental paragraph.

4. Finally, *the introductory paragraph should provide the kind of background information that a reader needs in order to comprehend the more specific material that lies ahead.* The kind of background information you need to provide varies widely, depending on the type of paper you are writing. If you were to do a personal paper about the qualities of a good friend, then background data for your introduction might consist of information about when the two of you met or some general comments about the person. In a paper with a more objective topic, you would bring up pertinent data to fill out a reader's knowledge or general perspective. If you were doing a paper on the use of vitamin A as an anticancer vitamin, your introduction might mention when this vitamin was first discovered and when its effect on certain forms of cancer was first observed by scientists.

ANALYZING MODEL INTRODUCTORY PARAGRAPHS

The introductory paragraph from the model five-paragraph essay illustrates how an effective introduction works. The assignment for this essay asked for discussion of a community area needing improvement. The introduction to the essay meets the four basic requirements just discussed. These criteria are indicated by notations in the left margin.

The writer starts with a <u>direct response</u> to the assignment.

Background information on the community is given showing the writer's awareness of it.

THESIS Responds to the assignment; gives the area needing improvement.

When I observe my community, there are a number of conditions that could use some improvement. It would be valuable to have a Neighborhood Watch on our block to prevent crime or to get better lighting near some of the wooded areas. But I think that the need to care for our younger generation is most important. This is why I believe that every elementary school in my community should have crossing guards at all intersections used by

Subthesis
Relates directly to
thesis; provides a
direction for the bulk
of the essay (2
reasons).

the school children. There are two excellent

reasons for such an action.

All four elements of the introduction serve important functions. Responding to the assignment helps the writer to stay on target, so to speak, while providing background information to prepare the readers, allowing them to understand a situation gradually. Without background of some kind, an introduction tends to be too abrupt. The thesis, of course, provides the key response to the assignment, but notice the assistance given by the subthesis (literally, material that appears after *or below* the thesis to clarify it further).

A subthesis of this kind has two functions: it is linked to the thesis and introduces information that controls the bulk of the essay. When we read that "there are two excellent reasons," we are prepared for a discussion of two supporting points mentioned in succeeding paragraphs. The reader is prepared for the development, and the writer has a clear road map for the content of the rest of the essay.

What if the thesis is placed near the *beginning* of the paragraph? Could the four elements appear in different order? Examine this second model introductory paragraph taken from the discussion of the three-paragraph essay. The assignment asked for a discussion of one aspect of married life. Notice the notations on the left.

THESIS
Responds directly to
assignment and
focuses upon one
aspect of married
life: need for <u>rituals</u>.

Psychologists and marriage counselors

emphasize the need for newly married couples

to establish rituals early in their

marriages. Essentially, these rituals

Background
Consists of a
definition of rituals
in a marriage and
commentary on the
nature of our society
(as pertains to the
thesis).

consist of long-term behavior patterns that

bring a couple closer together emotionally

and allow communication to flourish. The need

for regular contact becomes all the greater

considering that both men and women may now

work outside of the home; consequently, they

Subthesis
Returns to idea of
rituals and
emphasizes bonding.
Allows a smooth
move to second
paragraph where
types of rituals are
discussed.

```
tend to have less time and energy for each

other. If couples establish and preserve some

rituals, whatever they are, the two are more

likely to bond as a couple.
```

In the model paragraph on marriage, the characteristics appear in a different order than in the first example. Here the thesis begins the paragraph, followed by a certain amount of background information. Defining the term *ritual* is an important part of the background because the reader may not be familiar with the word. Commentary on the nature of our society as it influences the relationship between a husband and wife is also helpful. Although the subthesis sentence appears several sentences after the thesis, it once again appears as the last line. (A separation of this sort naturally occurs when the thesis is placed first.) The subthesis sentence achieves two important objectives for the introduction:

1. The *subthesis* keeps the essay *on course*. It is possible to get sidetracked and forget the major goal in a paper. In this case, the goal is a discussion of rituals and how they are important to a relationship. The presence of a subthesis keeps the writer on course and prevents straying into other areas such as overworked couples and inflation.

2. The *subthesis* provides a bridge or connection from the introduction to the rest of the essay. Because the essay is a multiparagraph structure, the connections between paragraphs become extremely sensitive. The transition between the introduction and the first developmental paragraph is particularly important, bridging introductory information and more specific developmental material. The subthesis allows for a smoother movement between the two sections because it introduces the path the discussion is to take.

Before beginning the exercises on understanding introductory paragraphs, review this pertinent information:

1. Introductions need various elements to be effective pieces of writing. These elements include (a) responsiveness to the assignment, (b) sufficient background information, (c) a thesis statement, and (d) subthesis material to provide a bridge to the rest of the essay.

2. Effective introductory paragraphs make good use of subthesis material (which usually appears as the last sentence in the introduction). The subthesis relates to the thesis and sets up the remainder of the essay—especially the developmental paragraphs.

FOR YOUR MENTAL FILE

If you have developed a habit of writing one-sentence introductory paragraphs, this discussion may help you see how important it is to write a longer introduction. Length is not needed for its own sake but to supply the kind of information that allows effective communication to occur. One sentence, no matter how well phrased, cannot contain all the elements of an effective introduction. If you were to put all the introductory material into one sentence, then the sentence would be entirely too long. When editing your drafts for content, watch to see that each introduction contains *several sentences* that work together to form a full, informative first paragraph.

 Exercise 3.21   THE EFFECTIVE INTRODUCTORY PARAGRAPH

Study the following hypothetical assignments and the introductory paragraphs written in response to them. Then answer the questions on a separate sheet of paper.

> *Assignment:* In a five-paragraph essay, discuss one negative aspect of your behavior as a student.

People can learn as much about themselves in college as they learn about computers, history, or psychology. Although I do have some strong points in my overall academic performance, the one area that I could drastically improve is my classroom attendance. Most college instructors do not take roll or make any issue out of coming to class; the choice is up to the student. I think that I may have abused this freedom. Irregular attendance has been costly to me in a number of ways, and I can see this clearly as the semester nears it end.

1. What is the thesis? Write it out.

2. What is the subthesis? Write it out.

3. Assuming the subthesis provides a smooth transition from paragraph 1 to paragraph 2, describe briefly what you would expect the writer to discuss in the next paragraph.

Read the writing assignment and the introductory paragraph that follows; then answer the question on a separate sheet of paper.

> *Assignment:* Respond to the following question with a five-paragraph essay. Do parents with adequate funds have a responsibility to pay for their children's college educations?

The question of obligation becomes a very complex and intricate one in today's era of changing social roles. In my estimation, parents, regardless of their wealth, have no <u>legal</u> obligation to educate their children beyond the senior year of high school; however, parents do have a <u>moral</u> obligation to do so. For me, at least, this distinction between legal and moral obligation is an important one that must be fully explored.

1. What is the thesis? Write it out.

2. Which sentence functions as the subthesis? Write it out.

3. What would you expect the next paragraph to contain?

 Exercise 3.22   THE EFFECTIVE INTRODUCTORY PARAGRAPH

In the following assignments, you will assume the identity of the person being described. Read the directions and write the introductory paragraph of what would be a five-paragraph essay in response to the assignment.

> *Assignment One:* Discuss one negative aspect of sports or athletics.

1. You are a woman whose husband loves to watch boxing matches.

2. When gathering data for the assignment, you recorded this information:

Too violent. Injuries to head (brain damage) or body (internal bleeding).

Violence then degrades a boxer's body and human nature spiritually.

My husband and many other men particularly, like the sport/do not see it as violent this way.

Begin to draft an introduction using this prewriting data. If you wish to supply any extra background information, use your imagination. Be sure that one of the sentences you generate is a thesis; try also to write a subthesis to indicate how the rest of the essay (if you were to write it) would proceed. Don't copy the words above verbatim; use your own ''voice.''

> *Assignment Two:* Discuss what you believe to be one important factor behind the difficulty experienced by men and women in communicating with one another.

1. You are a man in your midtwenties, unmarried, but with a steady girlfriend.

2. Because of certain experiences with your girlfriend, you jot down this remark in your data gathering:

women are too emotional when there is a problem.

You decide to pursue this choice as your writing focus.

3. As you see it, *emotional* does not mean temperamental, but it does refer to what you think of as an excessive display of emotion when there is a misunderstanding or disagreement.

Once you have absorbed this identity, begin your draft of an introductory paragraph. You may use any imaginative details to supply what you feel is necessary background. Be sure that your paragraph contains a thesis and a subthesis.

Exercise 3.23   THE EFFECTIVE INTRODUCTORY PARAGRAPH

Read the assignment below. Then decide which of the two introductory paragraphs following the assignment is more effective. When you have made a decision, write out a brief statement (2–3 sentences) on a separate sheet of paper, telling why you chose as you did. Use your knowledge of the elements of an effective introduction to support your evaluation.

> *Assignment:* Reflect upon your childhood or earlier years and focus on one person who stands out in your mind. In a five-paragraph essay, explain why this character is so memorable.

Introductory Paragraph 1

       My family lived in Texas for a number of years, and it was there

that I met a very special lady. Widow Morris was what everyone in town

called her, and now that I reflect upon it, I never knew her first

name. The Widow lived a few doors down from us, and I often passed her

house as I walked to school. Her house was very old, extremely small,

but perfectly tended. The paint was unchipped and shiny, the windows
were always clean, and the lawn was immaculately manicured.

Introductory Paragraph 2

When I reflect upon my past, many people come to mind for one
reason or another. The one to whom this paper is dedicated, however,
I really never got to know very well at all, yet the man's image and
behavior have always stayed with me. Mr. Morton actually lived next
door to us, but our homes were separated by a half-acre of land. He
was an older gentleman, of perhaps fifty or sixty. Although our
personal interaction was brief and infrequent, this man had one
unusual habit, a habit that totally fascinated and irritated me.

FOR YOUR MENTAL FILE

In addition to helping you control the content of your essay, your
introductory paragraph has great value as a stimulus to thinking. If at any
point you get bogged down writing the developmental paragraphs or find
yourself at a loss for words, try the following. Stop writing for a few
minutes to collect yourself; then reread your introduction (preferably
aloud) and whatever other material you have written. This kind of
rereading will remind you what you are doing (your goal) and where you
are in relationship to it.

If You Are Using a Word Processor

In this unit you will write three-, four-, and five-paragraph essays. Please follow
these general guidelines for all of the essay-writing exercises.

    1. *Prewriting.* For essays, you will need to do more prewriting than for para-
graphs because you will need to generate more ideas. Consider doing

your prewriting and then printing it out. Because you can only see a portion of your work on-screen it is difficult to keep scrolling back and forth to see what you've written. Doing so could seriously affect your concentration.

2. *Blocking Your Material.* When you block material, you must change the format of the model blocking sheet we show in the text. It is often difficult to do columns on the word processor, so just type your headings and then make your remarks *under* the headings, rather than alongside them. Refer to your word processing manual to find out how to do a page-end command so that your prewriting is on a separate page from your draft. Print out the blocking sheet to use when you write your rough draft. In this way, you can do all your work in one file, rather than opening new ones for each part of the process.
Note: You can set up a blocking-sheet form in a separate file and duplicate it each time you need one. This is called making a *boilerplate*. Once this form is entered, you can use a special command to insert a copy of the blocking sheet directly into the file on which you are working. Refer to your word processing manual to learn this useful skill.

3. *The First Draft.* Keep your printed blocking sheet beside you as you write your first draft. When you first begin writing essays, it will be worth the extra time to print out the first draft and edit it by hand. Because you cannot see the entire essay at once on the screen, you may have trouble knowing if all three parts of the essay are the way you want them. You eventually may be able to edit an essay entirely on-screen, but that may be difficult while you are learning essay structure in these initial exercises.

4. *The Second Draft.* If you don't have many corrections to make, you can revise your first draft without having to retype it. Refer to your first draft, and enter just the corrections, deletions, additions, and so on. Again, print this draft.

5. *The Final Copy.* After you have hand-edited your second draft, go back to the same file and refine your essay further. If you find any problem at all, you can easily fix it and reprint. For this reason, writing on a word processor is time-saving and efficient. If you were handwriting or typing your drafts, you would probably introduce new mistakes because you would have to redo the entire draft each time.

UNIT IV

Revising Your Work

- **IMPROVING YOUR CONTENT-EDITING SKILLS**
- **IMPROVING YOUR SENTENCES**
- **PREPARING THE FINAL COPY**

OVERVIEW

Improving Your Content-Editing Skills *provides a content checklist for paragraphs and essays and discusses four considerations in revising: responding to an assignment, developing the thesis, logically ordering the material, and supplying transitions.*

Improving Your Sentences *presents revision of language, point of view, sentence length, and sentence construction.*

Preparing the Final Copy *outlines a basic plan for submitting acceptable work to instructors.*

Introduction

When you have written a draft of a paper, you are at a critical point in the writing process. It is here that you switch roles, so to speak, from writer to editor or critic. What is your new concern? Mainly, you need to examine and evaluate what you have actually written so that any content deficiencies or mechanical errors can be revised or eliminated.

Unit IV is concerned with helping you edit and revise any content deficiencies and sentence weaknesses in your drafts. Because writing must rest upon a solid foundation of thought, the time you spend examining the content of your draft and the quality of your sentences is time well spent. The next unit will concentrate on the mechanical problems that need editing and revision.

Having to revise your drafts is not a sign that you are a poor writer. Professional writers draft, edit, and rewrite their work many, many times before any final version appears in print. This struggle to organize and refine our thoughts is the hallmark of anyone who wishes to write well.

IMPROVING YOUR CONTENT-EDITING SKILLS

This section includes both discussion and practice designed to improve your editing skills, especially in areas of content deficiencies. The content checklist and the technique of voicing are helpful in identifying weak spots. Strategies for revising are organized around four main topics: responding to an assignment, developing the thesis adequately, ordering material logically, and supplying transitions.

In the early stages of your college career, using a specific method of locating content deficiencies is an excellent idea. Once you have absorbed the basic points of the method, you may make whatever changes suit your individual needs. Then, as your experience with formal writing increases, you will discover less need for a strategy sheet such as the content checklist which follows.

The first part of the content checklist reflects the need for a paper to show a three-part structure: a beginning (introduction), a middle (development), and an end (conclusion). The questions in the second part of the checklist apply to all parts of a paper.

To make your editing efforts more noticeable and your revision easier, try using a colored marking pen. Some people who draft in pen prefer the contrast of pencil for their editorial comments. You may also wish to review some of the model rough drafts of a paragraph, basic essay, or longer essay featured in Units II and III; each shows how editorial remarks for content might look.

As you edit your papers, you may find that each one presents a different task. Sometimes your editing will show that one or two paragraphs are weak, and you may only have to rewrite these weak ones. At other times, all paragraphs will show deficiencies, and you will need to write out an entirely new draft. When you have rewritten your paragraphs or your second draft, review the checklist once again and make any further editorial remarks. If you find only minor content problems in the second draft, you can begin the final copy. If you are dissatisfied with some of the material in the second draft, rewrite that part before doing the final copy.

A CONTENT CHECKLIST FOR ALL DRAFTS

1. Focus on the beginning or introduction.
After reading it carefully, ask these questions:

   a. Is there a thesis statement?

   b. Does my thesis respond to the demands of the assignment?

   c. Have I provided sufficient introductory material in addition to the thesis?

2. Focus on the middle or development.
In a basic essay, this will mean one middle paragraph; in a longer essay, three or more middle paragraphs. Ask these questions:

a. Does each developmental paragraph have a clear purpose?

b. If the purpose is clear, then does each have enough explanation, specification, or discussion so that my reader can understand my line of thinking?

c. Does each developmental paragraph remain faithful to the thesis given in the introduction?

3. Focus on the last section or conclusion.
Ask these questions:

a. Is there a sense of an ending?

b. Did I fall into the trap of repeating my introduction?

c. Does this conclusion follow from the thesis statement?

4. After reviewing items 1 through 3, ask these questions about any part of your draft:

a. Is my material in the proper order? In other words, if it was important that ideas be presented in a certain order, have I done so?

b. Are there smooth movements or transitions between paragraphs?

c. How do my sentences look and sound? Are there repetitious words or sentence patterns that make my writing monotonous? Are any sentences overpacked or rambling?

d. Do I have enough material in the work as a whole? If you have drafted fewer than two pages (in average handwritten script), then you do not have enough material for a college essay. If this is the case, review the first three items on this sheet; you probably need some new material in all of the paragraphs.

ADDING VOICING TO YOUR EDITING STRATEGY

One of the best ways to improve your ability to locate content deficiencies is through the technique of voicing. Basically, voicing is the careful *oral* reading of your draft in order to hear as well as see various problems.

Voicing has a number of advantages. First, no special equipment is required. Secondly, reading your work aloud enables you to see and hear what you actually wrote (not what you *think* you wrote). Finally, voicing puts you in a more active posture with respect to your work and develops your awareness of writing performance.

How Voicing Highlights Content Deficiencies

Reading your work aloud is enormously beneficial when you evaluate the quality of your sentences. If most sentences are written in a similar pattern, the ear can pick up on this monotony better than the eye. Or, if you have used a word too often in a paragraph, the repetition tends to stand out if you hear it. Voicing may also help you hear when you didn't "say enough" and need to add information to a paragraph. If this leads you to develop an idea further, then the time spent on voicing has been valuable.

To dramatize the usefulness of voicing as an editing strategy, try the following sample voicing exercise. Follow its directions carefully so that you understand how helpful the human voice can be in evaluating writing.

A Sample Voicing Exercise

Examine the paragraph below. Although neatly typed, it has problems in content. First, read the paragraph *silently*, noting on a separate sheet of paper any problem that you see.

```
     Personal rituals can be extremely important in daily life.

Because people are different, there are all sorts of rituals, but for

me one of the most pleasing has been the one hour I reserve for doing

absolutely nothing. I go to school from 8AM to 2PM three days a week

and work part-time the other two days and other times I am either

cleaning, studying, and watching a little television. But from 3 to 4

PM each weekday, I get a cup of coffee, sit down in a comfortable

chair near the window, and do nothing but think or daydream. One of

the problems in modern life is the face pace, leaving people with no

time for themselves. In this 60-minute period, I can think through or

sort out any problems. I can reflect on a pleasant memory, or I can

just let my mind wander as I sip my coffee and gaze at the scene
```

```
outside. By 4 PM, I feel refreshed and can go on with the day's

activities.
```

The corrected version of the paragraph follows; notice the <u>underlined</u> words, for they highlight the various problems. Compare these areas with the ones you noted after the silent reading.

```
    Personal rituals can be extremely important in daily life.

Because people are different, there are all sorts of rituals, but for

me one of the most pleasing has been the one hour I reserve for doing

absolutely nothing. I go to school from 8AM to 2PM three days a week

and work part-time the other two days. Other times I am either

cleaning, studying, or watching a little television. But from 3 to 4

PM each weekday, I get a cup of coffee, sit down in a comfortable

chair near the window, and do nothing but think or daydream. One of

the problems in modern life is the fast pace, leaving people with no

time for themselves. In this 60-minute period, I can think through or

sort out any problems. I can reflect on a pleasant memory or just let

my mind wander as I sip my coffee and gaze at the scene outside. By 4

PM, I feel refreshed and can go on with the day's activities.
```

The third sentence has been broken into two shorter, more direct ones. This also eliminates the repetition of the word *and*. Correcting the misspelling of *fast* has made the meaning clearer. Finally, at the end of the paragraph, the repetition of "I can" has been removed. A silent reading may not make you as aware of such repetition as an oral reading would, for when you read aloud, you *hear* where such content problems occur.

Whenever you are editing, whether for content or mechanical problems, use both techniques. Continue to read silently so that you can study your draft more intently. However, add the dimension of your voice and the power of your ear to detect trouble spots. The two together greatly assist you in evaluating your papers.

FOR YOUR MENTAL FILE

For centuries, magicians have understood how easily the human eye can
be fooled. (So have special effects artists, fashion designers, make-up
artists, and pickpockets!) When you switch hats from writer to editor, use
the powerful combination of your voice and ear to help detect problems
and errors. Be sure, however, to read *exactly what you wrote as you wrote it.*

RESPONDING DIRECTLY TO AN ASSIGNMENT

When checking your draft for content deficiencies, your first point of focus should
be the actual assignment and your response to it. Most problems of this nature
appear in the introductory paragraph. Unfortunately, they influence the development and conclusion as well. To understand this type of editing concern, read
the sample assignment and then the sample essay stemming from it. As you read,
ask yourself: Is the writer responding to the assignment?

> *Sample Assignment:* Summer is a special time of year for many of us. Develop a three-
> paragraph essay based on one specific aspect of summer.

I genuinely enjoy going to the beach as often as possible. Being
a busy person--a student who works part-time--I don't get there as
often as I would like. To me, the beach is a special place, for it
offers so many possible activities, especially volleyball on the
warm beach sand.

Volleyball is probably my favorite beach activity because it
allows me to do a number of things at once. I can be very active and
keep in shape with all the moving around I have to do to keep the ball
in play. At the same time I'm playing, I am getting a tan and a much
healthier look than I otherwise have. Best of all, volleyball is a
sociable game that is great for me because it is sometimes hard to
make friends. Both men and women play, so I've had the chance to make
friends and even get some dates. If nothing else, I've had some
laughs and excitement.

I think that anyone who lives near enough to the beach should enjoy its pleasures. By getting out and involved in something like volleyball, a person can have so much fun. I know that I have.

This introductory paragraph makes no mention of summer. And, because summer was not mentioned in the introduction, it does not appear in either the developmental paragraph or the concluding one. If this type of problem is located during the editing stage, a second draft is needed, one which addresses itself immediately to the assignment.

Immediate response to assignment.
Thesis accurate

The summer brings with it a number of changes in lifestyle. I do hold a part-time job during the summer months, but I don't take any classes, so I have more free time than at any other time of the year. The highlight of any summer, though, is volleyball on the warm beach sand.

Volleyball is probably my favorite beach activity because it allows me to do a number of things at once. I can be very active and keep in shape with all the moving around I have to do to keep the ball in play. At the same

Refer to seasons to contrast with summer.

time, I am getting a tan and a much healthier look than I had as a pale student whose winter and spring were spent in the library or the classroom. Best of all, volleyball is a sociable game that is great for me because it is sometimes hard to make friends. Both men and women play, so there are chances to meet people and even get some dates. If nothing else, I've had some laughs and excitement.

I think that it is important for people to have changes and contrasts in their lives. I work and study

Reference to Summer { hard from September to June. But when that last class is finished, summer finds me on the beach where I can unwind with volleyball.

Most of your writing will be done in response to an instructor's assignment. Therefore, it is vital that you not only understand but also directly connect your introductory material with that assignment. You might feel that the original version of the volleyball paper was close enough, but consider this analogy. If you go to a restaurant and order a chicken dinner, you have a right to expect chicken, not turkey, even though the turkey is superb!

Exercise 4.1 RESPONDING DIRECTLY TO AN ASSIGNMENT

This exercise tests your ability to judge a direct response to an assignment. After reading the sample assignment, select what you consider to be the best response from among the three choices. Defend your choice.

Sample Assignment: Discuss one aspect of your first week of classes.

Response 1

In my opinion, the best aspect of school is being able to learn in so many areas. This semester, for example, I am taking photography for the first time, and it is a pleasure. But I am also taking a course in body-building and ceramics.

Response 2

When I think of my first week of school, I remember the crowds everywhere. Students jammed the bookstore, classrooms were packed, and lines at the enrollment window seemed endless. I can also recall the fact that construction workers were busy in the street right near my first class. The poor instructor had a terrible time lecturing with all that noise.

Response 3

> Although I have many memories of the first week of classes, I do recall one aspect of that time very well, and that was the crowded classrooms. Rooms that contained seats for only forty or so were jammed as overflow students stood at the sides and back of the room. This situation made me wonder whether this kind of teacher-student ratio per class is conducive to learning.

Exercise 4.2   RESPONDING DIRECTLY TO AN ASSIGNMENT

Write an introductory paragraph that responds directly to the requirements of the following assignment. Prewrite quickly and formulate a thesis. Be sure that your introductory paragraph contains between three and five sentences, one of which is a thesis statement.

> *Assignment:* What is your candid opinion of your first name?

Exercise 4.3   RESPONDING DIRECTLY TO AN ASSIGNMENT

Write an introductory paragraph for the following assignment. Notice that this assignment is a bit more complex than the previous one, so be sure to respond to its requirements as you construct the introductory paragraph.

> *Assignment:* Present two reasons why, in your opinion, many citizens do not vote even though they are eligible to do so.

Responding to an Essay Exam

The in-class essay exam is a special writing situation that demands a strong introductory paragraph. When you are writing under the pressure of the clock, you have little or no time to rewrite, so you must begin by doing a careful job of responding to the assignment in your introductory paragraph. Whether from tension or panic, many writers respond to an in-class essay assignment by producing poor or inadequate responses in their introduction.

Assume that the following is a midterm for U.S. history:

Fall Term

MIDTERM EXAMINATION

You have one hour to respond to this question:

The period following the Civil War is called
Reconstruction, a time when both the North and the South,
but particularly the South, recovered from the effects of
the Civil War. Many changes and developments occurred in
all areas of life in the South during this time. Focus on
two of these changes and discuss them thoroughly.

Do either of these two introductory paragraphs respond to the assignment?

Student 1

The Reconstruction period following the Civil War did have many changes and developments. One involved the rise of industrialism. A second was the growth of a mistrust or even hatred for the opposition, even though the war was officially over.

Student 2

The Reconstruction period was an especially turbulent one for the South. Many changes and developments were experienced, one being the growth of mistrust and hatred for the North. The Yankees, as they were called, were the victors who had ruined a genteel way of

life and an entire economy.

Unfortunately, both responses are inadequate. The first does not refer to the *South* as the site of the changes; the second writer does not mention *two* developments, only one. In the tension of that hour, both could forget these key elements.

To overcome this problem, use the first three to six minutes of an exam to focus on the assignment and jot down responses. Write on the exam sheet if it does not have to be returned. Otherwise use a separate sheet of scratch paper. Study the notations on the following exam sheet.

Fall Term

MIDTERM EXAMINATION

You have one hour to respond to this question:

The period following the Civil War is called

Reconstruction, a time when both the North and the South,

but particularly the South, recovered from the effects of

the Civil War. Many changes and developments occurred in

all areas of life in the South during this time. Focus on

two of these changes and discuss them thoroughly.

Reconstruction → South : Changes? Development?
  a) growth of industry – up to
      agriculture / cotton
  b) mistrust of north – carpet baggers
  c) Blacks – still taken advantage of

Choose a & b

With this type of guideline, a more specific and directly responsive introduction is produced.

> *During the Reconstruction period after the Civil War, the South*
> *experienced many changes and developments. One was the growth of*
> *industrialism in areas that had once been agricultural. The second*
> *was the development of a mistrust and even hatred of the*
> *Northerners ("Yankees"), who had defeated the South and*
> *interfered with Southern life.*

This introductory paragraph is far more responsive, for it mentions the *two
changes* requested in the assignment. The writer would now be ready to begin the
developmental paragraphs of the essay by explaining the two changes in greater
detail.

Guidelines for Responding Directly to an Assignment

Use the following four guidelines to help you check your drafts for any problems
in responding directly to your assignments.

1. If the assignment is in the form of a question, be sure to answer that question when you formulate your thesis.

2. Use some of the key words of the assignment in your own introductory
   paragraph to keep you on the right track.

3. Watch out for specific words, especially those that restrict your writing to
   one aspect or *two* reasons, and so on.

4. In longer essays, check that all paragraphs, especially the last several, are
   faithful to the thesis and assignment.

If your first draft does not respond to the assignment, it will probably have
to be completely rewritten.

DEVELOPING YOUR THESIS ADEQUATELY

As you revise your papers, you may find that a whole essay or parts of a paper
are inadequately developed. Such sections are often short and leave many unan-

swered questions in the reader's mind. Two ways to revise and solve this problem are by adding more information and by enriching your material so that it has more depth. Together, these two methods will help you improve both the quantity and the quality of the development you use.

Adding Information

The following sample essay dramatizes the problem of adequately developing a thesis. The notations in the right-hand margin call attention to a basic problem: all three paragraphs need additional material.

Being Prepared

Not having enough money with you can cause some *when?* *where?* pretty embarrassing moments. I experienced one of these *Occasion?*

moments at a restaurant.

Trying to impress a friend I was treating to dinner, *more details*

I ordered lobster and encouraged her to order whatever

she liked. We had appetizers before dinner and elaborate

desserts after the meal. Was I in for a shock when the *Why?* *Explain!*

waiter brought the bill!

Now I always carry extra money so that I can avoid

this kind of embarrassment. I can reflect on this *What was learned?*

experience and chuckle, but it wasn't the least bit

amusing at the time.

This effort is very thin indeed. The writer did little to encourage us to even finish reading, much less engage our interest in his problem. It is difficult for us to believe that the incident made a real impression because so little explanation is provided. In what way, for instance, was the writer shocked? Why was the dinner date worth impressing? What a thin paper ultimately suggests is that the writer has spent little time or effort on the assignment.

One of the goals of prewriting is to generate enough material to enable you to write an adequate first draft. If, however, your first draft is thin (for whatever reason) and editing highlights this deficiency, by all means set aside time to deal with these questions as you edit and revise the draft. Ask yourself the following questions when examining your draft:

1. Where can I add more explanation to make the scene, issue, or problem clearer to my reader?

2. At what points do I speak in generalities but fail to follow with specifics that would make the ideas clearer?

3. Where do I give an opinion or make a strong statement in only *one* sentence?

Once you locate these problem areas, you can add more sentences to develop the ideas. By the way, the same problem of thesis development occurs when you are taking a written examination in class. Improving your ability to develop a thesis will help you with your in-class examinations as well as with your take-home papers. To help you build this skill, the next eight exercises all work on adequate thesis development.

Exercise 4.4   ADDING INFORMATION

Problems with adequate development of an idea or thesis often begin in prewriting. Using your imagination, direct experience, or observation, add to these prewriting responses, following the directions in parentheses. Use a separate sheet of paper.

Assignment: Discuss one aspect of your first week of classes.

The writer generates these ideas to explore the assignment:

bookstore	*parking problems*
classes	*trouble finding classrooms*
lots of confusion	*homework assigned early*
new faces/eager	*I was nervous, tense*
old friends—a few	*cafeteria food not good*

Next the writer chooses the following topic:

Topic: *parking problems*

Now, data is gathered to develop the topic.

Had lots of trouble   (Why? Explain)

Too many cars/students   (Describe more specifically)

Got me very upset!   (Why? Give reason)

The school should do something about this.   (What? Give a pos-

sible solution)

Exercise 4.5   ADDING INFORMATION

Read the first draft of the introductory paragraph below; then study the editorial remarks made in the right margin. Using the remarks as your guide, supply sufficient introductory material. Add at least *two* sentences—one after the first sentence and a second after the last sentence. Write your revised, more developed version on your own paper.

> *Assignment:* Discuss one reason why parents and children often have trouble communicating.

First Draft Introduction

One reason why parents and children often experience problems communicating is the generation gap between them. As a result of this situation, discussions often end up in arguments with neither side able to appreciate or understand the point of view of the other.

→ Explain what generation Gap means. What does "gap" refer to?

Specify one area where the "g" gap produces problems.

Exercise 4.6

> *Assignment:* Evaluate the following introductory paragraph as acceptable or faulty on the basis of its development. The writer was asked to write about one particularly embarrassing moment. On your paper, give your rating and the reasons for giving it.

One of the most embarrassing moments of my life happened when I was quite young. I had been chosen to recite a poem with several other children in front of the entire school. If I live to be a hundred years of age, I will never forget how I accidentally confused my well-rehearsed lines and managed to throw off the entire group, causing all the students in the audience to laugh hysterically.

Exercise 4.7   ADDING INFORMATION

In this exercise, you will be the editor who writes the remarks about adequate development. As you read the essay, locate and mark poorly developed areas. Write brief instructions for improving each weak area. Use your own paper.

No!

One of the easiest words for a youngster to learn is <u>no</u>. It is interesting, however, that as a person grows older, it is often difficult or nearly impossible to say no in certain circumstances.

It is difficult for many people to say no to their friends. Rather than respond negatively to a suggestion or an activity, some people just agree with whatever their friends wish but usually feel resentful later on. It can also be difficult for a parent to refuse something a child desires. Rather than disappoint one's offspring, a father or mother tends to say yes.

Many psychological counselors find that this inability to say no causes a loss of self-esteem and a great deal of frustration. It then becomes part of their work to understand why a person behaves this way and what can be done to change the behavior.

Exercise 4.8   ADDING INFORMATION

In this exercise, you are to revise the sample essay "Being Prepared." Read the essay again; then read the directions which follow it, and write a second draft that is more thoroughly developed. Use your imagination, observation, or firsthand experience to fill in the details. Write on a separate sheet of paper.

Being Prepared

Not having enough money with you can cause some pretty embarrassing moments. I experienced one of these moments at a restaurant.

Trying to impress a friend I was treating to dinner, I ordered lobster and encouraged her to order whatever she liked. We had appetizers before dinner and elaborate desserts after the meal. Was I in for a shock when the waiter brought the bill!

Now I always carry extra money so that I can avoid this kind of embarrassment. I can reflect on this experience and chuckle, but it wasn't the least bit amusing at the time.

Directions for Development

Paragraph 1   You may either add sentences or rewrite those already given or both. Whatever you do, be sure to incorporate the following details:

1. when this incident occurred

2. whether or not it was a special occasion

3. who your dinner companion was (it's not necessary to give a name)

4. some details about your companion

Paragraph 2   Your main goal in this paragraph is to develop the incident by including further detail:

1. what the friend ordered

2. what appetizers were ordered

3. what desserts were ordered

4. the total bill for the meal

5. how much money you were short and what you did about it

Paragraph 3   Rewrite or add to this paragraph by saying specifically what you learned from this experience and how your friend reacted to the situation.

Enriching Your Material

In the earlier exercises, problems of development occurred in writings that were obviously "thin." Another kind of development problem you may encounter concerns the *kind*—rather than the *amount*—of information you supply to support a thesis in an essay or a topic sentence in a paragraph. Examine the following paragraph carefully.

```
                          Litter

     I am appalled by the littering in my neighborhood. I have lived

in the area for fifteen years, and it has never looked worse. When I

take a walk, I always seem to be dodging papers, bottles, and other

debris. If the article thrown away has any food on it, then flies add

to the problem. To make matters worse, some people have discarded

items in vacant lots. Who wants to see an old mattress or broken chair

lying around? I feel that it is important to exercise, so I continue

to walk every day, but many of my neighbors have stopped since the

environment is so unpleasant.
```

This paragraph is acceptable for a number of reasons:

1. It has a topic sentence (line 1).

2. It mentions specific bits of information: fifteen years, flies, broken chair.

3. It formally ends with a conclusion.

But this paragraph needs *enrichment.* More specifically, it needs additional information to develop the point of view in a deeper, more philosophical perspective.

How can you *enrich* an essay or paragraph? In this case, most of the writing is descriptive. Another dimension could be added with material that is philosophical in nature. Examine this second draft. The additional material is underlined.

```
                          Litter

     I am appalled by the littering in my neighborhood. I have lived

in the area for fifteen years, and it has never looked worse. When I

take a walk, I always seem to be dodging papers, bottles, and other

debris. If the article thrown away has any food on it, then flies add
```

to the problem. To make matters worse, some people have discarded
items in vacant lots. Who wants to see an old mattress or broken chair
lying around? When I stop to reflect on this change in the area, I
can't help but wonder about the effect on the youngsters. They don't
have the advantage of comparing today with yesterday as I do. What
happens to a person's soul or spirit when he or she never sees
anything of beauty? The long-term effects of neighborhood litter may
go far beyond the daily inconvenience and aggravation. I feel that it
is important to exercise, so I continue to walk every day, but many of
my neighbors have stopped since the environment is so unpleasant.

The bulk of the original paragraph remains, but as you can see, the writer
adds a human or philosophical dimension by sharing a concern about the effects
of littering on the young. This kind of development shows that the writer has
thought about the topic or thesis on a number of different levels.

When instructors talk about depth of discussion, they are speaking about
very much the same issue as enrichment. In other words, when instructors look
at your papers, they check to see if you have provided more than one dimension
to the writing and if you have tried to go beneath the surface to discover less
obvious ideas or thoughts.

 Exercise 4.9   ENRICHING YOUR MATERIAL

The paragraph below could profit by some enrichment. Read it carefully; then follow the directions about adding new material. Use your own paper to write your enriched draft.

A Memorable Place

One place that I remember fondly is our old city library. When my
family first moved to the town in 1951, I was only seven years old.
Because I enjoyed reading, I soon discovered the library where my
mother would take me fairly regularly. Part of its charm was its
size. I remember that instead of one huge area, which could overwhelm
a child, there were four or five small circular rooms filled with

books. The light wasn't too good because the rooms had few windows,
but I didn't mind. In the 1960s, the library moved to a new site: a
modern, large one-room facility, and the old building was torn down
to make room for a bank. Even though it is no longer there, I can still
see it in my mind's eye.

Directions for Enrichment

Use all of the material above but add three to five sentences after "but I didn't mind." In your
new sentences, mention what you did in the rooms and why you felt so comfortable. Consider
how and why a small old library would appeal to a seven year old. Did it offer an escape to a
fantasy world? Did it provide the freedom of no one watching the child's every move? Did it
supply something the child wanted or needed? Did it change the child's life in some specific
way?

Be sure to voice your revision to hear how well your additions blend with the material
before and after them.

Exercise 4.10   ENRICHING YOUR MATERIAL

Read the three-paragraph essay that follows. It consists of an introduction, one developmental
paragraph, and a conclusion. Follow the directions after the essay to enrich it. Use your own
paper to rewrite your enriched essay.

An Annoying Habit

Habits are interesting behaviors in that they can be very
constructive, or at the opposite extreme, highly annoying. For me,
at least, one irritating habit is bragging. In fact, I make a special
point of avoiding the person who brags.

People who brag usually want to display their strong points,
just in case you are not already aware of them. If the topic of
discussion is a restaurant, the braggart has already been there and
ordered the best of everything. If the issue is raising children, of
course the braggart has done the job better and will take the time to
tell you precisely how. After a minute or two of this performance, I

want to hit the person over the head with the nearest heavy object. Usually, I make a quick exit and try to relocate myself with people who are able to communicate in a less abrasive manner.

If people were only aware of what an annoying habit bragging truly is or if they could see themselves as their listeners do, then perhaps they could change this behavior. Without change, they are likely to find that only the most insecure people will want to listen to the bragging, for more well-balanced individuals will seek other companionship.

Directions for Enrichment

1. Keep all three paragraphs as they are, but **add a new developmental paragraph before the conclusion.**

2. Make your new paragraph speculative in nature: Why do some people have this habit or persist in behaving so badly?

3. In this new paragraph, suggest at least one reason but no more than two reasons for the behavior. Provide supportive material for each reason.

4. Your new paragraph should be between 5 and 10 sentences long.

 Exercise 4.11   ENRICHING YOUR MATERIAL

The following essay requires further development or enrichment. Read the essay and follow the directions for enrichment. Use your own paper to rewrite your enriched essay.

Film

Film is an especially powerful medium in our culture, especially now that people seem to be reading less and watching more for their entertainment. Films have been particularly effective in creating historical images in our minds. The portrayal of the cowboy and the Indian in film is a case in point.

The image of the cowboy was fairly consistent in the early

Westerns. Popular cowboy actors such as Tom Mix, Gene Autry, or Gary Cooper invariably played the role of the typical film cowboy--white, clean, modest (especially with women), brave, incorruptible, and fearless in pursuit of the treacherous enemy--the Indian, the original native American. Generations of American and foreign moviegoers have accepted the clean-cut image of the cowboy and the negative portrayal of the Indian. History books, however, present a different "typical" American cowboy. Cowboys came from many racial and ethnic backgrounds--white, black, and Hispanic. Because of the roughness of life on the frontier, the typical cowboy was usually dirty, unkempt, and no less corruptible than any other person in the Wild West. Likewise, historical Indians were part of complex social structures and were far from the savage, rootless people shown in many films.

To keep a balance between film fiction and historical fact, perhaps it would be a good idea to require students in junior and senior high school to study film in a more formal manner. In this way, people would have a more accurate understanding of a particular art form, be able to see it in its proper perspective, and be less likely to believe unrealistic images.

Directions for Enrichment

Keep all three paragraphs as they are, but **add a fourth paragraph to appear as the second developmental one.** Add material that discusses the possible *harm* that could result when popular film distorts historical facts. Use this first line for your new paragraph: This kind of distortion in film has produced a number of negative side effects in our society.

Guidelines for Developing Your Thesis Adequately

When editing your drafts, be sure to watch for the more obvious signs of inadequate thesis development—paragraphs of one to three sentences or a five-paragraph essay that has been handwritten in a page and a half. To pinpoint areas needing development, read your draft carefully and check where these are lacking:

1. Specific and detailed support of any general statement, opinion, or description.

2. A deeper level of discussion of your thesis: Is there room for enrichment of the thesis by looking at it from a humanistic, philosophical perspective?

Any paragraph that is inadequately developed should be *rewritten!* Don't try to save time by doing two activities at once: rewriting and final copying. Writing a second, expanded draft allows you to edit it to see how well your new material works and then to move on to the other editing concerns.

ORDERING YOUR MATERIAL

Well-organized writing is easy for a reader to follow because one point leads to the next. Depending on your topic and your point of view, you will need to organize different papers in different ways. Common ways of ordering material are based on time sequence, stages in a process, and order of importance.

Events in Time

When you narrate events, ordering the events in a proper sequence helps your reader understand the progression of activities. The paragraph below, for instance, includes many special details and develops its topic sentence well. However, there is a problem in the way in which the writer has presented events in time. Read the passage as well as the notations in the right margin.

```
     Shopping on a Saturday morning in the supermarket is

one duty that is a real torture for me. The checkout line

is always long, and I usually find that I am at least the

tenth shopper behind nine others whose carts are bulging

with items. Of course, I always manage to pick a line with

a slow or unusually talkative checker, and that slows

down everything and adds to my aggravation. When I

finally get out of the line, my feet ache, my head is
```

pounding, and my nerves are frayed. Walking through the aisles is also a problem because there are so many other shoppers. Whenever I turn, I seem to bump into someone or encounter the discourteous soul who leaves his or her cart dead-center in the aisle so that no one can pass easily. As a result of my Saturday shopping experience, I have decided to change my marketing to a day and time that might be less crowded.

Order?

To revise this paragraph, the events need to be rearranged in the order in which they occurred. A new draft would use the following order of events:

1. Topic sentence
2. 1st—Walking through the aisles
3. 2nd—Long checkout line and slow checker
4. 3rd—Physical discomfort at its peak
5. Conclusion

With the events ordered sequentially, the paragraph's development is far more coherent.

Exercise 4.12　EVENTS IN TIME

Read the following eight sentences. When properly ordered, they form a paragraph that narrates an incident involving two friends. After reading all eight, organize them into a unified paragraph. (Renumbering may help you work out the order.) Use your own paper to write out the organized paragraph.

1. I arrived at the museum an hour before it opened.

2. My friend and I decided to go to the museum for a special exhibit of Impressionist painters.

3. An hour later than scheduled, my friend arrived.

4. To avoid the crowds, we promised to meet early.

5. By this time, the museum was crowded and noisy.

6. She threw her catalogue on the floor, accused me of being too critical, and stormed out.

7. Unable to restrain myself, I told her how angry I was that she was so late.

8. I stayed for another hour but went home early since the incident not only spoiled my morning but my enjoyment of the exhibit as well.

Exercise 4.13   EVENTS IN TIME

Examine the following paragraph and mark any events that are out of order in terms of time. If it is helpful, number the events to be sure you have them in the proper order. Rewrite your properly ordered version on your own paper.

Tuesday is an especially hectic day for me. I am up at 5 AM and have to be on the freeway to get to work by 8. Once I am at work, I have the usual problems, but afterward, I have to get over to UCLA Extension for a night class. Parking on that crowded campus is always rough. When my class is finally over, there is still no chance to relax because it's back on the freeway for home, a trip that takes about forty minutes. By the time I reach my destination, it is nearly 11 PM, and I am exhausted! Having to take my daughter to the sitter before I go to work adds to the general rush. I am looking forward to the day when my Tuesday schedule ends, and I can get a better one.

Stages in a Process

Related to the logical ordering of events in time is the presentation of the stages in a process. Many college courses, such as those in the biological sciences, require a knowledge of processes such as cell division or photosynthesis. Although such processes do indeed occur *in time,* they tend to be more enduring, not unique to an individual.

Learning about such processes will be a primary part of many courses. Therefore, when you write about them, you will need to order the parts of the process correctly. Study the following process paragraph to see how its events or stages are ordered.

Some historians have written about the life of a civilization as having certain predictable characteristics. In its early stages is struggle, which has the effect of focusing energies toward goals such as independence from a ruler or unification of various subgroups. If the struggles are successful, the "golden years" can begin. It is here that the society experiences growth and an even

greater degree of unity. The arts often benefit greatly because of
the increased political stability. These golden years, however, do
not last indefinitely. At some point, a downward spiral begins.
Bureaucratic corruption often appears, the society's energy seems
wasted or even lacking, and many people are conscious of a change in
the times. With the lack of the cohesion that marked the earlier
periods, the society begins a decline--slow for some groups, rapid
for others. As for individual people, their fortunes depend largely
on which stage of society happens to dominate during their lives.

The three stages of this particular process include struggle, golden years (success), and decline.

When you are dealing with a process that is highly complex, it is all the more critical to present the stages accurately. Jumping from one stage to another or mixing them will disturb the reader who might conclude that you don't have a grasp of the overall scheme.

Exercise 4.14   STAGES IN A PROCESS

Write a one-page paragraph in which you describe a process. You might describe how to do an activity related to your home, yard, car, children, or social life. Or you may even wish to write about a process learned in one of your other courses—biology, psychology, or chemistry, for example.

To help order your paragraph, write out the process first so it is clear to you. Then list the various steps needed to undertake it successfully. If it is helpful, number the various steps and make sure they are in the proper order. *A word of caution:* select a process that is simple enough to describe adequately in one page.

Orders of Importance

The third method of ordering material does not relate to time or a process but to the point of view of the writer. The sample paragraph that follows discusses television violence. The first sentence is the topic sentence; the three underlined phrases mark the beginnings of the three groups of supportive material. Focus on the three underlined areas, for there is a problem in the order of presentation.

Unfortunately, violence has become a part of modern life,

but it is especially disturbing when it is glorified on so many   (1)

television programs. <u>Probably the worst side effect</u> is that   (2)
television violence desensitizes the viewer, regardless of age. We
become so adjusted to the sight of bullets ripping through the human
body or of a car plunging down a cliff that we feel cheated if there
aren't any "exciting" scenes. <u>In addition, violent films</u>   (4)
<u>tend to breed more violence</u> as special effects artists battle for
greater realism. Compare the gangster film of the thirties to any one
of the seventies or eighties and see which is more gruesomely
realistic. <u>Another vitally important side effect</u> involves the   (6)
influence violence has on human actions. For example, children
exposed to television violence tend to behave aggressively to their
peers. Violent crimes committed by adults often copy a type of crime
presented in a movie. Can we afford to stimulate this kind of
antisocial behavior in an already crowded and trouble-ridden world?
Certainly not! Unless filmmakers realize the enormous
responsibility they have to society, the overall situation in this
country can only worsen.

If you were to chart this paragraph's structure, this pattern emerges:

Topic Sentence—Sentence 1
Strongest Point—Sentence 2
Weakest Point—Sentence 4
Strong Point—Sentence 6

The writer indeed has specified a topic and expressed a point of view. The three supporting points, however, should be reorganized in one of two ways:

Descending Order	*Ascending Order*
Strongest Point	Weakest Point
Strong Point	Strong Point
Weakest Point	Strongest Point

Using such a structured order allows you to lead a reader smoothly through the developmental material. The proper ordering of your writing allows you to be in control of your paper, even if your paper is long and your strongest point requires several developmental paragraphs.

Exercise 4.15   ORDER OF IMPORTANCE

For this exercise you will be writing two versions of the same paragraph: one in *descending* order, the other in *ascending* order. Use your own paper to write your paragraphs.

> *Assignment:* Write a paragraph in support of this topic sentence—There are three reasons why I enjoy going to college.

For your first paragraph, arrange the three reasons in descending order: the strongest first, followed by the second in importance, down to the third and least important.

For your second paragraph, take the same three reasons and reverse them to use an ascending order. Now place the least important reason first, the second next, and the most important at the end.

Guidelines for Ordering Your Material

When you begin editing your draft, first consider whether the ordering of information is an issue. For the sorts of order discussed on the previous pages, use these overall guidelines:

Temporal ordering: Is every event in the proper sequence? To test this, walk yourself mentally through whatever activities you are writing about. Compare this review with your draft.

Process ordering: Mentally run through the process you attempted to describe before reading the draft; then compare this review with your draft to see how well you adhered to the order of events in the process.

Ascending or descending order: Be sure you know how many supportive points you wish to make. If necessary, number them as you read the draft. Then, make sure that these points do indeed follow one or the other of the orders.

If you have adequately developed your thesis, revising the order of your material may not be too time-consuming. For instance, you may only have to mark your draft with an arrow to tell you to move a sentence or two up or down in the text. If, however, ordering problems are complicated by poor paragraph blocking, then a second draft will be necessary to be sure that each paragraph has a clear purpose and appears in a logical place.

PROVIDING TRANSITIONS

Besides developing and ordering your material, adding transitions is another major method of helping a reader understand and follow your papers. Transitions are words or phrases that connect ideas. They are especially useful between sentences and between paragraphs.

Transitions between Sentences

Whether you read the following passage silently or aloud, you will notice that most of the sentences are choppy and disconnected. They are also repetitious: three of the four sentences begin with *I* and thus sound monotonous. In this type of writing the reader is forced to supply the connections between ideas and may often miss what the writer wanted to say.

```
        I have had a rough time in my economics class this

semester. I lack experience or familiarity with major   TRANS

concepts. The law of diminishing returns, supply and

demand, and theories of the stock market are all very
                                                        TRANS
foreign to someone who has never even held a real job. I

have to drop the course--for now--until I have matured a

bit in the ways of the marketplace.
```

These missing connections point to the need for *transitions,* phrases or words that link ideas. The prefix *trans-,* means a *going across* from one point to another and is the key here. A writer needs transitional phrasing to help the reader move from sentence to sentence within an individual paragraph or between two paragraphs. Examples of the different types of transitions are listed in the Guidelines for Providing Transitions on page 199.

Focusing on the sample paragraph above, you can see that the topic is the writer's "economics class," and the point of view is "rough time." By adding transitional phrasing to the already existing material, the quality and unity of the entire work can be improved. In the following revision the transitional words are underlined.

```
        I have had a rough time in my economics class this semester. The

main reason is that I lack experience and familiarity with major

economic concepts. The law of diminishing returns, supply and

demand, and theories of the stock market are all very foreign to
```

someone who has never even held a real job. <u>As a result of my
confusion</u>, I have to drop the course--for now--until I have matured a
bit in the ways of the marketplace.

Within a paragraph, the transitional words usually get their direction from the point of view in the topic sentence. In many paragraphs, transitional words tend to appear at the beginning of a sentence, thus telling the reader *how* the sentence connects back to the topic sentence or the thesis statement. Study the following paragraph: the topic sentence is underlined, the point of view is circled, and the transitional words are in brackets.

<u>Many people are (undecided) when it comes to the question of
marriage</u>. [On the one hand,] they may truly desire a loving and
faithful companion who will share in making a home and rearing
children. [But on the other hand,] they fear the enormous
responsibility and pressure that home and children bring, especially
if the marriage ends in divorce. [This wavering back and forth]
causes many people to remain single for as long as possible.

The transitional words allow the writer to unify the material around the key word—*undecided.* The result is a smooth and clear paragraph. But transitions can also occur in other parts of a sentence. In the following example, transitional words appear at or near the end of sentences 2, 3, and 4. Because these transitions relate to and link with "by myself," the paragraph is smooth and unified.

<u>For some reason, I have always had to bathe our large, shaggy
English sheepdog (by myself.)</u> My sister, who is always there when I
don't want her to be, disappears, [leaving me behind] to deal with
old Manfred. I once suggested that my folks might enjoy the
experience of bathing Manfred together, but the look they shot back
at me [told me, "You're it!"] A few times I have talked a friend into
helping me but [usually I do it alone.]

Exercise 4.16   TRANSITIONS BETWEEN SENTENCES

Examine the paragraph below and the notations in its margins; these marks highlight the need for transitional phrasing. Rewrite the paragraph on your own paper, adding the necessary transitional material. Voice your draft to hear its effectiveness.

There are several reasons why I would never eat   *TRANS*

restaurant food. I am very weight conscious and find that

restaurants tend to cook with the offenders: butter,

oils, lard, sour cream, and mayonnaise. If I ate out

regularly, I would probably gain too much weight. I do not   *TRANS*

trust anyone else to prepare my food because I am hard to

please. Chicken must be succulent, vegetables slightly

crunchy, and the pasta al dente. I rarely, if ever, dine   *TRANS*

out.

Exercise 4.17   TRANSITIONS BETWEEN SENTENCES

After reading the paragraph below, note those areas needing transitional phrasing. Then, use your own paper to rewrite the paragraph, adding appropriate transitions. Use voicing to hear how well your additions blend with the original material.

I think most personalized clothing is ridiculous. I saw a man the

other day whose pants, shoes, and jacket had the designers' names on

them. Why should I pay for the clothes and then give free advertising

to the designer? Personalized T-shirts can be very funny. Some of the

messages are very clever. Let's return to wearing clothing that is

without any form of advertising.

Transitions between Paragraphs

One of the requirements of an essay is that it have at least three paragraphs. In the process of moving from one paragraph to the next, however, problems may arise if you do not use enough transitions to bridge the gap between the separate

paragraphs. In the essay entitled "The 'Adult-Proof' Cap," pay particular attention to the underlined words and the arrows in the right-hand margin, for these
highlight transitional material.

The "Adult-Proof" Cap

Sometimes a product that was designed for the benefit of one
group of people can strangely upset the lives of another group. The
child-proof cap has no doubt saved many young lives, but it really
complicates mine. I can remember many frustrating times when I've
tried to pry open one thing or another, but <u>one incident stands out in</u>
<u>my memory.</u>

TRANS

Last spring, I decided to give my apartment a thorough cleaning
and, as part of the cleaning regimen, bought a rug shampoo in a child-
proof spray container. I should have realized when I saw all those
arrows and marks indicating which way to turn, then push, that I was
headed for trouble. I spent the better part of a half-hour following
every possible sequence of push down, twist, and lift imaginable. As
I went to the upstairs neighbor for help, I reminded myself that I
wasn't stupid and surely was smarter than the average child.
Wouldn't you know, Mrs. Casey's twelve-year-old son got it open
within seconds.

TRANS

<u>When I experience such a time-consuming problem as this one,</u> I
wish there were another way to protect young children. Those bottle
and can caps have proven to be such a source of frustration to me. The
problem is not so much that I can't open them but that I should be able
to open them.

In well-written essays, transitional phrasing will appear both *within* individual paragraphs to link sentences and *between* paragraphs to link these units to
each other, thereby unifying the entire essay.

Exercise 4.18   TRANSITIONS BETWEEN PARAGRAPHS

Watch for clear transitions between paragraphs as you read the following essay. Then answer the questions after it.

All of us want to spend money wisely so that we have enough to cover not only our debts but to pay for the little extras that make life so enjoyable. One way that many people overlook consists of saving every single sales receipt, whether a credit card slip, a restaurant stub, or cash register slip. There are a number of reasons why this can be a good policy to follow.

First of all, when people save receipts, they can get an idea of money spent over each month. By taking the time to separate all receipts into categories such as groceries, clothing, and restaurants, and adding them on a monthly basis, it is possible to know exactly what is spent in each area. Sometimes the totals will be a real shock, but they offer an incentive to change spending habits. Secondly, the process of categorizing and totaling sales receipts in different areas can be a good way to involve family members in real-life activities. Children in the family, for example, can practice addition skills and at the same time learn that food, clothing, and luxury items can be costly in today's world.

These two reasons may not seem impressive, but to me and my family they have proven invaluable. In the process of collecting, categorizing, and adding receipts, we have learned how we really spend our money and in what ways we might economize. I consider that a worthwhile return for the small investment of my time.

1. At the end of paragraph one, what are the transition words that allow the reader to move smoothly to the next paragraph?

2. In paragraph two, what are the two groups of transition words that hold the paragraph together and respond directly to the transition in the first paragraph?

3. At the start of the third paragraph, what transition words link the developmental paragraph?

Exercise 4.19   **TRANSITIONS BETWEEN PARAGRAPHS**

Read the following essay, noting its transitions; then answer the questions that follow the essay.

The Rabbit Effect

The first order placed in a mail-order catalogue will start what I call the "rabbit effect." Everyone knows how quickly rabbits multiply, and so do catalogues after a person orders even one small item. The multiplication process, as I recall, took about two years and had some startling results.

Because I've never been fond of shopping, I decided to order a dress from a Texas mail-order firm. I got the dress, which was lovely, and I was, of course, pleased. But within a month, I received a new catalogue, this time from Georgia. On the heels of this publication came one from Virginia, and so on. These catalogues showed a great deal of variety: some were slanted to sporty types, some to the elegant, affluent buyer, whereas others catered to campers, parents, or gourmet diners. As an experiment, I decided to write down the name of every catalogue I received over a three-month period prior to Christmas (the big season for catalogues). Nearly two years after that first order, I was astonished to discover that the total number being sent to me was 137! It was not long afterward that I moved and because bulk mail isn't forwarded, the vast majority of my catalogues didn't follow me to my new address.

Some people would be terribly distressed by this kind of expansion process. On the contrary, I rather enjoyed getting all the mail and being able to do out-of-state, tax-free shopping without having to struggle for a parking space or battle department store crowds. But the rabbit effect did and does hit two people with special "weight": my mail carrier and the trash collector.

1. What words at the end of paragraph one preview the development?

2. Which sentence in paragraph three allows the writer to comment on the material provided in paragraph two at the same time that the conclusion is begun?

3. Now go through the essay another time to note transitions. Look both for words that show the connections between ideas as you read from sentence to sentence and for words that connect back to the key words and ideas of the thesis.

Guidelines for Providing Transitions

Certain words or phrases are traditionally employed by writers as transitions. Study the following writing situations and the transitional words that could be used to unify a writer's ideas. Notice that when these phrases begin sentences, they are followed by commas.

1. To explain or develop a statement by using a specific incident, example, or illustration from your experience or observation, use these phrases to start your sentences:

   For example,   For instance,   To illustrate,

2. If you are giving a number of reasons to explain a point, use these words to introduce each reason in sequence:

   First of all,   Second,   Third,

   Next,   Finally,

3. When you compare and contrast ideas, situations, people, and so on, use these helpful terms:

   On the one hand,   Unlike. . . ,   On the other hand,

   However,   Similarly,   Conversely,

4. To draw a conclusion or to make a point, try these:

Therefore,   From this example,

In conclusion,   As a result,

Thus,   Consequently,

No matter where transitional words occur, they help to guide your reader and to keep the various portions of your paragraph, essay, letter, or report unified and easy to follow. Once your ideas are organized logically, transitions can be added to your draft quite easily.

IMPROVING YOUR SENTENCES

Revising the content of a paper requires you to evaluate and improve the way you responded to the assignment, developed your thesis, ordered your material, and provided transitions. Such revisions produce fuller, better organized, and more coherent paragraphs and essays. These paragraphs and essays, however, are collections of sentences.

Although the word is the most basic unit of both speech and writing, it is the *sentence* that forms the backbone of writing. Well-constructed sentences do much to present written ideas effectively and clearly. For this reason the next sections in this unit highlight the nature and revision of sentences, especially as they work to convey meaning in a reasonable and effective manner.

Whether you are asked to write a formal research paper, an essay, or the answer to an exam question, your final product must consist of sentences—groups of words that convey meaning and a degree of completeness to the reader. In constructing sentences, it is important to follow the rules of punctuation, spelling, and grammar. These are reviewed in Unit V, which also advises you about how to correct errors in mechanics. Nevertheless, it is not enough for sentences to be mechanically correct. They must also convey meaning—ideas, beliefs, and facts—and work together in the paragraph or essay to help the reader understand your train of thought.

The phrase "train of thought" points to a dual feature of sentence writing. Although each sentence is an individual unit (with a capital letter and an end mark of punctuation), *a sentence does not exist in a vacuum.* A train of thought is expressed in sentences linked in meaning, one after the other, just as the various cars in a train work together to transport people or products. Keep in mind, then, this double view. We may speak of a sentence as an individual unit, or we may speak of all sentences within a piece of writing as they work to transport ideas to the reader.

Four general characteristics support a sentence or sentences of high quality: (1) *suitable language,* (2) *reasonable point of view,* (3) *variety in length,* and (4) *variety in construction.* The first two are characteristics mainly of individual sentences whereas the last two concern themselves with the need for sentences to work together harmoniously.

FOR YOUR MENTAL FILE

Developing the ability to write effective sentences is crucial in communicating with the written word. To better experience what makes sentences effective, supplement your required college reading with a program of your own. Include serious newspaper reading such as the front page and the business or opinion sections and an ongoing reading project of your choice. For instance, you may find certain types of novels or specialized magazines both entertaining and relaxing. Although modern Americans are often described as "fitness oriented," we often neglect our minds. The mind, too, must be "exercised" to achieve maximum benefit. Reading is probably the single most effective mental exercise to reach your goal of writing sentences of solid quality.

USING SUITABLE LANGUAGE

Introduction

Examine the sentences in the following short piece of writing. Note the underlined portions, for they display various types of weaknesses in the writer's choice of language.

When I arrived in Minneapolis, I <u>looked up</u> my <u>old</u> high school friend Jeff. What a character! Even though Jeff was always <u>goofing off</u> and <u>getting into hot water</u> with everyone, he was <u>something else</u>. What a shock when I did finally <u>get hold of him</u>, for he had <u>turned around</u> completely.

Teachers have different ways of marking unsuitable language, but most tend to use the following terms:

Diction: a general term referring to choice of words. As an editorial mark on your paper, it means that your choice of words is weak in some way. The weakness may involve slang or any other type of unacceptable phrasing.

Slang: a more specific term for a word or phrase coined by or associated with a particular group of people or period of time. An expression such as "the cat's pajamas" illustrates how slang has become so dated that meaning is no longer clear.

Cliché: another more specific term used to refer to phrases such as "the early bird gets the worm." With time and usage, clichés lose meaning and dramatic impact.

Colloquial: a general term for language that is too casual or conversational for college writing.

Idiom/Idiomatic: refers to an expression that derives its meaning from usage, not from direct translation of individual words. Often, idioms involve verb phrases such as *pass out* (for faint) or *put up with* (for endure or tolerate). Although idiomatic language can be rich and powerful, too much may cause your writing to be both casual and wordy.

Other types of language to avoid include profanity or any type of expression that is vulgar in nature. Improper use of language, especially of more sophisticated words *(malapropism)*, is also a potential problem. The television character Archie Bunker is well known for his constant misuse of words, resulting in a great deal of laughter but poor communication. For example, he might use the word *sexagenarian* to accuse someone of being oversexed, but the meaning of this word is quite different—someone who is in his sixties. Finally, be on guard for non-words such as *upmost, orientate,* and *interpretate.* These words contain portions of existing words in our language, but they are not acceptable forms.

Rewriting Sentences to Improve Diction

Rewriting sentences with weak diction often produces a longer piece of writing, for you must usually add language that clarifies what you actually mean by a phrase such as "goofing off" or "getting into hot water." Compare the sentences below with the earlier ones written about Jeff. Note that the previously underlined portions have been rewritten.

When I arrived in Minneapolis, I located my high school friend, Jeff, whom I had not seen in fifteen years. What a character! Because he could not resist telling jokes or playing clever tricks on his teachers, Jeff probably set records for mischief during class. Certainly no one spent more time in the vice-principal's office. Despite his misbehavior, however, Jeff was my genuine and enthusiastic friend. What a shock when I met him years later to find that he was completely transformed.

The rewritten sentences are better, for they are characterized by a greater level of meaning. We learn:

> exactly how Jeff is an "old" friend; that is, he is a friend from the past.

> who Jeff bothered (specifically his teachers and the vice-principal) and how these people were annoyed.

> what made Jeff special to the writer in spite of Jeff's tendency to cause trouble.

FOR YOUR MENTAL FILE

Keep in mind the basic differences between speech (informal) and college writing (formal). One way to add formality to your writing is both simple and effective: Avoid contractions. Writing *I'll* for *I will* or *there's* for *there is* will make your writing sound conversational.

Guidelines for Revising Diction

If you are unsure about the quality of your diction or simply wish to expand your knowledge of language, consider the following suggestions:

1. First and foremost, pay close attention to all writing returned by your instructor. These papers are the best source of information about your current use of language.

2. Purchase a *thesaurus,* a specialized dictionary of synonyms (words of similar meanings) and antonyms (words of opposite meaning). Use your thesaurus to expand your word usage. For instance, if your teacher noted that you overused *good* in a particular paper, you could find the word in the thesaurus and note other, more suitable and precise terms such as *decent, just, honest,* or *worthy,* to replace it. Be cautious with the thesaurus, however. Use only words you understand and whose shades of meaning are appropriate. Otherwise, you are likely to add not only variety but also possibly inappropriate or stilted language.

3. Examine serious reading models such as your textbooks with an eye to their diction. Texts are generally written in formal language, so they can prove most helpful to you if you take the time to study them.

4. Set aside private time for speaking aloud. During this period (10–20 minutes), you could respeak your favorite slang expressions with more precise language. For example, if you tend to say or write "He's too much," rephrase the expression to pinpoint what you mean:

He has a strange sense of humor.

No one is as clever as Joe.

Joe could probably make a judge laugh.

In each case, the language is more precise, allowing meaning to be clearer. The think-and-respeak approach can provide insight for your rewriting efforts.

Exercise 4.20   REWRITING SLANG AND OTHER COLLOQUIAL EXPRESSIONS

On a separate sheet of paper, rewrite each of the following sentences by replacing the colloquial words or phrases (in italics) with more precise and specific language. Some terms are considered slang; all, however, are too casual to be effective in formal writing.

Example: Phil is too *uptight.*

Revision: Phil constantly worries about pleasing everyone, so he never can relax.

1. A cold drink on a hot summer day really *picks me up.*

2. My boss *blew his stack* when the *stuff* arrived too late.

3. The idea of a nuclear war *blows my mind.*

4. The committee made an even bigger *mess* out of the *deal.*

5. Some ball players make *big bucks.*

6. Doug *hangs out* at the beach.

7. The lottery winner *went out of her mind* because she won a *bundle!*

8. The boy was the *spitting image* of his father.

9. Some people *press the panic button* when they should *keep a cool head.*

10. Sometimes my little brother *drives me up the wall.*

11. Walter was a *real cheapskate* when we *went out on the town.*

12. I prefer someone who is *open.*

13. My geography exam was a *real bummer.*

14. That outfit is *totally awesome.*

Exercise 4.21   REWRITING CLICHÉS

Many of us use clichés rather than writing precisely. Clichés are especially disappointing when they replace authentic insights at key points in short writing. In this exercise, each short piece of writing ends with a cliché in italics. Use your imagination to remove the cliché, and replace it with more suitable language. Write the revisions on your own paper.

Example: My supervisor made many critical remarks about my work. Basically, though, he said that I had to *keep my nose to the grindstone.*

Revision: Basically, though, he said that I must *perform my duties with no distractions or interruptions.*

1. Last Tuesday, the refrigerator broke, the dog got sick, and the landlord raised the rent. All I could do was try *to keep a stiff upper lip.*

2. I maintained my calm until my roommate returned. I told her about the refrigerator, the dog, and the landlord and began to cry uncontrollably. My roommate sat down beside me and said that *into every life a little rain must fall.*

3. After this response, I contemplated getting a new roommate. How could she be so callous, so insensitive? However, she explained that she too had had a miserable afternoon at work and on the freeway, so I forgave her. After all, *tomorrow is another day.*

Exercise 4.22   REWRITING IDIOMATIC LANGUAGE

Each of the following sentences features a group of idioms in italics. In each case, the group can be more clearly written with *one* word only. Study the model; then, on a separate sheet of paper, replace the italicized phrase with the more concise, single word.

Example: I could not *make up my mind* what to buy.

Revision: I could not decide what to buy:

1. Ted did not *back up* his facts with footnotes.

2. Parenting *takes up* time and energy.

3. Jessica *stood up for* me during an argument.

4. My youngest son *took up* with an artistic group of people.

5. Early in my career, I had to *put up* with an egotistical supervisor.

6. People who *put down* others have few friends.

7. Jim tried to *wind down* after a hard day's work.

8. My children do not *own up to* their domestic responsibilities.

9. I *let him down* when I refused to help him.

10. When some people nag, they never *let up.*

Exercise 4.23   MISCELLANEOUS LANGUAGE CONCERNS

The following words or phrases in italics are unsuitable for formal college writing. Some feature objectionable terms such as profanity, and others use words too loosely or inaccurately. (When necessary, the problem is explained.) Write the revisions on your own paper. Either one or a few words will be necessary for a successful revision.

1. Jeff was unable to communicate with his *old man*.

2. Love is an amazing *thing*. (*Thing* refers to an object.)

3. My sister makes me *crazy* when she borrows my clothes. (The term *crazy* is insulting and prejudicial.)

4. The freeway was so *damn* busy this morning.

5. The *kids* were really well behaved today. (*Kids* is too casual.)

6. When the *cop* stopped me, I did not know what to expect. (*Cop* is an insulting term.)

7. Joy was a *neat* person to know. (*Neat* properly refers to tidy or orderly habits.)

8. Disneyland is a *fun* place to visit.

9. The downtown area of the city is filled with *bums*.

10. I had a *hell of a* time getting my children to try eating liver.

Exercise 4.24   MISCELLANEOUS LANGUAGE CONCERNS

The following paragraph is marked by inappropriate diction including slang, clichés, and casual, idiomatic language. Replace the underlined words with one or several words that are more specific. Write your revision on your own paper. To lessen the conversational tone, remember to expand all contractions (change *I'm* to *I am*).

Whenever I'm down, I always go to the movies. Light stuff is my favorite because I know I'll be laughing before too long. A few months ago, I was feeling low after taking examinations, so I took off to the movies. After about twenty minutes, I was laughing so hard I could cry. In the process I managed to forget about my exams and any worries about my grades. The movie theater is a neat place because other people join with you in laughing. Sometimes I've started chuckling just because other people were. I guess the mood kind of rubs off on a person. By the time the show is over, I've got my head straight and am up once again. Laughter really is the best medicine.

MAINTAINING A REASONABLE POINT OF VIEW

Introduction

Study the following paragraph, paying close attention to the italicized portion. Although the last sentence has no errors in punctuation, grammar, or spelling, its quality is poor because of the writer's point of view.

> This quarter, I am taking trigonometry to fulfill a mathematics requirement in my major. At the start of the course, I had confidence in my ability to do well, but now at the midpoint of the quarter, I am barely passing the quizzes and major tests. The reason I am doing poorly is the professor.

The writer may sincerely feel that the professor is the cause of the problem, but the statement is unreasonable in its point of view. *Why?*

This writer's point of view is weakened because it is not intellectually valid or fair to resolve a problem merely by assigning blame. If the student truly thinks that the fault lies with the professor, then specifics are necessary to provide a fair reason for the problem—in other words, to provide a reasonable point of view. Consider these two possible revisions of the faulty sentence:

> One reason I am doing so poorly stems from my instructor's habit of lecturing in a low, barely audible voice.

> My problem can be directly connected to the fact that in one month we have had four different substitute teachers because our instructor has been ill.

If, after a bit more thought, the writer decides that the problem does not involve the instructor, then other revisions are possible:

> Unfortunately, my work schedule changed unexpectedly and disrupted my ability to keep up with the reading assignments.

> This situation developed because I have missed half the lectures in the past month.

All four revisions are stronger because they provide reasonable explanations for the poor performance. Furthermore, all are believable, for they provide some analysis of the problem, not a superficial excuse.

Other problems with reasonable points of view involve *prejudice* or *stereotypes*. Examine the following statements, all of which are faulty in their reasoning and degree of fairness.

> Young people cannot be trusted.
> Old age brings disease, misery, and poverty.

Women are simply not good at mathematics.
My younger brother has been the cause of all our family's problems.

Other sentences are faulty because they are too obvious in their points of view:

I enjoy going to museums because of the art.
School is a place for a person to learn.

Guidelines for Locating Problems with Your Point of View

Locating this type of sentence problem may be difficult at first, for on the surface, nothing appears to be wrong. However, when you examine your sentences, watch closely for the following situations:

1. If your assignment asks for your *opinion* in any way or if you are asked to provide reasons for a problem, then focus on the sentences that express your point of view. Ask yourself:

   a. Have I given a *reasonable* explanation? Or have I too simply or unfairly blamed someone or something?

   b. Does my reason or explanation seem too simple for the circumstances? In other words, could I have decided too easily on an opinion about a complex issue or problem?

2. Be particularly attentive to assignments that are emotional or controversial. Writing assignments affect each of us differently, but if a response is highly emotional, then it is likely to lose the objectivity necessary for a persuasive response. If you find yourself in this situation, ask questions such as those provided for the earlier example. The very process of questioning will help you to achieve some intellectual distance and may keep your point of view reasonable.

Exercise 4.25   RECOGNIZING FAULTY THINKING

Dealing with the problem of an unreasonable or overly simplistic point of view is made easier when it is clear what the problem actually is. In this exercise, each sentence contains an unreasonable point of view. After reading each sentence carefully, write several short sentences, explaining on a separate sheet of paper what the problem is.

Example: Jogging is good for people.

Remarks: Jogging is not good for *all* people, especially those with medical problems. The statement is not true for everyone.

1. I failed the test because the questions were stupid.

2. A balanced budget is the solution to this country's problems.

3. Shoppers simply cannot trust salespeople.

4. The Christmas holiday brings out the best in everyone.

5. There is no point in discussing politics or religion because people will only argue violently.

6. Sports cars cause too many accidents.

Exercise 4.26   REWRITING UNREASONABLE SENTENCES

The sentences in this exercise are unreasonable or too simplistic. The analysis appearing beneath the first five sentences will help you recognize why their thinking is fuzzy and direct you toward a stronger, more reasonable revision. The last five sentences without any analysis will test your ability to see and correct the problems on your own. Rewrite all ten sentences on a separate sheet of paper.

1. One of my favorite television comedies was ''I Love Lucy'' because it was so funny.

Analysis: Comedies are meant to be funny, so this sentence does not say much about ''I Love Lucy.'' Your revision should focus on the words after ''because.'' Provide a concrete and logical reason why the show was funny.

2. I did not write a good essay because my heart wasn't in it.

Analysis: Using an overworked expression like ''my heart wasn't in it'' is much weaker than an honest analysis of the cause of the difficulty. In your revision, include a valid reason why the person wrote a poor essay. In addition, replace the word ''good'' with a word that is more specific.

3. Mathematics is an impossible class.

Analysis: This sentence is not true, of course, because many people do well in math. If you have a strong opinion about a class or an issue, it is not logical to assume that all people share it. Here, your revision should provide a specific focus. Try to specify whose frame of reference is guiding this statement or opinion, and also provide at least one reason why the course could be interpreted as difficult.

4. The problem is the government.

Analysis: Equating ''problem'' and ''government'' is too simplistic to be reasonable. After all, government is a necessity in civilized life. In your revision, focus on the specific complaint (inefficient, wasteful, or unfair) about some aspect of government (taxation, foreign policy, or personal liberty).

5. The problem with teenagers is that they are too irresponsible.

Analysis: The writer of this statement has certainly expressed an opinion—but not a reasonable one. Even if a person had known ten irresponsible teenagers, this statement does not hold true for everyone in this age group. For your revision, curb the effect of this sweeping generalization. Try, also, to specify some area of life where some teenagers may be irresponsible.

6. People behave foolishly when they are in love.

7. Television keeps me from reaching my goals.

8. I enjoy dramatic movies because they are so serious about life.

9. There was no way to get an *A* in that professor's class.

10. The biggest problem a celebrity has is being too well known.

Exercise 4.27   LOCATING FAULTY REASONING IN A TEXT

Read the following paragraph as preparation for class discussion. Watch for and make note of any thinking that is too simplistic or unreasonable. Consider, too, the effect this kind of writing would have on a reader.

> When asked to provide my opinion about a state lottery, I can clearly say that I am strongly opposed. As history and common sense illustrate, gambling of any sort has been the greatest source of evil imaginable. Consider the poor people who are persuaded or encouraged to gamble away the little money they have on the chance of winning millions. At the same time that tickets are being bought, children are starving, and bills are being left unpaid. If a lottery were in effect, who would monitor the proceedings? Crime is rampant in all areas of our society, so there is every reason to believe that corruption will reach lottery officials and backers. In conclusion, people should be content with forms of gambling now in existence and not bring in others.

VARYING SENTENCE LENGTH

Introduction

Read the following two paragraphs, both silently and aloud. Although the punctuation, grammar, and spelling are correct, each paragraph has problems with sentence length.

My most difficult class this past semester was psychology. It was just not what I expected it to be. The teacher discussed brain anatomy for a month. I thought we would be learning about unusual behavior. Instead we had anatomical terms. I really had to force myself to pay attention and to study so that I would not get behind or do poorly on tests.

Children often exhibit aggressive behavior after they have viewed violent programs on television or seen aggressive acts between their parents or older siblings, so we really need some form of censorship of television and better counseling agencies for families so that domestic problems in our society can be solved.

In the first paragraph, the first five sentences are similar in length, causing choppiness. If you read the paragraph aloud, the choppy and repetitious quality of the sentences will be even clearer. In the second paragraph, the opposite situation occurs. Here the writer has packed all the ideas into one enormous sentence of such length that the reader is left gasping for breath and struggling to absorb all the ideas.

How can you avoid sentence extremes in your writing? With writing as with life, *balance* is crucial. A blending of lengths will eliminate the monotony of too many short sentences and lessen the negative effect of too many long ones.

Balancing Short Sentences

Two basic and highly effective methods are at your disposal if you tend to write too many short sentences:

1. Combine two or more short sentences to create a single longer one.
2. When combining is not possible, add new material to an existing short sentence to lengthen it.

Watch what occurs when these two revision tactics are used to improve the first sample paragraph. The notations in the left margin indicate the types of change made.

	My most difficult class this past
Combination	semester was psychology <u>because</u> it was just
	not what I expected it to be. <u>From the very</u>
New Material	<u>first lecture</u>, the teacher discussed brain
	anatomy <u>and continued with this for an entire</u>
	<u>month</u>. I thought we would be learning about
New Material	unusual behavior, <u>especially in areas dealing</u>
	<u>with sex</u>. Instead, we had anatomical terms
New Material	<u>relating to the brain and its various parts</u>
	<u>and chemicals</u>. I really had to force myself to
	pay attention and to study so that I would not
	get behind and do poorly on the tests.

This revised version is stronger than the original for a number of reasons. First, it eliminates the choppiness that resulted from many short sentences placed together. Second, its meaning and communication are enhanced by the addition of specific, pertinent information.

Combining Sentences with Connectors   Certain words in our language prove useful for combining sentences to achieve balance in length. These words, called *connectors,* have the power to join separate sentences (groups of ideas) into a smoother train of thought. For example, what words come to your mind as possible connectors for these pairs of short sentences?

1. I wanted to eat.————It was my dinner hour.

2. Sheila did not like pizza.————She had a slice anyway.

For the first set of sentences, you may have thought of *because* or *for,* two major connectors in English:

I wanted to eat *because* it was my dinner hour.

I wanted to eat, *for* it was my dinner hour.

For the second set, you probably considered the connector *but* or *although.*

Sheila did not like pizza, *but* she had a slice anyway.

Sheila did not like pizza, *although* she had a slice anyway.

There are three major groups of connectors or conjunctions, as they are called in grammar: *coordinating, subordinating,* and *adverbial.* Although this unit does not focus on the grammar and punctuation of these elements, it is helpful to study them in the three categories.

Coordinating Conjunctions   join *equal* elements. The six that follow are particularly useful in combining short sentences into one unit:

> **and**: joins sentences (ideas) that have equality:
>> I went to the store, *and* Janet accompanied me.

> **but**: joins sentences but with a sense of contrast or the unexpected:
>> Janet applied for the job, *but* she was not hired.

> **for**: links ideas and suggests a reason or cause:
>> We should study history, *for* there are valuable lessons to be learned.

> **or**: signals a choice of some kind:
>> Do you want to go to the movies, *or* would you prefer ice skating?

> **yet**: is similar to *but;* however, it is not quite as strong:
>> I had trouble understanding calculus, *yet* I continued doing my homework.

> **so**: draws or indicates a conclusion or result:
>> The Christmas season brings a dramatic increase in the number of shoppers, *so* most stores hire extra personnel.

Other coordinating conjunctions include *nor* and *and so.*

Subordinating Conjunctions   also join sentence elements, but they make the material introduced by the conjunction *dependent.* In other words, subordinating conjunctions join *unequal* elements. The most commonly used connectors in this category include the following:

> **because** or **since**: similar to the coordinator *for, because* and *since* signal a reason; *since* can also refer to a particular event in time:
>> I wanted to move *because* my rent was too high.
>> My headaches have disappeared *since* I began taking that new medication in June.

> **while** or **as**: tend to join activities occurring at the same time:
>> He vacuumed the carpets *while* I dusted the furniture.
>> The sun was setting *as* I finally completed my project.

> **although** or **though**: are similar to *but* and indicate some contrast or unexpected situation:
>> I wanted that dress *although* I could not afford it.
>> Even *though* I warned him that it looked like rain, he went without an umbrella.

after or **when**: relate to time, especially connecting one event to another that follows:

> My little brother deliberately ate all the cake *after* I told him not to.
>
> He blushed *when* I unexpectedly kissed him.

until: suggests time but with the idea that a certain point or limit has been reached:

> I studied *until* I could not concentrate any longer.

if: is a wishful or hypothetical connector that allows you to set up many speculative constructions:

> I could retire *if* I were to win the lottery.
>
> Some believe that chaos will result *if* people are allowed to govern themselves directly.

Other subordinating conjunctions include *where, whereas, whether, that, so that, till,* and *than.*

Adverbial Conjunctions   show strong relationships between the elements they join. A semicolon is added when these conjunctions connect sentences:

therefore, thus, or **consequently**: signal that a conclusion is being drawn or some result has been achieved.

> The time limit had passed; *therefore,* I had no choice but to pay the penalty.
>
> The committee made an effective presentation; *thus,* its recommendations were accepted.
>
> My first handwritten paper was marked as "illegible"; *consequently,* I typed all of the other essays.

however or **nevertheless**: similar to *although* and *but,* these conjunctions signal some contrast or the unexpected.

> The American colonies felt that they were being overtaxed; *however,* the British were of a different opinion.
>
> On January 1, I resolved to budget my money; *nevertheless,* February 1 finds me short of cash.

in fact, furthermore, or **moreover**: introduce material that emphasizes and extends what was said in the first sentence.

> Fiona was a model student; *in fact,* she was the teacher's pet.
>
> To be eligible, contestants had to enter the sweepstakes promptly; *furthermore,*

their entry blanks had to be filled out completely and accurately.

The judge dismissed the case; *moreover,* he expressed dismay that the matter had ever been allowed to occupy the court's time.

Other adverbial conjunctions include *then* and *besides.*

For more detail on the punctuation of coordinating, subordinating, and adverbial conjunctions, consult the punctuation section of Unit V, pp. 312–332.

Exercise 4.28   USING COORDINATORS

The sentence pairs below are choppy because of short, repetitious sentences. Combine each pair into *one* sentence (one capital plus one period or question mark). Use one of these connectors:

, and   , but   , for   , or   , so

Before making your choice of a connector, read each sentence carefully to see what type of situation or meaning exists. To correctly punctuate your *new* combined sentence, add a comma *before* the connector. Write your revised sentences on a separate sheet of paper.

1. I ordered a small bowl of oatmeal. My stomach wasn't ready for it.
2. Some people use time constructively. They tend to accomplish a great deal.
3. I finally got into the checkout line. I had purchased all my groceries.
4. Tea and coffee are popular beverages. They both contain caffeine.
5. Exercise can help a person lose weight. I don't like to exercise.
6. He needed to borrow a car. I loaned him mine.
7. Do you want to eat dinner at home? Do you want to go out to a restaurant?
8. My daughter thought the school year was too long. I didn't think it was long enough.
9. Studying for three hours left me fatigued. I decided to take a short break.
10. Carmen ordered sushi. Then she ordered dessert.

Exercise 4.29   USING SUBORDINATORS

Combine each of the following pairs of short sentences into one smoother sentence, using a connector from this list of subordinating connectors:

because   when   although   after

Do not worry about comma usage at this time. Most of your combinations would not require a comma. Write your revised sentences on your own paper.

1. I was studying my physics text. Jack approached me to ask about lunch.

2. Birds will often fly into a closed window. They do not see the glass.

3. The runner raced for home plate. He saw the fielder drop the ball.

4. Phyllis wanted to get a concert ticket. She could not afford one on her budget.

5. My patience was exhausted. I had given the customer too much of my time.

6. Tina applied for the job. She did not have all the needed skills.

7. I started to devour the dessert. I saw the hostess take her first bite of it.

8. Howard resigned from his job. The situation at the office had become intolerable.

9. We ran for the parking lot. The ball game had not officially ended.

10. Deep in thought, I pondered my future. The doorbell rang.

Exercise 4.30   USING ADVERBIAL CONJUNCTIONS

Carefully read each sentence in the pairs below to decide which adverbial connector is suitable. Remember that adverbial conjunctions are preceded by a semicolon and followed by a comma *when they join sentences*. Choose from these adverbial conjunctions:

> ; in fact,   ; consequently,
> ; however,   ; therefore,

1. The doctor was not satisfied with the patient's progress. She decided to obtain a second opinion.

2. I took an auto mechanics course in the summer. I still did not feel competent to do major work alone.

3. I studied regularly and attended every class. My grades improved by the end of the term.

4. I did very well in my anthropology course. I earned my first *A* in college.

5. Harold was generally reclusive. He did manage to get out for an occasional visit with his family.

6. Irene refused Darrell's offer of marriage. She told him she never wanted to see him again.

7. The basketball team lost every game. The coach decided to increase the number of practice sessions next season.

✎ Exercise 4.31   USING CONNECTORS IN A TEXT

The following paragraph has too many sentences of a similar length; consequently, the writing is choppy. Using your knowledge of *connectors* (coordinating, subordinating, adverbial), rewrite the paragraph, combining sentences with an appropriate connector.

First, read the paragraph carefully, marking where you hear a need for a connector. Then decide which connector fits best. Try to use a variety of connectors; watch, too, for any necessary punctuation. Finally, rewrite the combined version on your own paper.

Visiting a world's fair can be marvelous. A person has an opportunity to visit many countries in one place. My first fair was in Vancouver in 1986. The experience was unforgettable. Not all nations were represented. There were enough to give me a sense of having been around the world. My favorite exhibit was from British Columbia. It presented a spectacular movie that took my breath away. The fair also made me realize the great diversity of human culture and expression. I have resolved to visit each world's fair, no matter where it is located.

Combining Sentences with Relative Pronouns   There is another way to combine sentences when you notice that too many of them are short and choppy. This second strategy works without using the connectors discussed earlier, but it is just as effective *when certain conditions are present*. Read the short paragraph below; pay close attention to the underlined portions, for these indicate where problems occur and what conditions are needed.

The "dumb blond" is a very offensive <u>stereotype</u>. <u>This stereotype</u> presents a standard image of <u>blonds</u>. <u>They</u> are shown as curvaceous, giggly, and unintelligent. The image appears on television and in film and seems to be a part of our cultural humor. The stereotype appeals to many <u>men</u>. <u>Men</u> tend to find a buxom, fluttery blond sexually attractive. But what about the harm this stereotype causes?

To study the trouble spots more closely, focus on the underlined words: *stereotype, This stereotype, blonds, They, men,* and *Men.* This type of writing situation—the repetition or *echoing* of words at the ends and beginnings of sentences—affects the quality of these sentences. In the first and third examples, the repetition is the most obvious because the same word is echoed at close range. In the second example, *they* refers to blonds, so repetition still exists. If you were to read the paragraph aloud, you would hear the effect of this type of echoing. When this sort of repetition begins to dominate a paragraph, the writing takes on a juvenile tone.

To lessen the negative effect of these short and repetitive sentences, the writer could use connectors: "The 'dumb blond' is one very offensive stereotype *because* this stereotype presents a standard image of blonds." However, the two *stereotypes* are still repeated, now in one sentence instead of two. Examine the following revision of the earlier paragraph and watch what has been done to remove the echoing; key areas are underlined:

The "dumb blond" is a very offensive <u>stereotype</u> <u>which</u> presents

a standard image of <u>blonds</u>, <u>who</u> are shown as curvaceous, giggly, and

unintelligent. The image appears on television and in films and

seems to be a part of our cultural humor. The stereotype appeals to

<u>men</u> <u>who</u> tend to find a buxom, fluttery blond sexually attractive. But

what about the harm this stereotype causes?

The key words used for this special type of combination are *which, that,* and *who.* In grammar, they are identified as relative pronouns; the fourth relative pronoun *whom* can also be used but in different types of combinations. Let's look more closely at what happened to the various sentences:

The "dumb blond" is a very offensive stereotype, ~~This stereotype~~ *which*

presents a standard image of blond women.

1. Remove the period from the first sentence.

2. Remove the echoed word (stereotype) and "This" from the second sentence.

3. Join the two units with either *which* or *that.* (These two relative pronouns tend to be interchangeable when preceding a dependent clause.)

4. The new unit consists of one sentence (capital plus period) instead of two.

The stereotype appeals to ~~many~~ men. ~~Men~~ tend to find. . . .

1. Remove the period at the end of the first sentence.

2. Remove the echoing word, the second "Men" from sentence two.

3. Join the two units with an appropriate word—*who*, in this case—because it refers to people.

When you examine your own writing, watch to see if there are repetitions or echoes such as these. Use good judgment as you edit. Sometimes repetition works well in connecting or emphasizing ideas or feelings. But, if you notice that echoing appears too often, especially several times in one paragraph, consider using this second combination strategy to eliminate it. Remember that using the relative pronouns *who, which,* and *that* to combine ideas will work properly *only* if there is the kind of repetition shown in the examples.

For additional information on relative pronouns, consult the subject–verb agreement section (p. 276) and punctuation section in Unit V (pp. 321–322); Appendix A contains specific information about the use of the pronoun *whom.*

Exercise 4.32   USING RELATIVE PRONOUNS

In the pairs of sentences that follow, the echoes or repetitions are highlighted by italics. Use one of the following three relative pronouns to combine each pair of sentences into one unit: *who*—use for people; *that, which*—use for objects, places, ideas, and nonhumans.

Choppy: I took *an economics class. It* was most informative.

Revision: I took *an economics class that* was most informative.

Follow this model as you work through this exercise. Remember that your goal is to combine two choppy sentences into a single smooth one. At this stage, do not worry about adding commas.

1. Young and old alike are fascinated by *dinosaurs. They* have been extinct for millions of years.

2. A fascinating group in the Old West was the Hole-in-the-Wall *Gang. It* included Butch Cassidy and the Sundance Kid.

3. Catherine of Aragon was the first wife of *Henry VIII. Henry* had five more wives before his death.

4. I bought a charming music *box. It* played "Stardust" when opened.

5. Three men and three women were accepted into the training *program. It* lasted for three months.

6. I try to avoid *Melanie. She* always manages to irritate me.

7. Some people prefer perennial *plants. They* bloom year round and do not require replanting.

8. I spoke to my travel *agent. She* told me of the new tour.

9. My most precious possession is my collection of photo *albums. They* contain the pictures of my beloved family down through the years.

10. I had trouble holding on to my small *daughter. She* kept squirming and wriggling.

Exercise 4.33   USING RELATIVE PRONOUNS TO IMPROVE A TEXT

The following text contains many short sentences which can be combined using relative pronouns. Read the text carefully and note where echoing occurs (the underlined portions). Combine repetitious sentences using one of these relative pronouns: *who* for people; *which* or *that* for objects, places, ideas, and nonhumans. Write your revised version (it should contain nine sentences) on a separate sheet of paper.

One of the most fascinating tourist spots in England is the <u>Tower of London</u>. <u>The Tower</u> is an especially rich historical site. My most memorable visit there was in 1964 when there were fewer tourists to crowd the area; in fact, I was among the first to enter that day. One special discovery was of a stone <u>tablet</u>. <u>The tablet</u> marked the spot where Anne Boleyn was beheaded. I remember trying to imagine the agony of this young wife and mother as she faced her death. Later, I saw a group of students with their <u>teacher</u>. <u>He</u> was lecturing on another of the Tower's grisly tales. Perhaps the most famous attraction of all is the crown jewel collection. Crowds form to see the brilliance of the <u>gems</u>. <u>The gems</u> flash and glisten in their royal settings. On each of my visits to London, I have visited the Tower. Despite the increase in the number of tourists, I love to contemplate this magnificent <u>building</u>. <u>It</u> speaks volumes of an era long past.

Adding New Material   If you were to combine too many sentences, a new sort of monotony and repetition could occur. Furthermore, in some instances it may not be possible to join sentences clearly. A second tactic, then, is to develop the length of a short sentence with additional information. Adding new material not only lessens choppiness but also provides your reader with new ideas, images, or facts.

Guidelines for Adding New Material   To add information to any of your sentences, use the following suggestions:

1. First, study the sentences in question very carefully. Technically, any sentence can be increased in length; however, some lend themselves more naturally to the process. In the following pair, for example, which sentence suggests the possibility or need for an effective addition?

   The instructor began her lecture promptly at 9:00 A.M.
   She discussed several areas.

      The second sentence has possibilities for expansion since a reader would be interested in knowing something about what was discussed. Consider these additions:

   She discussed several areas, *including the marriage customs of the Cheyenne.*

   She *then* discussed several areas *in a dramatic and mesmerizing hour-long lecture.*

      The first expansion focuses on one of the areas presented by the lecturer. The second highlights the way in which she delivered her message and the length of the talk. Both effectively expand a relatively short and potentially choppy sentence.

2. When you do start to add details or new ideas, be sure they are in keeping with the content of your paragraph. In other words, injecting fresh details or additional information is an excellent idea, but be certain that these additions fit into the overall purpose of your writing.

3. When you have added new material to an existing sentence, read the revision aloud to be sure that the addition blends to form one sentence, not two.

   Correct: She discussed several areas in a dramatic and mesmerizing manner. (one sentence)

   Faulty: She discussed several areas she spoke in a dramatic and mesmerizing manner. (two sentences run together)

      When two sentences are incorrectly written as if they were one, a major sentence error results: the run-together sentence or the comma splice. See the section on major sentence errors, pages 259–311 in Unit V for a thorough discussion of these problems.

Exercise 4.34   ADDING NEW MATERIAL TO AN EXISTING SENTENCE

Add new material to each of the following short sentences as indicated by the directions in parentheses. Study the example and write your expanded version on your own paper.

> *Example:* I spotted a gorgeous dress. (Add material that describes the dress.)
> I spotted a gorgeous blue dress *trimmed with sequins, lace, and ribbons*.

1. Sylvia's head ached. (Add material to describe further *how* her head hurt.)

2. Generally, Thursday is my roughest day. (Add a connector, and give a reason *why* Thursday is so difficult.)

3. I do not eat candy. (Add new material that gives at least *one reason* for not eating candy.)

4. Lisa gave an interesting talk. (*Why* was the talk interesting? Add some facts about the talk, such as the topic and some details about the topic.)

5. As a rule, I exercise. (Add a connector and give a *reason* for exercising.)

6. The store is closed. (*Why* is the store closed? Add a connector and a reason.)

7. I lost my key ring. (Add material to tell the reader *when* and *where* this occurred.)

8. Janet simply refused to date George. (Add a connector and give one reason *why* she refused.)

9. Gardening is my favorite hobby. (Add material to this sentence to tell *when* the person gardens and for *how long* the hobby has been maintained.)

10. The news report was filled with frightening bits of information. (Add material to give an idea of *what sort* of information was broadcast.)

Exercise 4.35   EXPANDING SENTENCES IN A TEXT

The paragraph below is marked by a number of short, ineffective sentences (underlined). To each underlined unit, add new material according to the guidelines in the right margin. Use either your own direct knowledge or your imagination to provide fresh information.

Write the revision on your own paper. Evaluate your first effort to see that the material you add does indeed work well within the sentence and in relationship to other sentences. Make whatever corrections are necessary for a final version.

Driving in heavy freeway traffic is an exhausting,

frustrating experience for most people. In my *Add material to give a reason why.*

experience, the worst period of time is mid- to late

afternoon. Drivers at this time will forget many of the

simple rules and courtesies of the road. Some are just

How are they careless? Describe

careless. Others take unnecessary chances. A few are *→ What chances? Describe*

simply rude. Sometimes, the thought of driving in the

↓ How is a driver rude? Describe

midst of all this confusion makes me use the surface

streets. Unfortunately, the situation there is not that

much better.

Balancing Long Sentences

Let us return to the earlier example of a sentence that is simply too long to be effective:

Children often exhibit aggressive behavior after they have

viewed violent programs on television or seen aggressive acts

between their parents or older siblings, so we really need some form

of censorship of television and better counseling agencies for

families so that domestic problems in our society can be solved.

This writer has presented a number of good observations and reasonable opinions, including the following:

that children behave violently when they see violent behavior on television or from family members

that television censorship is needed

that better counseling agencies are necessary

that censorship and counseling will help the domestic situation

When these ideas are packed between a single capital and a period, however, the reader is overwhelmed by too much information presented too quickly. The situation is comparable to being forced to eat a large quantity of food so rapidly that there is no possibility of savoring or appreciating individual flavors and textures of various foods.

Sentences that are bursting with too much information need to be broken down into smaller, more easily understood units. Logical breaking points would separate the various ideas. The fact that children do imitate violent behavior would form one sentence for the reader to process, and so on. Compare the effect of the following revision, consisting of five sentences. Notice that some material (underlined) was added so that sentences link smoothly or are complete.

Children often exhibit aggressive behavior after they have

viewed violent programs on television. In addition, aggressive acts

between parents or older siblings will also set a negative example

for a child. Because of these facts, we must first have some

censorship of television violence. Secondly, we must allocate more

funding for family counseling centers to be made available to all who

need them. In this way, we can better solve domestic problems.

By breaking up one long, packed sentence into five shorter ones, the writer's train of thought is better absorbed by the reader, who is no longer overwhelmed by too much material.

Guidelines for Balancing Long Sentences   When editing your own drafts, try the following strategies to detect problems with lengthy sentences.

1. Read your draft aloud, for this practice increases your awareness of rambling sentences. Be sure to read your sentences just as you have written them. If you are running short of breath, this is a strong indication that the sentence is too long.

2. Watch for the presence of too many connectors, especially *and* in one sentence. This word in particular causes some of us to string together too many ideas into a single sentence.

3. Visually examine your paper, focusing on capitals and periods or question marks. Do you see one sentence that looks like an entire paragraph? If the answer is yes, you have a sentence that needs pruning.

Exercise 4.36   BALANCING LONG SENTENCES

Each of the following sentences is too long and should be separated into two sentences. To split the large unit, focus on the italicized word (a connector) because it is here that the splitting can safely occur. When you rewrite the sentences, remove the connector and punctuate each of the remaining portions with its own capital letter and period. Use your own paper.

1. I wanted to go to the mall for the special summer sale on linens, *and* then I planned to stop off at the open air market for a fresh supply of vegetables.

2. Some schools experience difficulty providing adequate parking for their students because of insufficient space, *and* my college is no exception as I have never been able to park in the morning without a struggle.

3. Someday I may move to the country and live in a house surrounded by trees, *but* for now, I am happy to stay in my small apartment in the heart of the city because I am close to my job.

4. Parents who are concerned about adolescent drug abuse should attend the meeting Wednesday night *when* new ideas for drug abuse prevention will be presented to help curb this growing problem.

5. The stormy night seemed endless, and I thought I would never sleep *because* each time my eyelids closed, a resounding clap of thunder would awaken me.

6. My daughter's collection of small reptiles was beginning to be a problem *because* several of the lizards (plus a small snake) had managed to climb out of their terraria and hide somewhere in the house.

Exercise 4.37   BALANCING LONG SENTENCES

This exercise is similar to the previous one in that the problem area is italicized. However, after you have separated ideas and removed the connector, you will have to add material to the second portion to make it a complete sentence. Use your own paper.

> *Example:* For two grueling hours I climbed that hill to the very top where I could see for miles *and* be overwhelmed by the beauty of forest and sky.

> *Revision.* For two grueling hours I climbed that hill to the very top where I could see for miles. *All of my senses were* overwhelmed by the beauty of forest and sky.

The connector *and* is dropped entirely, but new material is added (all my senses) so that it is clear who or what is overwhelmed. The verb *be* is changed to *were*.

1. After my parents gave me a car for my birthday, I decided to take a class in car maintenance *and* learn to tune up the car and make minor repairs myself.

2. The first week of school is exciting *because* of the crowds of new students rushing to locate their classes, purchase books, and greet old friends.

3. Prewriting helps writers organize their thoughts *and* also provides a special time for experimentation with various topic sentences.

4. The bargain basement was crammed with holiday shoppers frantically trying to grab for bargains *while* at the same time holding on to their raincoats, umbrellas, and handbags.

5. I was mesmerized by the bright and colorful collection of children's toys in the department store window *and* was especially delighted to see several porcelain dolls that reminded me of my own childhood toys.

6. I had to walk across the crowded dance floor to the buffet table *but* unfortunately was kept from my goal by moving bodies blocking my path.

Exercise 4.38   BALANCING LONG SENTENCES

The following paragraph contains many sentences which are simply too overloaded with ideas to be processed by a reader. For your revision, break up the oversized sentences into smaller, more understandable ones. To make effective divisions, read carefully, noting where you think a separation might help. Write your final version on a separate sheet of paper. There is *no one correct way* to rewrite, so individual versions will vary.

One of the best ways to develop an interest in and an appreciation of history is to watch a well-made documentary on television, for when events are dramatized, they are better understood and even better retained for later reference or use in the classroom or general conversation. Modern history lends itself well to video documentary because we do have considerable film footage and photographs for use in special series that everyone can view. In my estimation, some of the most interesting programs have been devoted to the century's two major world wars. It is fascinating to watch people who lived in Europe and America seventy years ago and to see how they dressed, spoke, and behaved with one another in the various film clips we have of royalty or just common people. In a sense, the camera has kept them "alive" and given them a kind of immortality, for as long as the film is preserved and shown, modern people with their many different lifestyles and customs will have

```
something to reflect on. This combination of film and history is

indeed a powerful one, and it gives to us all much stimulation,

education, and entertainment.
```

VARYING SENTENCE CONSTRUCTION

Introduction

Study this next example, paying special attention to a new kind of repetition, not of length, but of sentence construction or pattern. Reading the lines aloud may help you recognize the problem.

```
     The restaurant opened in March of 1985. The owner and staff

struggled for a long time to earn a profit and keep the place open to

customers. They worked without success until a new amusement park

was built a few miles away. The tourists came by in droves, and soon

the restaurant was able to capitalize on this situation. The

restaurant has now expanded, and staff members are relatively secure

in their jobs.
```

One way to identify a sentence construction problem is to look for the repetition of certain words. In the preceding paragraph, the word *the* starts four sentences, forcing a pattern or rhythm that becomes noticeable to the eye and ear as shown in the following table:

	Who? What?	*Action?*
The	restaurant	opened
The	owner, staff	struggled
The	tourists	came
The	restaurant	has expanded

Grammatically expressed, the subject–verb pattern is repetitious. The repetition of this pattern in sentence after sentence weakens the quality of the paragraph.

Guidelines for Revising Sentence Construction

There are a number of strategies for you to use, if you notice that your sentences are dominated by a repetitious pattern of this type.

1. Reverse or relocate elements of the sentence.

   The restaurant opened *in March of 1985.*

   In March of 1985, the restaurant opened.

   With this relocation, there is less emphasis on the overused pattern. (A comma was added following the new introductory phrase.)

2. In sentences joined by connectors, especially the subordinators, reverse the sentence parts.

   They worked without success *until a new amusement park was built a few miles away.*

   Until a new amusement park was built a few miles away, they worked without success.

   Once again, the ideas remain, but the monotony of the pattern has been broken.

3. Experiment with new sentence patterns, especially those that minimize unnecessary repetition.

   a. *Since I finished high school,* I have been working as a clerk.
      Since finishing high school, I have been working as a clerk.
      This new pattern eliminates the repetition of *I.*

   b. George was a wonderful man. He was also *my neighbor.*
      George, *my neighbor,* was a wonderful man.
      This pattern eliminates the need to repeat *was,* while creating one stronger sentence.

   Consult Unit V (pp. 319–320) for material relating to introductory adverbial phrases and their punctuation.

Exercise 4.39   REVERSING SENTENCE ELEMENTS

Take the elements in italics at the end of the following sentences and place them at the front. If you hear a pause after the new introductory element, place a comma as was done in the model. Use your own paper for the exercise.

1. Many people visit the doctor regularly *because of a belief in preventive medicine.*

2. I sent out all my bills *at the end of the month.*

3. Tamara flew to Hawaii *to escape her hectic life in Sacramento.*

4. Many changes occurred in Western civilization *after the development of the iron-tipped plow.*

5. I marched into the courtroom *with a firm conviction of my innocence.*

6. The Rembrandt painting sold for a huge amount of money *at an auction in New York.*

7. The beach is a wonderful locale *for imaginative people.*

8. Massive Chinese vases were situated for maximum effect *at either end of the hall.*

9. The class signed up for diving lessons *after completing the lecture series.*

10. Chris tiptoed up the stairs *with a twinkle in his eye.*

Exercise 4.40   SWITCHING ELEMENTS JOINED BY A CONNECTOR

Other types of reversals are possible, especially in sentences joined by appropriate subordinating conjunctions or connectors. The conjunctions used in this exercise are:

if   because   when   although   after   as   since

For this exercise, reverse the entire section in italics and move it to the beginning of the sentence. A comma is placed after the last word of the reversed unit because there is a noticeable pause. The item below has been done as an example. Use your own paper for this exercise. Comma Rule 4 discusses use of the comma in such sentence constructions; see pages 319–320.

Example: I couldn't start the car *because the engine was flooded.*

Reversal: Because the engine was flooded, I couldn't start the car.

1. My husband bought twenty lottery tickets *after I told him of the fabulous sums we could win.*

2. Proceed with caution in this business *since the stakes are so high.*

3. Sally jumped to her feet *when she heard the bloodcurdling scream.*

4. A field of wildflowers is my enemy *because I am allergic to so many varieties of pollen.*

5. The angry customer loudly demanded a refund, *although he had no receipt for his purchase.*

6. It is a good idea to get a tutor *if you need additional help.*

7. I sat waiting for the plumber *as the minutes and hours rolled by.*

8. Some commercials are very clever *because they use animation imaginatively.*

9. The meeting was finally adjourned *after old business had been resolved.*

10. You should buy your ticket now *because prices will soon rise.*

Exercise 4.41   **EXPERIMENTING WITH A NEW PATTERN**

The following sentences allow you to practice a new pattern, one that lessens repetitions of similar words. Study the example below carefully, focusing on the italicized portions of each sentence:

>   *Original:* Before *I leave* my house, I always check my wallet.
>   (Repetition occurs with the two "I's".)

>   *Rewrite:* Before *leaving* my house, I always check my wallet.
>   (The first *I* is removed entirely, and the action word *leave* is changed to the *-ing* form *leaving*.)

Follow the same procedure with each of the following sentences; use your own paper.

1. After he invaded Poland, Hitler entered Holland.

2. Since I started this exercise program, I have noticed an overall improvement in muscle tone.

3. Because I failed the class, I decided to revamp my study habits.

4. After she graduated from the police academy, Maureen was assigned to a car patrol with an experienced officer.

5. Whenever I bake pastries, I am overwhelmed by the aroma of butter, brown sugar, and vanilla.

6. After I took my first sip, I knew that tea was the beverage for me.

7. Although I needed to save money, I decided to splurge on a new outfit.

8. Since she started her new job, she decided to open a savings account.

Exercise 4.42   **EXPERIMENTING WITH A NEW PATTERN**

One way to combine two choppy sentences is to take the major idea of the second sentence and graft it to the appropriate spot in the first unit. Study the following example:

>   *Example:* My aunt lives in Cleveland. She is *a kind and generous person.*

>   *Rewrite:* My aunt, *a kind and generous person,* lives in Cleveland.
>   (Since *kind* and *generous* refer to and describe aunt in the first sentence, the italicized unit can be moved closer to her. The subject–verb unit *she–is* is dropped.)

Try this same procedure with the sentences below. Take the italicized material from the second sentence and move it next to the word that it describes in the first. Use commas to surround the unit being moved because it forms an appositive. (Comma Rule 4—pp. 319–320— deals with this need for commas.)

1. The Kentucky Derby is traditionally held on the first Saturday in May. It is called *"The Run for the Roses."*

2. My microwave is the heart of my kitchen. It is *a true time-saver.*

3. Mount Everest is a magnet for an adventurer. It is *a rugged and challenging peak.*

4. The dictionary is useful to writers. It is *a major reference tool.*

5. The unicorn is written about in many mythological tales. It is *a one-horned animal.*

6. Pierre is a cuddly delight. He is *my stuffed polar bear.*

7. Acapulco attracts tourists from around the world. It is *an attractive seaside resort.*

8. Aspirin is used by many people. It is *a painkiller.*

SENTENCE SUMMARY

The sentence is the basic unit of writing, consisting of individual words that are well chosen and placed in such an order that they communicate meaning to a reader. High-quality sentences display four general characteristics: suitable language, a reasonable point of view, variety in length, and variety in construction.

Some Terms for You to Review

Diction: A writer's choice of words.

Slang: Inappropriate diction for college writing; too limited in its ability to communicate.

Cliché: A common expression such as "You can't beat City Hall"; inappropriate for college writing as it has been overused.

Colloquial: Writing that is too casual and conversational for use in college writing.

Idiom: Words or expressions that are often quite common and accepted in usage; the danger lies in their overuse, for idioms lend a casual tone to a paper.

Contractions: Contractions are abbreviations of subject and verb, such as *I'll* for *I will,* and are generally considered too casual for college writing, especially for papers written in the third person.

Point of View: The opinion or state of mind of the writer as it is expressed in a sentence. If a point of view is not reasonable (The president is to blame for everything wrong in this country), then the credibility of the writing suffers.

Stereotypes: Unfair judgments made against an entire group (meddling mother-in-law, the corrupt politician, and so on). In a paper, stereotyped thinking adversely affects the point of view.

Connectors: Words which allow us to join sentences that are short and choppy so that one smoother unit is produced. The majority of connectors are *conjunctions,* those words whose primary function is joining.

Variety: With reference to sentences, variety points to the need for a balance of length and of sentence construction. The lack of variety produces monotony.

Echoing: Echoing refers to the repetition of either the same word or a variation of it too close together, specifically at the end of one sentence and the start of the following one. (I enjoy reading fiction. Fiction allows my imagination to soar.) If overdone, echoing can be monotonous.

PREPARING THE FINAL COPY

NEARING THE END OF THE WRITING PROCESS

Compared with the work involved in thinking about an assignment, prewriting to generate ideas and a thesis, drafting, editing, and revising, the preparation of the final copy may seem insignificant. But, consider if you will, the following analogy.

You are a skilled and intelligent person applying for a job and must first be interviewed. Your qualifications are in order, your experience is more than adequate, and your general character is excellent—but you dress inappropriately for the interview, perhaps too casually. Despite all of your strong points, the visual impression you make is very weak—and you are not offered the position. In the same way, a paper may make a poor showing if it is sloppily written or typed. Even if the writing in it is good from the standpoint of development and diction, the reader cannot help but be influenced by its unprofessional appearance.

The idea underlying college level writing is a high degree of excellence—of thought, of language, and of presentation. As you reach the end of the writing process for any given assignment, be sure to allow enough time to produce a professional-looking paper.

Guidelines for Preparing the Final Copy

Use any or all of the following guidelines:

1. *Allow a sensible amount of time*, keeping in mind your particular situation. If, for example, you do not type well, it would be an unrealistic expectation to think that you could type a neat college essay in an hour. You may need to set aside perhaps two or more hours for typing. The worst situation is having to write or type rapidly because you lack time. You may unintentionally create new errors or cause the paper to look messy and unprofessional.

2. *Follow your instructor's directions* on the arrangement of the final copy.

3. *Get the final copy in on time!* Turning in a paper late may cause your work to be penalized or not accepted at all. What is more serious, however, is that late papers impair your overall performance and self-discipline as a student. Of course, it is possible that an emergency may cause you to submit work late. But for most students, lateness tends to show that time was used very carelessly. If you fall behind in assignments, then you tend

to fall behind in other course work—class lectures, and so on. When the situation is reversed and you are waiting for someone else to meet a deadline, you enjoy getting paychecks, important documents, and tickets to concerts on time. For the same reason your teachers appreciate and expect promptness from you.

Guidelines for the Physical Arrangement of Your Paper

Be sure that your papers display the necessary physical characteristics of a formal piece of writing. At the beginning of many classes, you will receive a syllabus which includes your instructor's directions for the form your papers should take. In addition, you may want to use the following general guidelines from the *MLA Handbook for Writers of Research Papers*, Second Edition:

1. *Maintain the spacing of the left and right margins.* Leave one-inch margins at the top and bottom and at the left and right.

2. *Number each page in the upper right corner* one-half inch from the top.

3. *Include your name and class information and title of the paper.* Type your name, your professor's name, the class, and the date on separate lines one inch below the top of the page in the upper left corner. Double space and type in the title, centered. Capitalize the first letter and each major word in the title (Love in Bloom). Leave four spaces between the title and the first line of the text for typed papers; one space for handwritten papers.

4. *Indent all paragraphs uniformly.* In typed papers, a five-space indentation is the rule. In handwritten papers, indent each paragraph approximately one inch from the left margin. For both typed and handwritten papers, at least an inch is desirable for side and bottom margins.

5. *Maintain spaces within and between lines.* When you type a period at the end of a sentence, be sure to hit your space bar *twice* before starting the next sentence. After typing a comma, press the space bar once. Double-space between lines.

6. *Use appropriate paper.* Use standard size (8½-by-11-inch) white paper. Avoid erasable typing paper as it tends to smudge when handled. For handwritten work, use *wide-ruled* lined paper (not narrow-ruled).

7. *Proofread carefully.* No matter how careful you are, there is always the possibility of making mistakes when writing or typing. Although you have already read through your work several times during the writing process, it is vital that you do so one last time, slowly. As you read your drafts, silently and aloud, watch for these trouble spots:

    a. missing letters and missing words

b. transposed letters

c. the wrong word altogether

8. *Correction of errors.* Use a liquid correction fluid or special paper to correct errors. If a page has too many corrections, retype or rewrite the page. Should you spot an error in class just before handing the paper in, correct it neatly in pen.

9. *Bind pages properly.* Follow your instructor's preference for binding your pages. If no directions are given, bind your pages with *one* staple in the upper left-hand corner. Be sure to number pages in the upper right-hand corner, including your name before the number on every page except page 1. This will prevent any confusion from pages being out of order and ensure that your pages are not mixed in with anyone else's.

Exercise 4.43   EDITING FOR THE HUMAN FACTOR IN ESSAY FORM

Voice this paragraph about burgoo very carefully. Locate the following problems: 13 missing letters   3 missing words   3 wrong words

A burgoo is a type of thick stew which was once quiet popular in America. In fact, the burgoo was served for many year during the late 19th century in Kentucky for the Kentucky Derby. Basically, a burgoo consists of an enormous variety of ingredient. It would not have been unusual for cook to put chicken, lamb, veal, beef, pork, and even squirrels in the stew. To add to the vegetables were tomatoes, butter beans, carrots, corn, okra, celery, onions, and potatoes. All of this ingredients were cooked slowly to enhance the wonderful medley of flavors. By the time it ready to serve, the burgoo was thick and hearty and a definite hit with the Derby goers. Unfortunately, most people today, especially those in the North or in the West, have heard of a burgoo. With our modern emphasis on fast foods, it is unlikely that the slow-cooking burgoo will ever have much of a future unless some company decide to put this stew in cans for easy use in American homes.

Exercise 4.44   EDITING FOR PROBLEMS IN FORM

Search for a variety of physical problems in the way the following text is typed. (You may wish to review the preceding few pages related to typed texts.) Make note of any weak spots on a separate sheet of paper.

Daniel Perez

Professor Barry

English 101B

April 21, 1988

Forms of punishment

As time passes, our ideas change, and in some cases, they change very dramatically, especially in the area of executions. In the Middle Ages, which spanned many centuries of Western

civilization after the fall of the Roman Empire, an execution was a public spectacle. Parents would bring their children and even elevate them in some way so the younger ones got a better view of the proceedings. Whether it was a public hanging, decapitation, or burning, an execution attracted people who were curious to witness the event. Rather than being repelled by it, most felt a sense of righteousness at the sight of justice at work. This behavior is in marked contrast to our more modern view of dealing with criminals. If someone were to suggest having executions in Times Square or at prime time on a major network, we might well call the idea outrageous and barbaric.

If You Are Using a Word Processor

The primary goal of this unit was to provide you with criteria for judging the content of your rough drafts and to give you practice in revising to meet these standards. You will be able to use the word processor for a number of exercises in this unit, especially those that require you to rewrite (for example Exercises 2 and 3). Use all of the guidelines concerning prewriting and drafting from the previous units. Along with your work on the exercises, you might begin a special spelling file to record words you have frequently misspelled from papers your professor has returned to you.

In the sentence exercises you will work on improving the quality of your sentences through the use of varying techniques. As you go through the exercises, it is a good idea to type the instructions for each so that you can keep your focus on the screen and not be distracted by looking back and forth from screen to paper.

After completing each exercise and before printing, check your work to be sure that you have followed the directions. Spend a little extra time proofreading your work. One disadvantage of using the word processor is that your work *looks* so good that it is difficult to spot errors. If you can, edit on screen before you print. You will find that when you edit in this way, you save time. However, be sure to proofread your final printed copy. You can easily go back into the file and correct any errors afterward.

In certain exercises, you will be working with problem sentences in paragraphs. You might want to triple-space the lines to be able to write comments between them. When you have finished each exercise, delete your comments, reset the machine for double space, and reformat your paragraphs. *Note:* Refer to the manual if you do not know how to reformat.

As you know, the word processor is an ideal tool for the process of rewriting. You can add material, delete, and move portions of the text, even whole paragraphs, to different locations in your paper. You can also write notes to yourself directly on your paper and then delete them when you are satisfied with your work. If possible, practice editing and rewriting directly on the screen. This procedure saves time and develops your ability to concentrate. However, if this proves too difficult, by all means print out copies of your rough drafts and work on them away from the computer. Whatever method you develop for rewriting, you will be able to save time, paper, and energy by working on the word processor.

Preparing your paper in proper form is also easy with a word processor. For example, you can indent your paragraphs the proper five spaces with just a keystroke. Your printer will usually have a preset left margin that is correct for most writing situations. You can also use a feature which justifies (aligns) all the words in the right margin, but this is not a useful function. Most programs create unnatural spaces within the lines in order to produce right justification, and this produces a paper that is difficult to read. Newer programs can right-justify without unnatural spacing, but unless you are using one of these more sophisticated models, do not use this feature. Be sure to learn the command that centers text. By using it, you can center your titles perfectly.

Correcting errors is one of the strongest features of the word processor. You can add to, change, or delete words, lines, and even paragraphs anywhere within the text, and then use a command to re-form the paragraph. This function will be very useful to you. For the more sophisticated user, the *block move* can help you to move entire paragraphs and sections of paragraphs within a text.

UNIT V

Understanding Grammar, Punctuation, and Mechanics

- **THE GRAMMAR OF THE SENTENCE**
- **MAJOR SENTENCE ERRORS**
- **A GUIDE TO PUNCTUATION**
- **A GUIDE TO MECHANICS**

OVERVIEW

The Grammar of the Sentence *focuses on the basic parts and forms of sentences from a grammatical perspective.*

Major Sentence Errors *discusses eleven major grammar errors involving sentences.*

A Guide to Punctuation *presents the three end marks and those marks which work within sentences to clarify meaning.*

A Guide to Mechanics *covers capitalization, italics, homonyms, numbers, abbreviations, and hyphenation.*

Introduction

Study the following brief conversation between friends, for it sheds light on any study of written language:

> "Going somewhere?" asked Joe.
> "To the store," replied Phil.
> "For what?"
> "Ice cream."

Joe and Phil managed to communicate clearly enough for their purposes *without ever using a complete sentence.* As long as these friends continue *speaking,* they need not worry about parts of speech, rules of grammar, punctuation, or spelling.

When, however, the two are required to write, as occurs in school or at work, the casual nature of the situation changes dramatically. It *does matter* how words are spelled, and errors involving word use (grammar) make writing *look bad.* Improper punctuation can also make the communication difficult to follow or highly misleading. In short, we are judged not only on what we write but on how we write.

You can probably remember a little of nearly every rule of English you have learned over your years of schooling. As a college student, however, the need to bring your knowledge of grammar and punctuation into sharper focus is vital. This refocusing is the goal of this unit.

THE GRAMMAR OF THE SENTENCE

GETTING FAMILIAR WITH SENTENCES

Focusing on sentences in general, we can say that they are very much like people in that both display great variety as well as certain common qualities. However, there are four basic criteria that all word groups must meet to be considered sentences.

1. All written sentences begin with a capital letter and end with a full stop to keep ideas from running into each other:

   The woman wanted caviar for her baked potato. Her date was in shock! How could she be so bold as to order the most expensive item on the menu?

   Watch what occurs when capitals and end marks are removed:

   the woman wanted caviar for her baked potato her date was in shock how could she be so bold as to order the most expensive item on the menu

2. Sentences fall into one of three general types, depending on the sort of message being sent:

   Command (Imperative): Get me a cup of coffee.
   See to that problem.
   Stop!

   Question (Interrogative): Will you get me a cup of coffee?
   Is the problem solved yet?
   Have you stopped smoking?

   Statement (Declarative): The coffee is ready.
   She has solved the problem.
   The rebels stopped fighting.

3. All sentences must send a message with some degree of completeness.

   Is this a sentence?—She hates him.
   If you said yes, you are correct. Although we know very little about the people, we have a "degree of completeness." *A* female strongly dislikes *a* male.

   What about this one?—After Mary screamed at Steve.

This unit is much longer, but it is not a sentence, for it is missing something important. The sentence never finishes the message begun with the word *after,* so we are left hanging—What *happened* after Mary screamed?

4. To achieve unity and transmit meaning, all sentences must contain two vital grammatical elements: a *subject* and a *predicate.* Examine the following sentences, in which the two basic parts are identified.

       S   ←P→
  a. My car | stalled on the freeway yesterday.
     ←S→   ←P→
  b. The man of my dreams | has not yet come into my life.
     P   S   ←P→
  c. Did | you | talk to my brother yesterday?
            ←P→   S
  d. At the top of my grocery list was | meat.

In most declarative sentence patterns, such as (a) and (b), the subject comes first with the predicate appearing after. But when sentences are in question form, such as in (c), the order is changed. In (d), we can actually see the reversal of subject and predicate. No matter what the type of sentence, however, the two elements must be present.

To bring this discussion of general sentence characteristics to a close, study this definition:

In written communication, a *sentence* consists of one or more words working together to convey a message with some degree of completeness. A sentence must contain a *subject and a predicate.* It must also begin with a *capital letter* and end with some *appropriate mark of punctuation.*

The majority of the sections that follow present material that will bring you to an understanding of more specific sentence elements. If you feel at all uncertain of your grasp of terminology, take some time to review the appendix, starting on page 346. The appendix reviews the seven major parts of speech.

UNDERSTANDING SUBJECT AND PREDICATE

In terms of grammar, subject and predicate represent the foundation of sentence structure and provide a pathway for the understanding of more technical, complex sentence architecture. Rather like the two sides of a coin, the subject and predicate are different elements yet inextricably related. Examine the following sentence dealing with an *action:*

      Complete
      Subject   Predicate

My little brother broke his toe yesterday.

The term *complete subject* is used to indicate all those words that relate to the *doer* of the action—the party responsible for the event occurring. It is clear that *brother* is the main part of the complete subject, but the words *my* and *little* are included because each gives additional information about the brother. The predicate consists of those words that complete the sentence and tell us what the brother did; in this case—*broke his toe yesterday.* The key element of the predicate is *broke* (past form of break). But the words *his toe yesterday* are included because we know *what* he broke and *when* the incident occurred.

Let's examine a sentence which expresses a different predicate situation— that of *being.*

> Complete
> Subject   Predicate
>
> Mrs. Carson was my teacher in the fifth grade.

The complete subject, *Mrs. Carson,* consists of one name and is the focus of this sentence. As we move along, however, we see that Mrs. Carson is not doing anything. The predicate starts with the word *was,* the past tense of the verb *to be,* and takes in these words: *was my teacher in the fifth grade.* Immediately, the reader of this sentence grasps the idea of someone who existed at an earlier period of time. The verb form *was* establishes this situation as having occurred in the past. *My teacher* tells us what role Mrs. Carson had; *in the fifth grade* tells us when she was the speaker's teacher. It is an excellent idea to become familiar with the principal parts of the verb *to be,* which is responsible for our being able to express existence: *am, are, is; was, were; be, been.*

Exercise 5.1   LOCATING COMPLETE SUBJECT AND PREDICATE WITH ACTION VERBS

Read each of the following sentences carefully to note what is actually happening and who or what is responsible for the activity. Copy each onto a separate sheet of paper, drawing a line through the point where subject and predicate meet. Write **S** above the subject and **P** above the predicate.

←S→   ←P→
Example: My entire family | cried all through the wedding.

1. A huge shark swam through the ocean's depths.

2. My closest friend lives only a few doors away.

3. Alice offered a helpful suggestion about my diet.

4. I asked him for a small loan of $5.00.

5. The sleek Mercedes raced down the street at top speed.

6. Several of the dissatisfied customers wrote to the manufacturer.

7. His bad table manners annoy everyone in the dormitory.

8. My mother and I shopped for new fall clothes all weekend.

Exercise 5.2   LOCATING COMPLETE SUBJECT AND PREDICATE WITH THE VERB
_TO BE_

After reading each of the following sentences carefully, copy them onto a separate sheet of paper. Draw a line through the point where subject and predicate meet, and write **S** above the complete subject portion, **P** above the predicate. In all sentences, however, watch for the verb of existence or being (forms of the verb *to be*). These are not action-oriented; instead, they allow us to place ourselves, objects, or ideas in a particular time.

S   ←**P**→

Example: Today | is the first day of the rest of your life.

(*is* puts us in the present. What *is?*—*today,* a word naming a 24-hour period occurring as the sentence is written or spoken.)

1. One of my photo albums was especially precious.

2. My six children are all extremely talented.

3. I have been in sales for twenty years.

4. Any major celebration such as a wedding is usually very expensive.

5. My lipstick shade and my nail polish were in harmony with my new outfit.

6. The police department is in a sensitive position in the community.

7. Some people are unable to compromise on any issue.

8. I am so delighted about your promotion!

FOCUSING ON THE SIMPLE SUBJECT AND THE COMPLETE VERB

Study the subject and predicate portions of the sentence which follows. Within the two major parts, it is possible to isolate the basic essence of each: the *simple subject* and the *complete verb*. The process, by the way, is rather like reducing a fraction to its lowest common denominator.

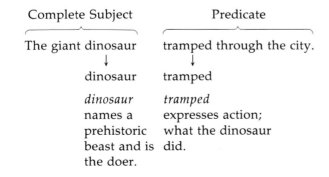

Complete Subject	Predicate
The giant dinosaur	tramped through the city.
↓	↓
dinosaur	tramped
dinosaur names a prehistoric beast and is the doer.	*tramped* expresses action; what the dinosaur did.

The words *dinosaur—tramped*, the simple subject and the complete verb, are the most important words in the sentence. All others, though informative, are secondary in importance. Let's work through another sequence that is a bit longer:

The actor in my workshop has been studying for two years

    ↓   ↓   ↓   ↓

   actor   has been studying

There are two nouns, *actor* and *workshop*. Because *actor* is responsible for the action, it is the simple subject.

has been studying expresses the activity of the actor. All three words work to get across *one activity* that started in the past and has continued to the present.

In sentences such as the preceding one, where more than one noun appears in the complete subject, you must take care to distinguish which person, object, or idea is responsible for the activity. When working to find the complete verb, remember that most verb constructions require the use of several words (as many as four) to express one action or state of existence. Study the following brief series, which illustrates how parts of a complete verb cooperate.

I *will go* tomorrow.

Will, a helping or auxiliary verb, suggests the future. *Go*, the main verb, supplies the actual activity.

I *am going* tomorrow.

Am, the helping verb, matches *I* in number and works with *going* to suggest future. *Going*, the main verb, supplies the actual activity.

She *has been* a student for five years.

Has, the helping verb, matches the subject in number and establishes a sense of present; *been*, the main verb, suggests the past element and the fact of existence over time.

I *should have prepared* myself.

Here there are two helping verbs: *should* indicates judgment; *have* matches the subject in number and suggests a past situation. The main verb, *prepared*, supplies the actual activity.

I *will have been married* for five years next month.

Three words now work to help the main verb: *will* suggests that the event is to occur in the future; *have* and *been* work to complete the action at a point in the future. The main verb, *married*, supplies the

actual activity which is to be completed in the future.

Understanding complete verbs is very important to your work in the grammar of the sentence. You may wish to consult the appendix, under Verbs (pp.
351–352), to better understand how auxiliary and main verb forms work to
express action or existence.

Let us now examine another sequence featuring a being verb:

Chihuahuas are my favorite dogs.

    ↓   ↓

Chihuahuas are

Chihuahuas—are may seem to be a strange pairing, but remember that a verb can
express more than action; it may also, with some form of the verb *to be*, express
existence. We know from the use of *are* that this sentence expresses a current point
of view of the writer. If someone writes, "Chihuahuas *were* my favorite dogs," we
would assume that the breed is no longer preferred and that some other type of
dog is probably the favorite. Without the verb *to be*, communication would be
difficult, for we could not locate ourselves or anything else, for that matter, in
time: "I *am* a conservative." "The government *is* complex." "The times *were* violent." All these verbs are forms of *to be*; imagine trying to express ideas without
them.

 Exercise 5.3   LOCATING SIMPLE SUBJECT AND COMPLETE VERB

All of the sentences in this exercise are simple declarative types. That is, they make statements
and have one subject–verb relationship. After finding the complete subject and predicate, focus
on the simple subject and complete verb and write them on a separate sheet of paper.

Complete Subject	Predicate
Example: The man at my left	sneezed loudly.

Simple Subject: ___*man*___ + **Complete Verb:** ___*sneezed*___

Test your choices to see that they work together reasonably. In the sentence above, *man–left,
left–sneezed,* and *sneezed–loudly* do not work, for there is no actor–action or actor–existence
relationship.

1. Two of my friends are going to Europe.

2. The directions on the label are very easy to understand.

3. That young couple has no money in the bank.

4. Dating customs have changed drastically over the past decades.

5. Anyone in the room could have been involved in this incident.

6. We will celebrate our silver wedding anniversary soon.

7. The beast rose from the primeval slime.

8. A day by the seashore can revitalize a busy city dweller.

9. One of the accident victims is being treated at the hospital.

10. I was an employee of that company for fifteen years.

Compound Subjects and Multiple Verbs

One particular group of words adds to our ability to form effective sentences: the coordinating conjunctions—*and, but, for, or, yet, so,* and *nor.* Most of these words can be used in both the subject and predicate portions of sentences to extend communication and increase the size of the simple subject and the complete verb. Remember, however, that *for* and *so* join whole sentences together.

Compound Subjects

The conjunction *and* joins equal elements as subjects. When this occurs, the combination is called a *compound subject.*

>   S   S   V
> Chemistry *and* physics are my favorite courses.
> The conjunction *and* allows for the expression of the fact that two courses, not one, exist as favorites. The word *and,* however, is not a part of the simple subject.

Awareness of compound subjects becomes particularly helpful when you study subject–verb agreement in the upcoming section on major sentence errors. The two subjects, as equals, must be matched or joined to a plural verb as shown above.

Multiple Verbs

A multiple verb occurs when a coordinating conjunction brings in more than one activity or state of being for the simple subject. Study the difference between the following two sentences:

>   S   S   V
> My *dog* and *cat are playing.*
> There are compound subjects in this sentence—*dog, cat*—but only one verb—*are fighting.* Although two words are needed to express this action, they function as one verb. You can test whether there are two verbs by trying to write the sentence with only one of the words—My dog and cat *are.* My dog and cat *fighting.* Neither version makes sense. The two words are one verb, not two separate verbs.

Watch what happens when a conjunction is used to add another action that the dog and cat can perform:

>   S   S   V   V
> My *dog* and *cat are playing* and *ruining* my flower bed.

We now can see two separate actions—*playing* and *ruining*. The helping verb *are* serves both of them and establishes the action as occurring in the present tense.

Other conjunctions can be used effectively to join two sorts of actions. Study the following examples:

    S V   **V**
I *lied* but *confessed* later.
    S   **V**   **V**   **V**
You *can* either *pass* or *fail*.
    S   **V**   **V**
I *hesitated* once yet *continued* on my journey.

The conjunction *but* suggests a contrast in the two types of activities; *or* suggests that there is an option or choice; *yet* also brings with it an idea of contrast. In all three examples, the multiple actions were undertaken by one subject.

Using multiple verb constructions can help you improve your sentence style. If you see choppy sentences such as these on a draft—

I thanked George. I wished him good luck.

Rewrite the sentence by combining major actions:

    S   **V**   **V**
I *thanked* George and *wished* him good luck.

This multiple verb construction is far more effective than the two choppy sentences.

 ## Exercise 5.4   LOCATING COMPOUND SUBJECTS AND MULTIPLE VERBS

There are two types of sentences in this exercise. One type has *compound subjects* joined by the conjunction *and;* the other has *multiple verbs* joined by various conjunctions in the predicate portion. Rewrite the sentences on your own paper, marking **S** above each subject and **V** above each verb. Circle all conjunctions. Refer to the preceding discussion for a full list of conjunctions.

1. The moon and stars have inspired many songs over the years.

2. Marge wanted a refund but lost her receipt.

3. I gave and received many gifts at the holidays.

4. The students and tutors worked together at the start of the term but now have finished their activities.

5. I am and will be your friend always.

6. The snow in the mountains and poor road conditions prevented our departure.

7. The canary flew through the window and disappeared from view.

8. My aunt and uncle always prepare a delicious Christmas dinner and invite all of the family.

Verbals

Verbals are words or phrases that resemble verbs in appearance, but nevertheless do not express action or existence. Of the three types of verbals, two are particularly important in the identification of simple subject and complete verb—*gerundive* and *infinitive* phrases. The third verbal, the *participle,* is discussed in Appendix A under Adjectives.

Gerundive Phrases

Examine the following sentences closely; the gerundive phrases are in italics.

$$\overset{\text{V}}{\text{\textit{Worrying about money}}}\text{ is common in an inflationary time.}$$

$$\overset{\text{V}}{\text{\textit{Going to school and working}}}\text{ can make a student's life hard.}$$

Both phrases begin with a word that ends in *-ing,* and each of these words brings with it a phrase, a related group of words. These characteristics traditionally mark the *gerund,* a verbal that *acts as a noun* in a sentence. Because it is free to function as a noun (naming people, places, ideas, and so on), the gerund can serve as the subject when it is responsible for the action or state of being. If the gerund is receiving action—"I do not enjoy *worrying about money*"—then it acts as a noun but as the direct object of the verb, not the subject.

If it is not clear to you how all of the words of the gerundive phrase form a simple subject, try an experiment. Take each word of the phrase by itself to see how it works as a subject:

Worrying is common in an inflationary time.
This version sounds good to the ear, but it is not accurate in its content. There are other areas of worry involving taxes, children, crime, disease, death, and so on. *Worrying* by itself is too general.

Money is common in an inflationary time.
This does not make sense even though it sounds like a sentence; there is no mention of worrying, and this word is a vital part of the message. The complete phrase—*worrying about money*—is necessary to convey the meaning.

Infinitive Phrases

The second verbal phrase which may serve as a subject in a sentence is the *infinitive phrase.* These units begin with an *infinitive* (the preposition *to* plus any *verb*), along with several other words attached to it to form a phrase. Watch this progression to see how these phrases form and work in sentences:

Infinitive: *to be*

$$\text{Infinitive Phrase: }\overset{\text{V}}{\text{\textit{To be a successful student}}}\text{ takes discipline.}$$

We can see how the whole infinitive phrase unit works to express the subject. Isolating any of the individual words would not produce a sensible alternative. *Student takes discipline,* or *Successful takes discipline* do not make sense.

Exercise 5.5   LOCATING GERUNDIVE AND INFINITIVE PHRASES

The simple subject of each of the following sentences is either a gerundive phrase (*ing* construction) or an infinitive phrase (*to* + *verb* construction). Copy each sentence onto your own paper and underline each phrase carefully, marking **GS** for gerund subject and **IS** for infinitive subject.

> **GS   V**
> *Example: Being rich* is my major goal in life.

For additional practice, mark **V** above the complete verb.

1. Starting my own business was not a simple procedure.

2. To annoy me seemed my little sister's mission in life.

3. Keeping my temper is sometimes difficult.

4. To have every modern convenience does not always lead to happiness.

5. Completing my research paper required two long months of work.

6. Working with small children is especially rewarding.

7. To work with small children is a career goal for me.

8. Being dishonest can only lead to unhappiness.

LOCATING SUBJECT AND VERB IN SPECIAL SITUATIONS

Command Sentences

Command or imperative sentences tend to be short because an order is far more effective when delivered quickly:

> Leave me alone!

> Open your books to Chapter One.

This type of sentence has a unique feature in that the subject rarely appears in the sentence. In command sentences, the subject is *understood,* meaning that it is held in the mind of the person giving the order and the party receiving the order. If, for instance, you tell someone to "close the door," it is understood between the two of you who is supposed to do the activity. It is not necessary to say "*You* close the door."

Because of this situation, the subject in a command sentence is called the *you understood.* The *you* usually can be written in parentheses near the beginning of the sentence:

> **S   V**
> *(You)* Leave me alone!
> **S   V**
> *(You)* Open your books to Chapter One.

Exercise 5.6   LOCATING SUBJECT AND VERB IN COMMAND SENTENCES

All six of the following items are command sentences. Copy the sentences onto your own paper and write their *understood* subjects (you) in parentheses to the left of each. Then write **V** over each verb.

$$\overset{V}{}$$

Example: (You) Be quiet.

1. Come with me to the party on Thursday.

2. Tell me the latest gossip.

3. Do me a favor.

4. Get me those books from the top shelf.

5. For heaven's sake, lower the volume on the radio!

6. Deal me out of this hand.

Question Sentences

When you pose a direct question, the position of the subject and verb is changed. When the question involves a one-word verb, the verb appears first and is followed by the subject:

$$\overset{V}{}\qquad\overset{S}{}$$

Are those *dresses* for sale?

$$\overset{V}{}\;\overset{S}{}$$

Is she your sister?

When you ask a question using a two-part verb construction, you can see a **V–S–V** pattern emerge as the two-part verb surrounds the subject:

$$\overset{V}{}\quad\overset{S}{}\quad\overset{V}{}$$

Can Eleanor *keep* the kitten?

$$\overset{V}{}\quad\overset{S}{}\quad\overset{V}{}$$

Have you *seen* my son?

Native speakers have no trouble generating questions; however, in analyzing questions to identify the subject and verbs, it is important to know that questions differ from the common pattern of subject first, verb second.

Exercise 5.7   LOCATING SUBJECT AND VERB IN QUESTION SENTENCES

Locate subject and verb in the following questions. Remember that in all of them, the positions of the key elements will be *mixed* or *reversed*. Copy the sentences onto your own paper and write **S** above each subject and **V** above each verb.

V   S   V

Example: Can you lend me five dollars?

V S

Is he here?

1. Do you believe that incredible story?

2. Has Harold taken his dog to the groomer on Fifth Street?

3. Will you stretch your arm farther to the left?

4. Where is my shoe?

5. Do you know the route to follow to Des Moines?

6. Might I go with you on your adventure?

7. Were they the suspects in the crime?

8. Did she leave a note on the refrigerator?

9. Should we get extra food for the holiday weekend?

10. Is my backpack in your way?

Sentence Reversals

Posing questions causes the subject and verb to assume different positions from the normal pattern. However, it is also possible to have a reversal of subject and verb in declarative sentences that are statements, not questions. Study the following pair of sentences. The message is identical, but the word order is not.

S   V

Regular: The grand *marshal rode* at the front of the parade.

V   S

Reversed: At the front of the parade *rode* the grand *marshal.*

Switches of this kind can be quite effective in writing, for they provide variety in sentence construction. Sometimes, however, these sentences are confusing because we expect the subject to be first, the verb second. As you work through the next exercise, make a point of reading each sentence carefully to absorb what is actually happening, especially if it is a reversal of subject and verb.

Exercise 5.8   LOCATING SUBJECT–VERB IN REVERSED DECLARATIVE

Locate subject and verb in the following sentences, all of which have a reversed pattern: verb first, subject after the verb. Copy the sentences onto your own paper; then write **S** for subject, **V** for verb, as shown in the example.

V   S

Example: At the end of the line *was* a little *boy.*

1. Near the school was an abandoned winery.

2. After a brief pause came the announcement of his resignation.

3. Somewhere in this box of cereal is a surprise.

4. Here lies the body of a notorious pirate.

5. There were many people in the room.

6. At the end of the street stood a statue of Colonel Motley.

7. In a remote corner of the auditorium sat two tired teachers.

8. There is only one bathroom in the house.

Complex Sentences

Sentences are called *complex* when they contain more than one subject–verb relationship. Technically, we explain this construction by saying that the sentence has one *independent clause* (a unit that could be a sentence on its own) joined in some way to a *dependent clause* (a unit that cannot be on its own or separated). Examine the following complex sentences and notice the presence of a subject–verb relationship in each.

INDEPENDENT	**DEPENDENT**
Life is never dull	when a person has children.
S **V**	**S** **V**
(Life–is)	(person–has)

DEPENDENT	**INDEPENDENT**
When a person has children,	life is never dull.
S **V**	**S** **V**
(person–has)	(life–is)

INDEPENDENT	**DEPENDENT**
Many Americans buy cars	that are fuel-efficient.
S **V**	**S** **V**
(Americans–buy)	[(cars) that–are]

In the final example, we cannot switch clauses, because the dependent element is joined by a relative pronoun, not a conjunction. In addition, the subject of the dependent clause is dual: The pronoun *that* sits next to and refers to *cars*, which is plural, therefore requiring the plural verb *are*.

Since there are two sets of subjects and verbs in each complex sentence, which would have greater grammatical importance? The independent portion rules, so its subject–verb pair is considered primary, and the other becomes secondary. When you work with these longer sentences, especially on quizzes or in your own drafts, take care to read them carefully so that you are indeed aware of the two sets of related activities.

The use of commas to separate independent and dependent clauses is treated in the punctuation section, Comma Rule 4 (p. 319).

Exercise 5.9   DISTINGUISHING BETWEEN INDEPENDENT AND DEPENDENT CLAUSES

Rewrite each of the complex sentences below onto a separate sheet of paper; then circle the dependent clause and draw an arrow from it to the independent unit. Label each clause.

| **Ind.**   **Dep.**
Examples: I got a job (because I needed the money.)

                    Dep.   **Ind.**
            (When flu season arrived,) Mabel panicked.

1. As night fell in the desert, the coyotes began to howl.

2. I decided to read about space creatures because the setting was eerie and stimulating.

3. According to the book, many sightings have occurred in the desert, which is a relatively quiet, unpopulated area.

4. After I read this interesting fact, I heard a strange noise in the backyard.

5. The sound got louder as it moved closer to the back of the house.

6. In sheer terror, I focused my attention on the door, which suddenly blew open!

7. I never did see anything because I fainted right on the spot.

8. When I regained consciousness, there was nothing or no one to be seen.

Exercise 5.10   LOCATING SUBJECT–VERB SETS IN COMPLEX SENTENCES

Copy the complex sentences below onto a separate sheet of paper; then label subjects with **S** and verbs with **V**. Remember to look for two **S–V** relationships. The last three sentences feature two dependent portions, totaling three sets of **S–V** each.

1. When the last worshiper exited, the pastor closed the enormous front doors of the church.

2. Michelangelo was a painter who exerted an enormous influence in his lifetime and afterward.

3. The tree which stood for so many years fell in the storm.

4. What is your opinion of a class that requires no homework?

5. Cockroaches are durable creatures which have plagued many a home dweller over the ages.

6. When my last goldfish died, I vowed never to get another fish because their lifetimes are so short.

7. The candlesticks that I bought last year cracked before I could use them.

8. Because I couldn't bear the heat in the apartment, I moved out to the patio where I felt a breeze.

ADDITIONAL SENTENCE ELEMENTS

Predicate Constructions

Awareness of three sentence elements appearing in the predicate (verb) portion of sentences can add to your knowledge of sentence construction. These three elements are the direct object, the predicate nominative, and the predicate adjective.

The Direct Object

In many sentences, the presence of a simple subject plus a complete verb is not sufficient to complete meaning. This occurs when the verb is of the type called *transitive,* meaning that it reaches across to some other word. Therefore, the sentence needs a predicate element called a *direct object* (a noun, pronoun, or gerund) to receive action from the transitive verb. The following contain examples of transitive verbs.

> Lean meat contains—(Contains *what?*)
>
> I found—(*What* did the speaker find?)
>
> Sue enjoys—(Enjoys *what?*)

If we add direct objects to receive action, the messages will be complete.

Lean meat *contains* valuable *proteins.*   (**DO** = a noun)

I *found him* at the library.   (**DO** = a pronoun)

Sue *enjoys running in the early morning.*   (**DO** = a gerundive phrase)

The word order in the preceding declarative statements is consistent:

1.	2.	3.
Simple Subject	Verb	Direct Object

The **S–V–DO** order will be changed a bit if a question is formed:

Can you *see me* later?   *Have* you any *ideas?*

As you work with sentences, take special care not to confuse the object with the subject. Both can be nouns or pronouns, but a *subject does the action,* and the *object receives it.*

I took my seat.

Ask yourself *who took?* The *I* did the taking and is the subject or doer. But *what was taken? Seat* is the receiver of the action.

The Predicate Nominative

Although its name sounds formidable, the predicate nominative is relatively simple. Like the direct object, the predicate nominative appears in the predicate portion after the verb. However, its job is to *name the subject;* hence the term *nominative* for *naming.* Study the following sentences:

     S⌒   **PN**
I am a freshman.
Freshman renames *I* in an academic context.

     S⌒   **PN**
Money is the root of all evil.
Root renames *money,* saying that it is a source.

     S⌒   **PN**
Fred became a doctor.
Doctor renames *Fred* in terms of his profession.

In the majority of instances, the predicate nominative will be a noun (freshman, root, doctor) or a pronoun—"It is I." *I* in the predicate renames the subject *it.* "It is me" or "It's me" is incorrect because *me* is the objective case, and the nominative must match the subject in case. (Refer to the appendix under pronouns, p. 347).

This is the pattern that emerges in these sentences:
Simple Subject →Verb   Predicate Nominative
    1.   2.   3.
             1. *equals* 3.

Transitive verbs do not appear in the predicate nominative construction. Instead, the verbs belong to special groups of intransitive verbs called *linking verbs.* The most common are *be, seem,* and *become.*

The Predicate Adjective

The linking verbs mentioned above, including others such as *feel, sound, smell, taste, look,* and *appear,* may be used with a *predicate adjective,* a word in the predicate part of the sentence that describes the subject. Describing nouns and pronouns is the function of the adjective. Although most regular adjectives appear in front of nouns, the predicate adjective does its work from a distance:

     S⌒   **PA**
Janet appeared *listless.*
(Who is *listless?* Janet. She is being described.)

S   PA
The test seemed very *easy*.
(What is *easy*? The subject, test.)

S   PA
I was *exhausted*.
(*Exhausted* describes the physical condition of the speaker, *I*, a pronoun.)

The pattern which emerges is similar in some ways to the other predicate constructions, but notice the difference in relationship between 1 and 3.

Simple Subject   Verb   Predicate Adjective
1.   2.   3.
            3. *describes* 1.

Exercise 5.11   DISTINGUISHING THE THREE PREDICATE ELEMENTS

The three elements (*direct object, predicate nominative,* and *predicate adjective*) are in italics in the sentences below. Copy the sentences onto a separate sheet of paper; then label each unit on the basis of its function.

direct object (DO): when the unit *receives the action of the verb*

predicate nominative (PN): when the unit *renames the subject*

predicate adjective (PA): when the unit *describes the subject*

1. My partner congratulated *me* on my victory.

2. I played many *hunches* in Las Vegas.

3. Blackjack is my favorite *game* of chance.

4. Some forms of gambling are too *complicated* for me.

5. The betting system of roulette, for instance, confuses *me*.

6. The excitement of the casinos is so *contagious*.

7. On an average I spend at least three *weekends* in Las Vegas.

8. Even if I lose, I have a terrific *time*.

9. Some people, however, do not like *gambling*.

10. My father is one *person* in this category of nongamblers.

MAJOR SENTENCE ERRORS

Introduction

The eleven errors featured next are serious problems, for they damage the grammatical quality of sentences.

When your instructor returns papers to you, study all the editorial comments. If there are symbols on your paper, refer to Table 5.1 on page 260 for their meaning. Decide what problems seem to occur most often. Then, review the related material in the text on a regular basis. If you go over returned papers consistently, working out one grammatical error at a time, you stand a good chance of rooting out the problems. Another method for improving your understanding of grammar is to review the parts of speech in the appendix because a knowledge of these terms helps you avoid potential trouble spots.

FRAGMENTS

Fragments are nonsentences or incomplete thoughts masquerading as sentences. This particular error is one of the most serious of the group, for it calls into question a writer's ability to produce sentences, the basic units of writing. Examine the following sentences; the first three are relatively brief, whereas the fourth is more fully developed:

> She laughed.

> She laughed loudly.

> She laughed loudly at my joke.

> She laughed loudly at my joke because it was really funny.

Focusing on the fourth sentence, consider what would occur if a writer felt that the line was too long and added a period.

> She laughed loudly at my joke. Because it was really funny.

If the period is not edited out but allowed to appear on the final copy, the instructor would mark the sentence with *brackets* to indicate a fragment.

> She laughed loudly at my joke. [Because it was really funny.]

The first sentence can stand by itself, for it is complete; however, the unit starting with *because* is incomplete or dependent upon the previous one for completion.

Table 5.1   Symbols for Problems in Sentences

Symbol/Abbreviation	Problem
[ ]	**Fragment:** a nonsentence or incomplete thought. The marks are called brackets.
RT	**Run-Together:** two sentences incorrectly joined with no punctuation in between.
CS or CF	**Comma-Splice** or **Comma Fault:** two sentences incorrectly joined with a comma.
S–V ag	**Subject–Verb Agreement:** the subject and verb do not agree in number (singular or plural).
Pro ag	**Pronoun Agreement:** a pronoun does not agree in number with its noun.
Pro ref	**Pronoun Reference:** there is confusion about the reference of a pronoun; the meaning is unclear or inaccurate.
VT	**Verb Tense:** your choice of verb form is faulty.
P ✓	**Possession:** an apostrophe is used incorrectly, or you have omitted one entirely.
DM	**Dangling Modifier:** one part of your sentence does not clearly relate to another. It dangles instead of describing or relating.
MM	**Misplaced Modifier:** a group of words has been incorrectly positioned in a sentence.
FP	**Faulty Parallelism:** groups of words that should be harmonious in comparison or pattern are not.

Editing Your Drafts for Fragments

When editing your own drafts for fragments, watch closely for the following situations.

Sentences Beginning with Dependent Words

Because, after, when, although, if, since, as are all common subordinating conjunctions and signal potential trouble spots.

Who, which, and *that,* the relative pronouns, may also be involved in a fragment.

[*If* I had saved some money.] I could have bought that new stereo. But I borrowed the money from Steve. [*Who* is a good friend.]

To cure this sort of problem, look at the unit in front of the dependent element or the one behind it. Most fragments can easily be added to the independent unit to complete its message.

If I had saved some money, I could have bought that new stereo. But I borrowed the money from Steve, who is a good friend.

For the reasons for using commas in the preceding examples, consult Comma Rules 4 and 5 (pp. 319–323)

Sentences Beginning with *-ing* Words and Infinitive Phrases

[Danc*ing* the night away in my new gown.]

[*To spend* too much money on fancy outfits.]

To remedy this problem, follow the technique described above; that is, see if you can combine the fragment with the sentence in front or behind it. If that is not workable, then add new material to finish the message started by the fragment.

Dancing the night away in my new gown, *I felt so glamorous!*

To spend too much money on fancy outfits *is not always smart, but this occasion was an exception.*

Sentences Starting with Added Detail Words or Phrases

Look for these words or phrases: *especially, for example, for instance, such as*

I wanted a number of items. [*Especially* lettuce and mushrooms.]
Sue tried a number of tactics to help her friend in math. [*For example,* tutoring her in more difficult numerical concepts.]

You can usually add *especially* and *such as* to the preceding sentence to remedy this problem.

I wanted a number of items, especially lettuce and mushrooms.

However, the phrases *for example* and *for instance* usually require that you add material, specifically a subject and a verb.

Sue tried a number of tactics to help her friend in math. For example, *she tutored* her in more difficult numerical concepts.

Sentences Starting with *and*

As a rule of thumb, don't use *and* to start sentences, for this practice can lead to overuse and very poor quality sentences.

I visited the Philadelphia Museum of Art. [*And* was most impressed with it.]

Instead, see if you can add the *and* portion to the sentence preceding:

I visited the Philadelphia Museum of Art *and* was most impressed with it.

By all means, use voicing as you edit. Fragments are often relatively easy to hear, for they sound incomplete. In the previous unit, we discussed this practice at great length.

 Exercise 5.12   RECOGNIZING FRAGMENTS

Copy the sentences below onto a separate sheet of paper. Among them are five fragments. Place a bracket [ ] around the entire fragment, and write *F* to the left of the sentence. If the unit is a grammatically complete sentence, write *C* to the left of it.

1. Celebrities often have difficult lives.

2. Because some fans go to great lengths to touch or see their favorite.

3. Even with disguises and intricate systems of personal security.

4. The famous individual still has a problem maintaining privacy.

5. Some well-known people respond by becoming recluses.

6. Hiding within the walls of their private homes between films or public appearances.

7. To live in this manner and fear going out.

8. A person truly does pay a high price for fame.

9. The fact that celebrities are people is something we should all remember.

10. Especially the fans who need to use restraint when trying to see their idol.

 Exercise 5.13   RECOGNIZING FRAGMENTS

Each item below contains a pair of "sentences." One of the pair, however, is a fragment. Copy all eight pairs onto a separate sheet of paper. Read each pair carefully, then enclose in brackets the one which is incomplete.

1. As it allows a regular flow of current. A dimmer switch can save electricity in the home.

2. Having suffered all day from a migraine headache. Eloise left the party early.

3. When people eat and drink to excess. They can expect to suffer the consequences.

4. I was upset because I was late. In addition to the fact that the hostess was waiting for me to help her.

5. To ensure your reservation for next weekend. You should send a deposit for half the amount as soon as possible.

6. I wanted a new car. Which would allow me a greater degree of freedom and independence.

7. Running along a country road. A small stream gurgled and bubbled merrily.

8. If I had invested in real estate earlier. I might be a millionaire today.

Exercise 5.14   LOCATING FRAGMENTS IN A TEXT

There are five fragments located in the paragraph below. Mark them with brackets. Then, using your own paper, rewrite the entire paragraph, correcting the fragment errors in one of the two ways suggested earlier.

Note: You must evaluate each group of words from capital letter to period.

Incorrect: I went home [to my mother.]

Correct: [When I went home to my mother.]

I believe that all companies should offer child care to the working mothers they employ. Since the cost of living is so high today. Many mothers are forced to work in order to afford the bare essentials. Let alone the luxuries. Large companies usually have space that could be converted into areas for children. The initial cost of converting and equipping the space would soon be recovered in the increased efficiency of the workers. Who no longer have to take days off when their children are ill. When working mothers are no longer worried about their children's well-being. They will work faster and with better concentration. Knowing that just a few steps away their children are in good hands.

Exercise 5.15   LOCATING FRAGMENTS IN A TEXT

Bracket the three fragment errors in the following paragraph: then rewrite the paragraph, and correct fragments by using one of the methods suggested. Use your own paper.

Recently, I learned of an interesting new vacation concept. Which involves senior citizens. The program is patterned on the youth hostels that are very popular in Europe. When senior citizens join. A schedule of trips is sent to them. Most of the hostels are located on college campuses, and short study courses are planned for the travelers. Like the youth hostels, the facilities are dormitories, but more comfortable beds are provided. There are more bathrooms, and a nurse is in residence at each hostel. Colleges all over the world are participating and offering both relaxation and education to people who may be old chronologically but who still have a youthful attitude. And a love of travel and adventure.

Exercise 5.16   LOCATING FRAGMENTS IN A TEXT

Locate and bracket the ten fragments in the following essay, but make no changes or additions.

Living in a dormitory was an experience I hope never to repeat. At first, I felt that dorm life would be exciting. And different from home. New friends would be available to me, and I could develop good study habits. But my ideas turned out to be completely wrong. Because of my lack of knowledge.

When I moved into my dorm, music was blaring, people were shouting in order to be heard over the music, and showers were running. Day and night the music played while the showers ran. And never stopped. I knew that I would have a hard time settling down. To study carefully and well. It was clear that a plan must be developed to deal with this noisy and unpleasant environment. Especially for final examinations. After thinking for a while. I decided that my first purchase would be a pair of earplugs. Which I purchased the very next day.

I stuck it out in the dorms. For one long, difficult year. But I vowed that never again would I try to live and study in what seemed to me to be a zoo for humans. Because my grades were bad that year. I realized that I needed a more controlled and quiet environment. Although my home was familiar and even boring, at least I could tolerate the noise level. And concentrate. I'm more aware now, and I know that I will never be attracted to dormitory living again.

Exercise 5.17   LOCATING FRAGMENTS IN A TEXT

There are five fragments in the essay below. Mark each one by enclosing it in brackets, but make no changes in the text unless your instructor wants a revision.

A person can suddenly become aware of his or her age in the most unusual places imaginable. Not long ago, I ws driving home on the freeway. When I happened to glance casually at the vehicle to my left. There in the adjacent lane was a police car.

Immediately, I checked my speedometer. Which was fortunately registering under the speed limit. Then, for some reason, I clearly noticed the face of the policeman sitting in the passenger seat. A position which made him very close to me. Much to my surprise, there didn't seem to be a wrinkle on his face. In fact, my first thought was that he looked like a teenager in an officer's uniform. In nearly every movie I have ever seen or every policeman I noticed. The law officers were definitely older with wrinkles and crow's feet that gave a sense of dignity and maturity. I found myself rather upset by the fact that suddenly I was the older party.

From that time on, I have tended to compare my age with the ages of other people. Especially if they belong to a group which "should be" older. Such groups include not only law enforcement officers but members of the clergy and the medical profession.

RUN-TOGETHER AND COMMA-SPLICED SENTENCES

Run-together (RT) and *Comma-splice* (CS) errors incorrectly join two or more sentences. When run together, two sentences are written as one with *no* punctuation between; in a comma splice, a comma is used to separate sentences.

Notice that this writing error involves sentences or complete thoughts, making the problem the opposite of the fragment.

Correct: My back hurts *because* it is weak.

Correct: My back hurts, *for* it is weak.

Run-together: My back hurts it is weak.

Comma splice: My back hurts, it is weak.

The same elements appear in all four units. In the correct versions, however, "my back hurts" and "it is weak" are connected with a subordinating conjunction *(because)* and a coordinating conjunction *(for)*.

Editing Your Drafts for Run-together and Comma-spliced Sentences

When editing your own drafts, watch for these situations:

Look for commas, especially those in front of these personal pronouns, *I, you, he, she, they, we, it,* for there is a tendency for writers to forget that pronouns can be subjects.

CS

Sentence→   **Sentence→**
I enjoyed Mr. Field's class, *it* was so enlightening.

Watch for commas in front of the adverb *then;* it is not a conjunction and should be avoided as a connector between sentences.

CS

Sentence→   **Sentence→**
First, I went to the movies, then I had my dinner.

To avoid a comma splice or run-together error, choose one of these options:

1. Use a connector (an appropriate conjunction) to join the two sentences:

   I enjoyed Mr. Field's class *because* it was so enlightening.

2. Separate the two sentences with a period. This option is useful when the sentences are long or not directly related.

   First, I went to the movies. Then I had my dinner.

3. Change the comma to a semicolon. Use this option sparingly, for overuse leads to choppy sentences. First, I went to the movies; then I had my dinner.

The comma splice is relatively easy to spot since you can double check your commas. The run-together, however, gives no such visual clues. Therefore, the best way to discover the run-together is to read your draft aloud. If you read attentively, you will probably hear where these problems occur.

I find myself unable to resist peanuts ∧ they are so tasty.

When you locate this error, use any of the three options highlighted for the comma splice. A note of caution: When you do find a run-together, don't try to correct it with a comma. Why? You will have exchanged your run-together error for a comma splice.

Exercise 5.18   RECOGNIZING AND MARKING RUN-TOGETHER ERRORS

Four of the sentences below contain run-together errors. Copy all of the sentences onto a separate sheet of paper, marking the spot where the error occurs with **RT.** Write **C** to the left of those sentences which are correct.

> *Example:* I love my dog $\overset{\textbf{RT}}{\wedge}$ he is so faithful.

1. The painting sold for a fantastic price far exceeding my budget.

2. His words flowed on the paper they refused to stop.

3. We need a budget because we are always in debt.

4. June, July, and August are my favorite months these three represent the end of school and two months of total freedom.

5. Why should I help him he was always so rude.

6. Can you imagine my surprise when Emily walked in?

7. The clock struck twelve as the wolves began to howl.

8. First, I went to the bank then I drove to the day-care center.

Exercise 5.19   RECOGNIZING AND MARKING COMMA SPLICE ERRORS

Copy all of the following sentences onto a separate sheet of paper. There are *four* comma splice errors among them. Whenever you spot one, be sure to mark the trouble spot and write **CS** above it.

> *Example:* I love my dog$\overset{\textbf{CS}}{,}$ he is so faithful.

Remember not to add commas; you must evaluate the commas already there. If the sentence is correct as written, write a **C** to the left of it.

1. Collecting china was my hobby, but it soon got out of hand.

2. The first problem was space, there was too much china and not enough cabinets in my home.

3. I overcame that difficulty by rearranging my cabinets, however, another problem then appeared.

4. After about a year and a half of collecting pieces, I realized that I had spent quite a bit of money on this activity, too much actually.

5. I had two options, should I stop collecting, should I have other people buy pieces for me?

6. I decided that from then on, my parents and close friends could give me gifts of china for Christmas or my birthday.

7. That way, I could finish out my collection, people giving me gifts would also have an easier time selecting them.

8. When my china collection is complete, I can then start with crystal and silver.

Exercise 5.20   LOCATING RUN-TOGETHER AND COMMA-SPLICE ERRORS IN A TEXT

There are three comma-splices and one run-together error in the following paragraph. Locate and mark them. Then rewrite the entire paragraph using any of the three methods presented earlier to correct the errors. Use your own paper. Reread your revision carefully to be sure sentences are separated or joined correctly.

When my husband and I were first married, he always looked forward to the weekend, this was the time he could watch whatever game was being televised. I figured that with all of his anticipation, he would never move his eyes from the set, however, this was not true. Within moments of placing his head on the couch, he would fall asleep there I would be wondering what happened. While he slept, though, I could do chores and even make quite a bit of noise without ever waking him. But let me change the channel to a romantic movie, and guess what would happen? His eyes would pop open, then he would ask me what the score was.

Exercise 5.21   LOCATING RUN-TOGETHER AND COMMA-SPLICE ERRORS IN A TEXT

Read the following paragraph carefully, aloud if possible, to hear where the sentences are joined incorrectly. Using your own paper mark **RT** above each spot where sentences are run together without any punctuation; mark **CS** above each comma used incorrectly to join two sentences. There are seven **CS** errors and one **RT** error.

Henry VIII is one of history's most fascinating figures, he boosted the prestige of England, enriched the national treasury, and created his own church. But what he is most remembered for is his marital record instead of one wife, Henry had six! Each of the six relationships is fascinating, Henry changed both in character and outlook with every new wife. Certainly the most tempestuous and historically influential relationship was with his second wife, Anne Boleyn was a strong-willed woman who wanted to be more than a mistress, and she did manage to become the queen of England. Unfortunately, she did not remain so for long, in order to marry her, Henry broke with the Catholic Church, he also divorced his first wife. The offspring of their short marriage is perhaps the most famous British monarch: Elizabeth I, it was in her reign that Shakespeare wrote his finest plays, and England sent ships of exploration to far-off lands, later one of these areas would be called the United States of America. How interesting to think that so much can happen from one love affair.

Exercise 5.22   LOCATING RUN-TOGETHER AND COMMA-SPLICE ERRORS IN A TEXT

Read the following essay carefully; locate and mark one **RT** and five **CS** errors.

After reading a number of articles on health, I have decided to become a vegetarian. I plan to do this gradually, eliminating one category of food at a time. Red meat will be the first to go, it's the worst for the body. Steak and hamburgers have an extremely high level of fat they contain far too many calories for my already plump shape. I can't imagine what meals will be like without meat, I really love it.

   To maintain good health as a vegetarian, it is important to learn how to replace animal protein with other sources of protein by combining foods. For example, whole grains combined with nuts provide high protein. A sandwich made from whole wheat bread and peanut butter is a good choice. Beans and rice topped with cheese also are high in protein and a good bargain, they are inexpensive. There are many different food combinations that are healthy, economical, and do not saturate the body with fats and cholesterol.

   Before I made the decision to become a vegetarian, I read a number of books, then I shopped for my new diet. Although I am only just starting, I have high hopes and great expectations, I have come to realize how vital it is to do whatever I can to ensure my good health.

✎ Exercise 5.23   LOCATING RUN-TOGETHER AND COMMA-SPLICE ERRORS IN A TEXT

Write **RT** and **CS** above each incorrect joining in the following essay. Locate two **RT** errors and six **CS** errors.

   Last year my parents sold our family home and moved to a small apartment. It was time for me to find a place of my own. I was lucky in finding a small cottage right at the beach it was perfect. Living by the ocean was new, and I looked forward to the experience little did I know what experiences awaited me!

The cottage in summer was perfect, the place was cool and pleasant. Each morning I put on a pot of coffee and then walked the few steps to the ocean and swam. When I came back, I drank my coffee, then I got ready for work. Sunsets were unbelievably beautiful, and I usually had my dinner right on the beach. The gradual change of summer to winter, however, took me by surprise. One day was warm and pleasant, the next day the rains came. There were leaks in my roof, they flooded the floors. Shingles blew off the roof in the high winds, and I could never get warm enough. The tides were so high that there was no beach for my daily walks. I decided to see if my parents had room for me, the beach cottage was unlivable in winter.

When I think back to my time at the beach, I don't regret the experience, but I wish I had gotten more information before I made the decision. I should have been suspicious at the low rent I paid, it was really too low for that location. I would live at the beach again, but this time I'd be more careful.

SUBJECT AND VERB AGREEMENT

Subject–verb agreement errors occur when these two major parts of the sentence do not agree in *number.*

Within any sentence, the subject and verb work together to deliver the main idea; therefore, it becomes critical that the two work together harmoniously. In the case of subject and verb, the two can conflict with respect to *number*—that is to say, whether they match in being singular or plural. Study these two sentences:

Correct: They have worked all day.

Incorrect: They has worked all day.

The subject–verb relationship is harmonious in the first sentence because both subject *(they)* and verb *(have worked)* are plural; the helper portion *have*, controls the number. But in the second sentence, the subject is plural, but the verb *(has worked)* is singular; hence, they do not agree in number.

Editing Your Drafts for Subject–Verb Agreement Problems

When editing your own writing, watch for four potential trouble spots.

Check Your Subject–Verb Agreement

When you see singular indefinite pronouns at the start of your sentences: *each, one, any, anyone, someone, somebody, either, neither, anybody, none,* look for possible subject–verb agreement errors.

    S   **S–V**
Each of the nurses *are* present.
    S   **S–V**
One of my brothers *use* my car.
    S   **S–V**
Somebody in this room *have taken* my wallet.

Because these indefinite pronouns are by definition singular (though they may sound plural), they require a singular verb:

    S   **SING**
Each of the nurses *is* present.
    S   **SING**
One of my brothers *uses* my car.
    S   **SING**
Somebody in this room *has taken* my wallet.

This type of grammar problem is not easy to solve, for it usually involves retraining your pattern of speech. However, by calling attention to the indefinite pronouns, especially those you have not written in the standard way, and by drilling yourself orally on the correct words, you have a good chance of working out the difficulty.

Your first source of drill work is your corrected exercises. An additional source of drill is Exercise 5.25 (pp. 273–274).

If verbal practice seems silly, remember the situation we are all in when we learn a foreign language. We are usually sent to a language laboratory where we are required to practice the various sentence patterns and individual vocabulary words. In a sense, the problems seen in the examples above are foreign to the native speaker who is unaware of the difficulty. If you can retrain your speech and brain, you stand an excellent chance of correcting your written performance.

Exercise 5.24   AGREEMENT WITH INDEFINITE PRONOUNS

Each of the following sentences contains an indefinite pronoun as subject. On a separate sheet of paper, number from 1 to 10. Choose the verb given in brackets that agrees with the subject.

    S
Example: [is, are] *Any* of these ideas **is** workable.

1. One of my dogs [has, have] eaten a hole in the corner of my new carpet.

2. Each of these books [go, goes] back to the library.

3. Everybody in those two groups [hate, hates] that kind of problem.

4. One of my brothers [is, are] leading the race.

5. No one in those two families [is, are] able to get along for more than five minutes at a time.

6. Any of these classes [transfers, transfer] to the University of California.

7. Everyone in my group of skiers [expects, expect] me to take that big jump, but I'll fool them.

8. Neither of my options [has, have] materialized, and I am frustrated.

9. Either of these roads [brings, bring] you to Tonawanda, so take your pick.

10. Both of the children [loves, love] working with clay.

Exercise 5.25   AN ORAL DRILL IN SUBJECT–VERB AGREEMENT

Practice the following verbal drill for 15 to 20 minutes three to four times per week. As you speak the sentences, add slight emphasis to the verb (in italics). Be sure to accentuate the -s at the end of the verb, for it is the key to singular agreement. Work on this somewhere private so that you can speak without being disturbed.

1. Each *is* informative.
   Each of the speakers *is* informative.
   Each of the speakers on accounting practices *is* informative.

2. Either *is* acceptable.
   Either of these ideas *is* acceptable.
   Either of these ideas on profits *is* acceptable.

3. Everyone *was* chatting.
   Everyone in the rooms *was* chatting.
   Everyone in the rooms on the second floor *was* chatting.

4. One *runs* gracefully.
   One of my dogs *runs* gracefully.
   One of my dogs *runs* gracefully and *obeys* perfectly.

5. Any *works*.
   Any of these solutions *works*.
   Any of these solutions *works* for this problem.

6. Somebody *has* taken my figurine.
   Somebody in this group *has* taken my figurine.
   Somebody in this group of tourists *has* taken my figurine.

7. One *is* strong enough.

One of those pills *is* strong enough.

One of those pills for headaches *is* strong enough.

8. Not one *is* cooperating.

Not one of those workers *is* cooperating.

Not one of those workers or managers *is* cooperating.

9. None *suits* me.

None of these styles *suits* me.

None of these styles of dresses *suits* me.

10. Everybody *needs* help.

Everybody with problems *needs* help.

Everybody with problems or questions *needs* help.

Check Your Subject–Verb Agreement

Notice prepositional phrases between the subject and verb. At the same time that prepositional phrases provide valuable information, they tend to separate the subject from the verb. Examine the following sentences in which the prepositional phrases are in parentheses.

$$\overset{\textbf{S}}{\text{The stain}} \text{ (on the hem) (of my pants) } \overset{\textbf{V}}{\text{is}} \text{ permanent.}$$

$$\overset{\textbf{S}}{\underline{\text{A request}}} \text{ (for money and supplies) } \overset{\textbf{V}}{\overbrace{\text{was issued.}}}$$

This kind of separation sometimes confuses a writer who may remember the noun closest to the verb and choose the wrong form:

$$\overset{\textbf{S–V}}{\text{The }} \textit{stain} \text{ on the hem of my } \textit{pants were} \text{ permanent.}$$

A subject–verb agreement error occurs here because the writer has mistaken *pants* for the subject instead of stain.

Make a point of reviewing the material on prepositional phrases in the appendix (pp. 354–355), especially if your instructor marks **S–V ag** by a verb that has been separated from its subject by these units.

Use the oral technique to drill yourself on the corrected material in the next exercise.

Exercise 5.26   WHEN A SUBJECT AND VERB ARE SEPARATED

The following sentences contain subjects and verbs separated by prepositional phrases. On a separate sheet of paper recopy all the sentences, enclosing any prepositional phrases with parentheses to help you locate the subject. Then circle the appropriate singular or plural verb to fit the subject.

Example: The paint (on these walls) (is, are) peeling.

1. The day of my final examinations (is, are) not yet announced.

2. The print on all of those bottles (bothers, bother) my eyes because it is too small.

3. The law of diminishing returns in economics (is, are) an important concept.

4. An institution in such dire financial straits (has, have) to enlist the services of top consultants in the field.

5. An athlete with those talents and gifts (sets, set) a high standard for all the others.

6. The best time for many who are full-time students (is, are) semester break.

7. The books on my shelf in the library (was, were) old and dusty.

8. His remarks about salespeople (makes, make) me furious.

9. That lecture on the eating habits of hyenas and vultures (has, have) upset my stomach.

10. Communication between temperamental spouses sometimes (becomes, become) stormy.

Check Your Subject–Verb Agreement
when you see *and* forming compound subjects.

Chicken and beef *taste* delicious.

Sometimes a writer hears only the last subject, the one closest to the verb. Examine the following sentence:

S–V
Chicken and beef *tastes* delicious.

A subject–verb agreement error occurs because *tastes* is singular and not in agreement with the plural *chicken* plus *beef* subject.

Care in editing will help you to locate any compound subjects. If this type of agreement error occurs in your writing, practice reading aloud the corrected version of the next exercise. You may also wish to review the material about compound subjects appearing in the first part of this unit (pp. 248–249).

Look carefully at sentence subjects when you check agreement. Some subjects appear to be plural but are singular.

S   **V**
Correct: The *lawyer,* along with my doctor, *is entering* the room.
   (*lawyer* and *doctor* are not equal grammatically; there is no conjunction to join them.)

S   **S**   **V**
Correct: My *lawyer* and my *doctor* are entering the room.
   (With the coordinating conjunction *and, lawyer* and *doctor* are grammatically equal and will take a plural verb.)

Exercise 5.27   AGREEMENT WITH COMPOUND SUBJECTS

Six of the sentences below contain compound subjects joined by *and* for which you must circle the plural verb in parentheses. If the subject is not compound, then circle the singular verb. Write your choices on a separate sheet of paper.

1. A walk on the beach and a picnic in the woods (is, are) delightful to me.

2. An introverted person and an extroverted person (has, have) a certain amount of attraction for each other because of their opposite natures.

3. My English teacher, in addition to a special counselor, (is, are) attending the conference.

4. My begonia and my pothos (seems, seem) to be drooping.

5. An oil spot and a life raft (was, were) all that floated on the surface of the water where the boat sank.

6. Poverty and poor health (afflicts, afflict) many people in today's world.

7. The mayor, along with two council members, (is, are) holding a press conference.

8. Watching your weight and getting enough exercise (tends, tend) to increase your life span.

Check Your Subject–Verb Agreement

Look for *who, which,* and *that* used as relative pronouns. Relative pronouns form dependent clauses and may appear next to any noun. When sentences contain such units, however, there are two sets of subjects and verbs.

> **S   V   S   V**
> Stuart works with *people who pay* him well.

Basically, the verb in the relative pronoun clause should agree with the noun nearest the relative pronoun; hence, the verb *pay* must agree with *people* for agreement to occur.

Awareness of relative pronouns will be very helpful in remedying any agreement problems. In addition to the discussion above, you might also review material in other sections on relative pronouns: Unit IV (pp. 218–219), where they are used in combining sentences; the punctuation of relative pronoun clauses featured with Comma Rule 5; and the appendix (pp. 347–349), specifically pronouns.

Exercise 5.28   RELATIVE PRONOUN CLAUSE AGREEMENT

Each sentence below has a relative pronoun clause and a choice of either a singular or a plural verb in parentheses. To decide which verb form is correct, look first at the italicized relative pronoun, then back to the noun next to it. Write your verb choices on a separate sheet of paper.

> *Example:* The *profit which* (comes, come) from my investment is minimal.

1. A flock of *birds which* (is, are) flying south is a sight to behold.

2. Each of the *flowers that* (blooms, bloom) nearby emits a wonderful fragrance.

3. His *laughter, which* (pierces, pierce) our eardrums, is shrill enough to make me leave the room.

4. This plane has one of those *designs which* (is, are) unusual.

5. Many people get bogged down in details *which only* (serves, serve) to confuse the issue.

6. Any of our bad *habits that* (leads, lead) to health problems should be broken.

7. She prefers *flowers which* (blooms, bloom) all year round.

8. Jeff is the sort of *individual who* (plans, plan) every detail of a vacation.

Exercise 5.29   LOCATING SUBJECT–VERB AGREEMENT ERRORS IN A TEXT

There are eight subject–verb agreement errors of all types in the following paragraph. Mark **S–V** directly above the incorrect verb. Reading sentences aloud may help you detect errors. On your own paper, rewrite the entire text and correct the errors you have located.

Travel to a foreign country for any length of time involve some careful planning, especially with respect to luggage. First time travelers often do not realizes just how annoying and burdensome excess baggage is. It is often impossible to convince a person who wish to look special that only a few comfortable items are really necessary. The traveler who overpack, however, soon find out that there is just too many garments and often will mail back the excess. It take a while for some people to realize that in a foreign country, no one know you and can't criticize you for wearing an outfit several times.

Exercise 5.30   LOCATING SUBJECT–VERB AGREEMENT ERRORS IN A TEXT

There are seven subject–verb agreement errors in the text below. Mark **S–V** directly above the incorrect verb form. Rewrite the corrected paragraph on your own paper.

Every language contain colorful expressions which relates to various areas of life such as birth, marriage, and death. In English, for instance, there is many expressions which has developed over the years to refer to death. One of the quaintest phrases are "pushing up daisies" or for those more playful, "cashing in your chips." Who could leave out the unforgettable "kick the bucket"? Some of the phrases have arisen from war, such as "he bought the farm." In a religious vein, we can say that a person have "gone to his or her final reward," "met his Maker," and "crossed over Jordan." Words or phrases which are used to lessen the negative effect of an unpleasant situation such as death are called euphemisms. Instead of saying "she died," a person could say euphemistically that "she passed away"--a phrase that sound less disturbing and final.

PRONOUN AGREEMENT AND REFERENCE

Pronoun Agreement

Pronoun agreement errors occur when pronouns and the nouns to which they refer (or which they replace) do not agree in number. In the same way that subject and verb must agree in number, so must a pronoun agree with the noun to which it refers or which it replaces. Many inaccuracies have crept into our language in this area, and even well-educated individuals are unaware that pronoun agreement problems exist in their speech or writing.

> *Correct:* The *college* established a special fund since *it* wished to buy new equipment for *its* nursing department.

> *Incorrect:* The *college* established a special fund since *they* wished to buy new equipment for *their* nursing department.

Another way of describing the need for pronoun agreement is to say that the beginning of each sentence sets a standard for the words that follow. If you start with a singular noun, you must refer to it in the singular throughout.

Editing Your Drafts for Pronoun Agreement

When editing your own writing for pronoun agreement, try looking at the beginning of each sentence to see whether you started it with a *singular or plural noun.* Let's say that this was the first line of your draft:

> Every *person* I know seems to be involved in exercising and caring for *their* body.

Although *person* is singular, the possessive pronoun *their* is plural, so there is disagreement.

There are two ways to correct this problem. You can keep *person* and change *their* to the singular form *his* or *her*.

> Every *person* I know seems to be involved in exercising and caring for *his* body.

> Every *person* I know seems to be involved in exercising and caring for *her* body.

Traditional English grammar has used the masculine singular relatives for words such as a *person* or *someone* unless speaking specifically of a woman. Many people, however, object to this usage because they feel it emphasizes men at the expense of women.

One alternative to the traditional treatment is to change *person* (singular) to *people* (plural). Then *people* will agree with the plural pronoun *their* (which is either masculine or feminine). To balance all elements, change the verb to *seem* and make *body* plural, too.

$$\overset{\mathbf{S}}{} \quad \overset{\mathbf{V}}{}$$

People I know *seem* to be involved in exercising and caring for *their bodies.*

Exercise 5.31   SELECTING PRONOUNS FOR PROPER AGREEMENT

On a separate sheet of paper, number from 1 to 10. Write the correct pronoun from the pair in parentheses. To assist you, the key noun or pronoun governing the choice is in italics.

1. When a *person* has to leave a class early, (he, they) should be very quiet and unobtrusive.

2. If a *person* is not quiet, (she, they) might well disrupt the *class* and (its, their) concentration.

3. Every *one* of these suspects must supply (his, their) version of the crime.

4. The *firm* gave (its, their) support to the new proposal.

5. *Either* of these choices is a good one, for (it, they) will save money in the long run.

6. Because my *team* lost, (it, they) paid for everyone's lunch.

7. The *Internal Revenue Service* often appears to be heartless because (its, their) ultimate aim is to collect money.

8. The *history department* gave (its, their) consent for the special collection to be exhibited in (its, their) offices.

9. Each *girl* on the basketball team must supply (her, their) own warm-up suit.

10. After the first week of school, *people* who want to add classes must take (her, their) cards to the office.

Exercise 5.32   LOCATING PRONOUN AGREEMENT ERRORS IN A TEXT

The paragraph below contains five errors in pronoun agreement. Write **Pro Ag** above each incorrect form, and underline any verb which may need to be changed. Rewrite the entire paragraph with pronoun errors corrected and verb forms revised as necessary.

Parties can be tiring, for it makes my husband and me clean the house in an extra-thorough manner. Our home contains hardwood floors, which are lovely, but it does get dusty. Tending to this area is my husband's specialty. For me, windows are important because it lets light enter and makes the interior more pleasant. Plants are cleaned by both of us. Each individual leaf gets washed until they shine. We want every guest to enjoy themselves in a bright and shining environment.

Exercise 5.33   LOCATING PRONOUN AGREEMENT ERRORS IN A TEXT

Locate six pronoun agreement errors in the paragraph below. Write **Pro Ag** above each incorrect pronoun form. Underline any verb that would have to be changed to match the correct pronoun.

Often, a person who diets does not realize that they will not achieve their goal if the diet is a fad or extreme in any way. The human body responds to any deprivation of its necessary proteins, minerals, and carbohydrates in a dramatic way. For example, when a person starts a high-protein diet or the "drinking man's" diet, they will lose weight, but the loss is misleading! Most of the time, a fad dieter loses water and muscle tissue, not the fat tissue they are trying to shed. Interestingly, the dieter's body holds on to fat tissue and resists burning them. At the end of a week or two, there is weight loss, but very little of it is fat. To make matters even worse, the person generally regains the lost weight and a few pounds more before very long. Anyone who goes on a diet should consult with their

physician to plan a dietary program that not only maintains good

health but works to remove fat permanently.

Pronoun Reference

Pronoun reference errors occur when pronouns do not clearly refer to or replace nouns. The problem of pronoun reference is more complex than that of pronoun agreement. The four forms of this problem covered here include (1) ambiguous references, (2) nonexistent references with *they*, (3) problems with relative pronouns, and (4) the misuse of *you* to refer to the reader directly.

Ambiguous References

Stating an idea in an ambiguous way creates a problem because two equally valid conclusions can be drawn from the same sentence. Read the following example of ambiguity very carefully.

N/pl   **N/pl PRO/pl**

Ambiguous: When *people* discuss their *problems, they* should be objective.

There is no agreement error here because *people, problems,* and *they* are all plural. Nevertheless, there is ambiguity because a reader does not know to which noun the pronoun refers. *Who* or *what* should be objective—the *people* or the *problems?*

When you are working out your ideas for an essay or any kind of writing, the last effect you want to produce is confusion.

Editing Your Drafts for Ambiguous Reference   Read especially carefully any sentences with this pattern: two nouns in the front of the sentence with a pronoun following them. Check to see whether the pronoun reference is clear or ambiguous.

Once you have located this problem, you must decide what you really mean. In other words, which interpretation fits your point of view? If you had intended in the example about people and problems that the *people* should be objective, then write:

People should be objective when *they* discuss their problems.

Now it is clear that the pronoun *they* refers back to *people* because the noun *problems* has been moved to the back of the sentence.

If the *problems* should be objective, then write:

The *problems which* people discuss should be objective.

This version replaces the pronoun *they* with the relative pronoun *which* and moves *problems* to a more prominent position as the sentence subject.

Exercise 5.34   SPOTTING AMBIGUOUS PRONOUN REFERENCES

Four of the following sentences contain ambiguous reference errors. Mark **Pro Ref** above the offending pronoun. If a sentence has no ambiguous references, write **C** for correct.

1. After my brother told Kyle the news, he had to leave.

2. When I dropped the salmon mousse on the carpet, it looked dreadful.

3. We like Hank and Joe, for they are wonderful men.

4. Parents and children often have trouble communicating because they are too busy to talk.

5. Cynthia needs to speak to her friend, for she is at her wit's end.

6. I bought a bird and a fish, but they both got sick.

Exercise 5.35   LOCATING AMBIGUOUS PRONOUN REFERENCES IN A TEXT

There are three instances of ambiguous pronouns that affect the interpretation of the following paragraph. Mark **Pro Ref** directly above the pronoun.

Taking a physics and a chemistry class in the same semester was not smart because it was just too difficult. I had not realized the enormous workload with chapters to read and complex problems to solve. My part-time job also complicated matters by leaving me with less time to study. My instructor and the lab assistant told me to persist and that he would provide any extra help needed. Although I certainly appreciated the offer, I have learned that students should be careful when enrolling in classes. Otherwise, time and energy are wasted, and it is too precious to be squandered.

Nonexistent References with *They*

Read the following brief passage to see how a pronoun reference problem emerges from the faulty use of the pronoun *they.*

As a returning student, I very much enjoy going to college and feel that I am learning a great deal in the process. However, I have noticed one problem, and that involves the library. How wonderful if

they would do something to improve the building and make it a better

place to study.

After reading the last sentence, a reader might ask, *Who* are *they? Who* is supposed to improve the library? There is no noun to which *they* can refer, so the reader is left wondering.

This pronoun problem has become a habit of many writers and speakers. Although there is no harm in using *they,* this word must have a plural noun to which it can clearly refer.

Editing Your Drafts for Misused *They*

When you read your draft, circle every *they;* look at the material surrounding it to be sure that the preceding noun is plural. If there is no reference noun (as in the example given earlier), remove *they* completely and replace it with an appropriate word:

> How wonderful if the *school administration* could do something to improve the building and make it a better place to study.

As a bonus this remedy will force you to use more accurate vocabulary and, in turn, write more specifically.

Exercise 5.36   CORRECTING THE MISUSED *THEY*

All of the sentences in this exercise use the pronoun *they* incorrectly. Using your own paper, rewrite each sentence, and replace *they* with a more specific noun. (You may have to change some of the verbs to make them match your noun choices.)

> *Example:* The invitations were ruined because *they* were incompetent.
>
> *Rewrite:* The invitations were ruined because *the printer was* incompetent.

1. When I had my car serviced, they overcharged me.

2. At tax time, I get the feeling that they want all of my money.

3. With respect to drunk drivers, they are very strict in this state.

4. My accounts have been botched since they installed that new computer at the bank.

5. I tried to add new classes to my program, but they said that the classes were filled.

6. Because of an error, they brought me spaghetti, not chicken.

Exercise 5.37   LOCATING THE MISUSED PRONOUN *THEY* IN A TEXT

Write **Pro Ref** above each pronoun error in the following paragraph involving the misused *they* or its objective case *them*. Then rewrite the paragraph so that each misused *they* or *them* is replaced by a specific noun. There are three pronoun reference errors.

> Because I did not do well on my job interview, I was really frustrated. One of the problems which I can now clearly see is that I let them frighten me when I first walked in. Instead of remaining calm, I got nervous because I hadn't realized how hard the interview situation could be. Next time, though, I will know what to expect, and they will see a more confident applicant. In addition, I will take a brief course in public speaking to improve my overall communication skills. They offer such classes at my local college.

Problems with Our "Relatives"

The relative pronouns are *who, whom, which,* and *that.* One of the group, *which,* is often misused.

> *Incorrect:* I lost my *job, which* really angered me.

Because a relative pronoun must relate to the noun just before it, this sentence says that *the job angered* the speaker. Yet we know that this is not the case. What angers the speaker is the fact that the job was *lost.*

Another misuse of *which* occurs when no noun at all is next to the pronoun.

> *Incorrect:* I had to *leave,* which was disturbing.

The relative pronoun clause, *which was disturbing,* seems to point back to *leave,* but *leave* is not a noun, so this sentence is not grammatically harmonious.

Editing Your Draft for Relative Pronoun Problems

As you read the draft, circle every *which* appearing within a sentence. Then check the word that sits to the left of *which.* The noun must be responsible for the action or existence expressed in the clause following *which.*

> *Correct:* Tennis is a *game which* invigorates me. (game–invigorates)

> *Correct:* I do not enjoy *dishes which* are too salty. (dishes–are)

If you spot a relative pronoun–noun relationship that is inaccurate or illogical, it is easiest for you to eliminate the *which* clause entirely and rewrite the sentence:

Incorrect: I lost my job, which really angered me.

Revision: When I lost my job, I was angry.

Revision: Losing my job made me angry.

If no noun is adjacent to the relative pronoun, follow the same procedure. Remove the *which* clause completely, and rewrite the sentence:

Incorrect: I had to leave, which was disturbing.

Revision: Because I had to leave, I was disturbed.

Revision: Having to leave disturbed me.

The second revision in each case uses a gerundive phrase as subject; gerundive phrases were discussed earlier in this unit on page 250.

Exercise 5.38   CORRECTING FAULTY PRONOUN CLAUSES

Each sentence below contains a faulty *which* pronoun clause that has been italicized. When you decide what the meaning should be, rewrite the sentence on your own paper, and correct the reference problem. Remember to remove the *which* clause altogether.

1. I love being in the woods with my family *which sometimes takes weeks of planning.*

2. Dahlma overpaid for the dress *which made her upset.*

3. We bought our house *which was the right move at the right time.*

4. They want an end to the quarreling *which would bring peace once again to their home.*

5. People should not overuse medication *which could result in their deaths or in serious side effects.*

6. I enjoyed Uncle Al, *which made our time together very special.*

7. At dinner, I had too much to eat, *which made me sick.*

8. Ted bought a cheap suit *which was a terrible mistake.*

Exercise 5.39   LOCATING PRONOUN REFERENCE ERRORS IN A TEXT

Find the single pronoun reference error involving the faulty use of *which* in the following paragraph. Write **Pro Ref** above the error, and then rewrite the paragraph on your own paper.

I have always enjoyed my visits to sunny Mexico because it has

so many activities which interest a tourist. The beaches are

beautiful, the historical monuments are impressive, and the food is

delicious. Mexico seems to have everything which a tourist could

want. I have never been disappointed in Mexico, which is the highest

compliment I could pay to any country. If I had a choice between any

other nation and Mexico, I would choose Mexico. I only wish that my

vacation, which is only two-weeks long, were extended to include the

entire summer.

Misuse of the Pronoun *You*

When we write, our material can be described in general from the standpoint of persons.

> ***First-person* writing:** features personal and possessive pronouns *I*, *me*, and *my* for one writer or reference point; *we, us,* and *our* for two or more writers or reference points. This kind of writing is *personal* and *subjective*.

> ***Second-person* writing:** features the pronoun forms *you* and *your* and is specifically directed *to the reader.* Cookbooks, reference or instruction manuals, and this textbook are examples of writing dominated by the second person because the author or authors are telling *you,* the reader, what to do.

> ***Third-person* writing:** includes pronoun forms *it, he, him, she, her, they, them,* and *their.* It is considered more objective than the first or second persons, for its focus is outward to people or situations in general. The articles in most newspapers, textbooks, and scholarly journals feature this impersonal, objective type of writing.

A common error is to slip into the second person, specifically *you,* instead of maintaining either the first- or second-person viewpoint with which the piece started. Study the following passage and watch the effect when the writer switches to *you* in the third sentence.

When <u>I</u> was a small child, <u>I</u> loved to play in the mud. The fall and

winter seasons were best for <u>me</u> because of the rainy weather. <u>You</u>

could play for hours shaping and reshaping the wonderful, mushy

dirt.

Switching abruptly from first to second person is inconsistent with the established pattern of writing. In addition, when a writer uses *you*, this pronoun refers to a specific reader directly, not to the general reader, and can cause writing to be illogical. By writing "You could play for hours shaping and reshaping the wonderful, mushy dirt," this writer has put the reader in the dirt—literally. Remember that the experience is the writer's, not the reader's.

Editing Your Drafts for Switches to the Second Person

First, establish what person you are writing in. Are you writing a personal essay about some event or person in your life? Or, have you written an objective discussion about some problem in our society or situation of which you are aware?

Now, check your paper for any inclusion of the pronoun *you* which is inconsistent with your choice of the subjective, first-person viewpoint or the objective, third-person viewpoint.

To eliminate confusion in first- and third-person writing, remove all usage of *you*. Rewrite such cases to match whatever person the rest of your writing uses. In the example discussed earlier, a revision would return to the first person.

I could play for hours shaping and reshaping the wonderful, mushy dirt.

This revision is reasonable because it is the writer, not the reader, who used to play in the mud; the revision is consistent because it maintains the established first-person pattern.

Exercise 5.40   EDITING FOR MISUSE OF *YOU*

The following paragraph was begun in the third person, but the writer was inconsistent in this viewpoint. As you read this short paragraph, mark each *you*. Then, rewrite the paragraph, replacing each *you* with a better word (a noun or pronoun) that returns the text to the third person. Use your own paper.

The home computer has become a boon for many people, especially students. Once a student has learned the various functions and commands, there are so many ways you can use the machine. Essays and reports may still be hard to think through, but how much easier they are to correct, rewrite, and print. At many schools, you don't even have to buy a computer, for machines are made available in the various study centers.

VERB TENSE PROBLEMS

Verb tense errors occur when a writer either uses an incorrect tense form or switches tense forms unnecessarily.

Incorrect Tense

The following sentences illustrate the problem of incorrect tense choices made by a writer.

> *Incorrect:* He *brung* me a gift.

> *Correct:* He *brought* me a gift.

In this case, brung is a nonstandard form. In formal college writing and standard English, *brought* is the correct form for the past tense.

> *Incorrect:* They *have broke* every rule.

> *Correct:* They *have broken* every rule.

With the helper *have*, the verb tense becomes past continuous; therefore, *broken* is the correct choice. *Broke* would be correct for the simple past: I *broke* my foot.

Tense Switches

Read the following paragraph to see how verb tense switches can weaken writing.

> I will never forget the day my pants <u>split</u> at work. It <u>was</u> six months ago, but the thought can still bring a blush to my face. I <u>knew</u> I shouldn't <u>have worn</u> those pants because the seam in the seat <u>was</u> weak, but I <u>figure</u> it would be all right. As I <u>am</u> bending over to pick up a paper, I <u>hear</u> the awful sound: rrrrip! That kind of ventilation <u>is</u> definitely not what I had in mind.

You can see how the writer begins in the simple past *(It was six months. . . .)* because the incident did occur only once. However, about midway through the paragraph, the writer switches tenses to the present as if the incident were occurring right now.

Editing Your Draft for Verb Tense Problems

Focus on all verbs to check for accuracy. Decide which tense best expresses the event you are relating to your reader; then be sure you stick to it.

Review any previous writing marked by your teacher. If there were tense errors in the past, be alert to them in your current writing, for they tend to reappear.

To build a solid understanding of verb tense, refer to the irregular verb table on pages 356–357 of the appendix. Irregular verbs such as *break* or *bring* tend to cause incorrect forms.

If you have a weak spot, such as writing "has broke" for "has broken," drill yourself orally to overcome the problem.

Exercise 5.41 GENERATING THE CORRECT SIMPLE PAST TENSE

The sentences below require the simple past tense of the verb in the brackets. Decide on the correct verb forms (one verb, no helper), and write them on a separate sheet of paper.

Example: He [to go] to the optometrist. ___*went*___

1. He [to leave] his hometown when he was 17.

2. The winter [to begin] to change to spring.

3. I hesitated because I [to feel] that he was pushing me to make a decision.

4. Where were you when I [to need] you?

5. The Titanic [to sink] into the ocean's depths and remains there to this day, despite a recent attempt to raise it.

6. When I [to drive] to Albuquerque, my air conditioner malfunctioned.

7. The romantic suitor [to steal] her heart.

8. When we [to fly] a small airline, we found the experience refreshingly different.

9. They [to be], without a doubt, the happiest couple on the block until their divorce.

10. We [to have] only two weeks to do this project.

Exercise 5.42 GENERATING THE CONTINUOUS PAST TENSE

The sentences below require the continuous past, or past participle form, of the verb in brackets. The past participle uses a helping verb (*have* or *has*) with the past perfect tense of the verb. If reading a line aloud does not give you the correct answer, consult a dictionary for the past perfect form of the verb.

As with the previous exercise, write your answers on a separate sheet of paper.

Example: I have [to be] rich in my day. ___*been*___

1. Have you [to go] to see that new show?

2. She has [to begin] a new life for herself.

3. According to that critic, the movie industry has [to sink] to a new low.

4. We have [to fly] with this airline for ten years.

5. That celebrity has [to have] his fill of reporters and photographers.

6. Through the years, poverty has [to drive] some people to the brink of despair.

7. The wind has [to blow] for days and shows no signs of stopping.

8. Wallace has [to take] his complaint to the president.

Exercise 5.43   SPOTTING VERB TENSE SWITCHES

Three of the sentences below have unnecessary verb tense switches. Write **VT** above each verb that is switched to the wrong tense. Write **C** for a correct verb tense form. On a separate sheet of paper, number the sentences with unnecessary tense shifts and write the correct tenses.

1. When I saw the monster, I gasped and take one step back.

2. Years ago, I studied piano but was never very good.

3. My little nephew loves spinach, but he hated peas.

4. I gave the project my best effort because I have always had great integrity.

5. Last semester I took anthropology, and it seems to me very challenging and worthwhile.

6. As I left the stage, I turned and bowed to the audience.

Exercise 5.44   LOCATING VERB TENSE ERRORS IN A TEXT

Read the following paragraph carefully with special attention to the verbs in each sentence. There are five errors involving the construction of tenses. Mark **VT** above each.

Having the whole family together for a holiday such as Thanksgiving has always gave me a special thrill. Even though the house is pack with relatives (about forty), there is nothing as enjoyable as watching everyone chatting and reminiscing. Some of the family have even came from other states to attend. Last year, in fact, my cousin flew in from Maryland and brang several special game birds as an alternative to the turkeys. Everyone pitches in in some way. Of course, pictures are took so that we have a more permanent record of all those happy faces.

Exercise 5.45   LOCATING VERB TENSE ERRORS IN A TEXT

Study the following paragraph carefully and mark the eight verbs which switch tense incorrectly. Mark **VT** above the incorrect verb form. After you have marked the eight errors, use your own lined paper to rewrite the paragraph with proper verb forms.

Birds can be surprisingly aggressive and hostile for their small size. Last summer, I was home nearly every morning and became fascinated by the behavior of the birds nesting in our Spanish tile roof. As I was drinking my coffee one morning, I hear a whole assortment of tweets, chirps, and squawks. I look up to see two birds fighting furiously. Interestingly, they are about a yard above our German shepherd's head but are totally unaware of the dog as they actually drop onto the bricks about a foot in front of her. Our dog, by the way, is so surprised that she did nothing. When they realize precisely where they were, the birds flew higher--and then begin fighting again!

Exercise 5.46   LOCATING VERB TENSE ERRORS IN A TEXT

Study the following paragraph and mark the six verbs which switch tense incorrectly. Mark **VT** above the incorrect verb form; then, using your own paper, rewrite the paragraph in proper verb form.

Last year, the job I had been working on came to an end. I tried to find another job close to home, but there were none to be had. Finally, I was forced to become a long-distance commuter. The first morning I got into my car and started out. I'm driving along at a pretty fast pace when I look into the rearview mirror and see a motorcycle police officer. I step on the brakes and soon realize that this drive is going to take me a long time. One advantage, though, is that my drive is on a highway that runs along the oceanside. The view is very beautiful and keeps the drive from being a complete bore.

INCORRECT OWNERSHIP OR POSSESSION

Possession errors occur when a writer either misplaces or leaves out the apostrophe needed to indicate ownership. There are several ways to indicate ownership in English, without using an apostrophe.

> He took *my* seat.
> (*My*, a possessive pronoun, indicates that the seat belonged to the writer or speaker.)
>
> The hat *belonging to Karen* looked awful.
> (The participial phrase, *belonging to Karen*, indicates who owns the hat.)
>
> The problems *of our society* are many.
> (The prepositional phrase, *of our society*, indicates the owner of the problems.)

However, the most common way to indicate ownership is by using a small mark called the apostrophe between or after letters in various words. The apostrophe method is a shorter, more direct way to indicate the owner–object relationship. But, the writer must be able to place the apostrophe accurately so that communication is clear.

Singular Ownership

If an owner (person, place, object, idea) is *singular*, then the apostrophe appears *after the last letter*, and an *s* is inserted *after the apostrophe*.

> *Example:* Karen's hat looked awful.

What if Karen owned two ugly hats? Would there be any changes in the way that we expressed ownership? The only change would be to *hat*; if Karen had more than one ugly hat, we would have to write *hats*. The rest remains the same because there is only one owner.

> Karen's hats looked awful.
>
> Our *society*'s problems are many.

Words that have an *s* at the end but are singular, include *bus, Texas, Dolores, Olympics, economics*, and *physics*, to name just a few. These words form the possessive in the same way as words that end in other letters.

> *Los Angeles's* freeways are often jammed with cars.

Plural Ownership

If an owner (person, object, idea) is *plural*, then write the word in its plural form and add the apostrophe *at the end* of the word. (Do not add an *s* after the apostrophe.)

My *sisters'* friends were rude.
(The person speaking has two or more sisters with rude friends.)

The *buses'* tires were flat.
(*Buses* is the plural of *bus;* with the apostrophe after the plural form, we know that the writer is referring to two or more buses with flat tires.)

My *parents'* home is large.
(This writer has two parents who together own one home.)

Just as with singular forms of possession, the plural owner is written first and whatever is owned comes next. The form of the owners does not change, no matter how many objects are owned; two people, for instance, could own one house. Adjectives may also appear between the owner and the object.

> **ADJ**

My *parents' new home* is large.

Some nouns are made plural, but not by adding an *s* as is typical in English. Examine these words:

Singular	*Plural*
man	men
woman	women
child	children
goose	geese
mouse	mice

Add *'s* when these plural forms become owners: *men*'s lounge; *women*'s liberation; *children*'s department, and so on. Although these plurals seem to be exceptions to the general rule, in fact the rule is followed to the letter ("Write the word in its plural form and add the apostrophe.") Then all you need to do is to add the *s* because that sound is not already part of the word. If you were to write "The *childrens'* department," the form would suggest that the plural of child is *childrens* as in "I have five childrens."

Editing Your Draft for Possession Errors

Focus on any apostrophe that you see in your writing. Make sure that it serves one of three roles: *contraction* (*there's* for *there is*); *abbreviation* (*A's* for more than one *A*); or *possession or ownership*. Apostrophes are not used to make simple plurals.

If your draft has missing apostrophes—or none at all—read it carefully to listen for any owner–object relationships. Apostrophes are used when owner words appear before the item owned.

The *cats* of my *mother* were cute.
(No mark; owner is after cats.)

My *mother's cats* were cute.
(Must have mark, for owner appears before cats.)

From your earliest returned papers, establish what, if any, are your weak spots in using the apostrophe. Whether you overuse or underuse the mark, review the possessive rules and examples several times.

Exercise 5.47   SHOWING OWNERSHIP FOR A SINGULAR OWNER

Each of the following sentences shows ownership without the use of an apostrophe. Switch the owner–object relationship in each so that an apostrophe has to be used to indicate singular possession. Rewrite the sentences on your own paper.

> *Example:* The *collar* of my *cat* is too tight.

> *Switch:* My *cat's collar* is too tight.

1. The words of the lecturer grew louder and louder.

2. The taste of my friend in clothes is very trendy.

3. I watched the baby of my sister because no one else would.

4. The antique couch that belonged to my mother was recovered.

5. The two lizards of my brother Harold escaped somewhere in the house.

6. On the day of St. Patrick, I always wear green.

7. The oil painting that your friend has is absolutely stunning.

8. The stuffed animal collection belonging to my sister was getting too large for her bedroom.

9. The problems of our country are not easily solved.

10. The cover of this hardback dictionary has been ruined.

Exercise 5.48   SHOWING OWNERSHIP FOR PLURAL OWNERS

Switch the objects and owners in the following sentences so that the plural owner appears in front of whatever is owned. Add apostrophes as needed. Watch for any nouns which do not form plurals in the typical manner. Use your own paper to rewrite the sentences.

> *Example:* The *room* belonging to my *boys* is too small.

> *Switch:* My *boys' room* is too small.

1. The marriage of my parents has thrived for twenty years.

2. The foreign policies of those countries should be revised.

3. The speeches given by the delegates soon became boring.

4. A revolt of the taxpayers seemed near.

5. The decision of the committee members is highly debatable.

6. The behavior of my guests was admirable.

7. The dog owned by my next-door neighbors has ruined my begonias.

8. The play area for the children is being expanded and updated.

9. The movement of the women has caused many changes in society.

10. The clothing section of the men is temporarily closed.

Exercise 5.49   DISTINGUISHING BETWEEN POSSESSIVES AND PLURALS

Read each of the following sentences carefully to understand the relationships between the various words. If ownership is expressed, then put the apostrophe either in front of or behind the *s*. If a word is a plural, not a possessive, simply leave it alone and do not add an apostrophe. *All* sentences require *one* apostrophe.

1. After doing my last two term papers, I got writers cramp.

2. The strange yellow pillows did not match the rooms overall color scheme.

3. Millions of tourists have visited the nations historical buildings in Washington, D.C.

4. The winners names were drawn from huge boxes filled with tickets.

5. The parishioners rose and said the Lords Prayer in unison.

6. I took Harolds side in the argument even though I disagreed with most of his ideas.

7. Since patients needs were not being met, many of the hospital workers went on strike.

8. Piles of plates filled the sink in Doris apartment.

Exercise 5.50   LOCATING POSSESSION ERRORS IN A TEXT

The writer of the following paragraph has omitted nine apostrophes: seven to indicate singular possession and two for plural possession. When you locate a word which shows ownership but has no apostrophe, write **P** above it and add the necessary mark directly to the text.

Certain films have captured the hearts of Americans for

generations. The film The Wizard of Oz is the story of a young girls

adventures after she receives a blow to the head during a tornado.

Who could forget the Scarecrow, the Tin Man, and the Cowardly Lion as they try to help Dorothy get to Oz? These characters adventures have delighted young and old alike. Another of Americas favorite films is Gone with the Wind, the story of a willful Southern belles life and loves during the turbulence of the Civil War. The drama of Scarletts unrequited love for Ashley Wilkes and of Rhetts long-unreturned love for Scarlett will probably remain etched in all moviegoers hearts forever. With color television and new inventions such as the video cassette recorder, these two films can be enjoyed in the privacy of ones home and seen again at a persons convenience.

Exercise 5.51   LOCATING POSSESSION ERRORS IN A TEXT

This exercise is more complicated than the previous one. Some apostrophes must be added to show possession as in the previous exercise. In addition, some apostrophes are incorrectly used because no possession is shown or because singular and plural ownership forms have been confused and an extra apostrophe has been added incorrectly. These errors need to be corrected. Add four apostrophes directly to the text. Circle or cross out the four apostrophes that are used incorrectly.

I have always known that ivy is a durable, fast-growing plant that often kills surrounding plants by growing over them and damaging their root systems. The person who uses ivy as a ground cover must then be sure that it is trimmed at regular intervals. However, the full extent of this plants strength was dramatized to me when my wife and I moved into our home, an older structure built in 1932.

Not too long after we moved in, I noticed that the two tall fir trees at the edge of our property were overgrown with ivy. The plants vines had literally grown up along the tree trunks and reached upward almost to the top, a distance of more than forty feet! We didn't attend to the trees' right away, for we were busy moving into the house. When our lives calmed down, I went out to the trees with a childs innocence, thinking that all I had to do was cut a few vines, let them dry, and then pull them off. But when I pulled back the outer vines and got to those actually stuck to the first trees bark, I was horrified! The ivy's vines weren't vines anymore but trunks. I measured one of these "vines" as having an eight-inch circumference!

My days' adventure ended because I couldn't cut such enormous segments with the tools I had, so I hired a professional. Hundreds' of dollars later, our trees breathe freely, so to speak, and I now make sure that the ivy stays' in its place.

DANGLING AND MISPLACED MODIFIERS

Dangling Modifiers

A dangling modifier is a word group that does not relate clearly or reasonably to the closest noun or pronoun in a sentence. It "dangles" rather than modifying or describing the noun or pronoun nearest it.

Any group of words that modifies needs specifically to describe something or someone in the sentence. When using modifiers in your own writing, be sure that they clearly and reasonably point to the closest noun or pronoun. Here are several examples of modifying units that work effectively.

Correct: *Trying his best to look calm,* Roberto began to whistle.
(The italicized modifier clearly points to *Roberto,* the closest noun and the one trying to look calm.)

Correct: *Circling above,* the hawk was a majestic sight.
(*Circling above* points clearly to the nearest noun, *hawk.*)

Sometimes the relationship between the modifier and the closest noun or pronoun is confused. When this occurs, the problem is called a *dangling modifier.*

DM

Incorrect: *Walking down the street,* a trash can blocked Joe's path.
(The closest noun to the modifier is *can.* The sentence suggests that the trash can is walking down the street.)

DM ⌐━━━━┐

Incorrect: While eating my dinner, a fly landed in my salad.

(The closest noun to the modifier is *fly*. The sentence suggests that the fly is eating the writer's dinner.)

Editing Your Draft for Dangling Modifiers

Evaluate every sentence that starts with an *-ing* word or features an *-ing* word close to the start of the sentence. Many times, this type of word signals a modifying unit and a potential dangler.

If you locate a dangling modifier in your writing, use one of these two strategies to remedy the situation:

1. Leave the modifier portion as it is but *add* a reasonable noun or pronoun to which the modifier can relate.

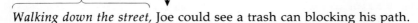

Walking down the street, Joe could see a trash can blocking his path.

In this version, *Joe,* the real "walker," is closest to the modifier.

2. Change the modifying portion to a dependent clause by adding a subject and verb. Leave the rest of the sentence intact.

    S   **V**

While Joe was walking down the street, a trash can blocked his path.

In this version, the *Joe–was walking* unit makes it clear who was walking—the person Joe, not the trash can. We can also see the creation of a complex sentence with two sets of subjects and verbs.

Comma usage with modifying units is covered in Comma Rule 4 on pages 319–320.

✎ Exercise 5.52   IDENTIFYING DANGLING MODIFIERS

In the exercise below, six of the ten sentences are flawed because of dangling modifiers. Recopy the ten sentences onto your own paper. When you identify a problem, write **DM** above the dangling modifier. Write **C** beside a correct sentence.

> *Example:* When I got off the bus, bees swarmed about me!   **C**
>
> (*Correct:* It is reasonable for a person, not the bees, to get off the bus.)

          DM

Getting off the bus, bees surrounded me!

(**DM.** It is not clear who is getting off the bus. Are the bees getting off the bus? Or is it "me"?)

1. Licking the envelope, the flavor wasn't very tasty.

2. When I study for a test, notebooks prove very useful.

3. To plant a garden, gloves should be worn at all times.

4. Properly cooked and not overly seasoned, children will usually eat what is placed before them.

5. Smiling broadly at her pupils, Ms. Jenkins began her lecture on epidemic diseases.

6. While reading my book, my husband entered the room and interrupted me.

7. To speak impressively, words should be enunciated clearly.

8. In searching for a dangling modifier, a student must see the internal logic of a sentence.

9. When you are fishing, the pole should be held properly.

10. Safely tucked away at the back of her drawer, Marcia figured no one would locate it.

 Exercise 5.53   REWRITING DANGLING MODIFIERS

Each sentence below contains a dangling modifier. Rewrite each in *two* ways as the example illustrates. Use your own paper.

DM

Example: To plant a garden, gloves should be worn.
  1. To plant a garden, a person should wear gloves.
  2. When a person plants a garden, gloves should be worn.

DM

1. Approaching the freeway ramp, the sign was hard to read.

DM

2. Seated at their desks, the professor handed everyone an exam.

DM

3. Craving some chocolate, the bonbons looked all the more tempting.

DM

4. Shining splendidly in the evening, I could see the distant star.

DM

5. To win the prize, a special form is needed.

DM

6. While eating my pizza, my stomach growled loudly.

Exercise 5.54   LOCATING THE DANGLING MODIFIERS IN A TEXT

Read the following selection, and watch for three dangling modifiers. Mark them by writing **DM** directly above them. Use your own paper if your instructor asks you to revise the errors.

> Going to a book review at a local library is an educational and enjoyable use of a person's time. I always try to attend at least one a month so that I can be up to date on new publications. Scanning the cultural section of the newspaper, book review dates are easily seen. By writing the dates on my master calendar, I can be sure not to forget them. One of the major benefits has been learning about those books I would want to read. Listening to and evaluating the reviewer's comments, the choice of which book to read is made easier. Time and money are not wasted buying books that I later discover are not what their titles indicated. Reading as much as possible, my life is enriched and expanded in so many ways.

Misplaced Modifiers

A misplaced modifier is a group of words improperly or confusingly located within a sentence. The hallmark of the **MM** error is that it can be easily fixed by moving it to the place where it logically belongs. Rewriting is not necessary.

Read the following sentence carefully, noting the italicized words.

> I called a man about a job *on Saturday.*

This writer wanted to say that the *call was made on Saturday.* The phrase *on Saturday* is misplaced here, however, for it suggests that the job involves *work* on Saturday. This occurs because the noun *job* sits next to the modifier. This misplaced modifier is easier to correct than a dangling modifier because the writer only needs to move the phrase *on Saturday* to a different spot in the sentence.

When a modifier is so placed that it can be interpreted in two different ways, it is called a "squinting" modifier.

> Men and women who smoke *often* die of lung cancer.

This placement of the adverb *often* suggests two ideas:

> If people smoke too often, they die of lung cancer.

> People who smoke at all will die of lung cancer.

Unless the sentence is rewritten, a reader would not be sure which interpretation is intended.

Editing Your Draft for Misplaced Modifiers

Read all sentences carefully to see if any phrases or clauses are in confusing or awkward positions. To find squinting modifiers, watch for words such as *often,* *frequently,* and *sometimes* to be sure they do not support two interpretations. Squinting tends to occur when such words appear midsentence.

To correct a misplaced modifier, *relocate* the awkward element to an area that makes your intention clearer.

On Saturday, I called a man about a job.

To correct a squinting modifier, you must first decide what you actually want to say. Look again at the earlier example.

Men and women who smoke often die of lung cancer.

If you felt that *too much* smoking increases the chance of death by lung cancer, you could add a word to indicate this.

Men and women who smoke *excessively* often die of lung cancer.

If, however, you believed that *any* smoking is likely to cause the problem, you could add a helping verb to make your meaning clearer.

V   V
Men and women who smoke *will* often *die* of lung cancer.

Or you could relocate *often* and add a modifier to it.

Quite often, men and women who smoke die of lung cancer.

Exercise 5.55   LOCATING MISPLACED MODIFIERS

Examine all the italicized elements in the following sentences, making sure they are placed properly to ensure a logical interpretation. If you see a misplaced modifier, write **MM** above it. Write **C** beside a correct sentence.

1. I sent a letter to the bank *about* a job.

2. I visited with my aunt in a convalescent home *for a* few hours.

3. People who smoke *occasionally* will develop circulatory problems.

4. Last week, I sent a get-well card to my neighbor, *who was hospitalized.*

5. I don't enjoy the company of people at parties *who talk a great deal.*

6. Vince took a seat at the ballpark *in the upper row.*

7. My husband loves to hear those old songs on a laser disc player *from the fifties.*

8. I developed a nasty bruise on my leg *which was tender to the touch.*

9. The detective spotted a man in a parked car *acting strangely.*

10. When people run *often,* they develop great levels of stamina.

Exercise 5.56 CORRECTING MISPLACED MODIFIERS

All six sentences below contain misplaced modifiers; in fact, sentence 3 contains two misplacements. In each sentence, locate the problem word or phrase, decide where it belongs, and rewrite the sentence on your own paper.

1. I detailed a complaint to the supervisor concerning holiday pay.

2. Jan studied for a biology test on Monday, so she feels prepared.

3. Suds got into my eyes from the shampoo, making them water.

4. I wore a wide-brimmed hat in August for its protection from heatstroke.

5. The title of my report appeared on the title page in italics.

6. People who gamble frequently become addicted to this activity.

Exercise 5.57 LOCATING MISPLACED MODIFIERS IN A TEXT

Locate and mark three misplaced modifiers in the following paragraph. Write **MM** over each problem word group and circle it. Rewrite the paragraph on your own paper, being sure to move each modifying group of words to the proper location.

Well-known people are often made more famous at a young age when they die. Rudolph Valentino is one example of a film star who died in his early thirties. Because he died so young, his fans were doubly grieved and openly mourned his passing for weeks. The interest has continued in Valentino to our own day. However, would Valentino or James Dean be as popular with later generations if these actors had lived to a ripe old age? As long as films remain, we can involve ourselves in the mystery of what might have been. In their seventies or eighties, we might not think of stars as being at all attractive or mysterious.

FAULTY PARALLEL STRUCTURES

Faulty parallelism includes two types of flaws: an illogical comparison of two unlike (unparallel) things or an unharmonious, imbalanced structure in which key elements are not presented in parallel form.

Faulty Comparisons

Examine the italicized parts of the following sentences to see the imbalance caused by faulty comparisons between people, places, objects, or ideas.

> Joe wanted a *salary* higher than his *brother Bill.*

> America's foreign *policy* was every bit as complex as the *Soviet Union.*

Since comparisons bring together two elements, it is necessary that the two be *like* quantities: apples compared to other apples, not to chickens. One salary needs to be compared to another salary, not a human being. One country's foreign policy can't logically be compared to another country.

Editing Your Draft for Faulty Comparisons

Watch for sentences using *than,* signaling the comparison of elements. Watch also for an *as . . . as* construction in an individual sentence, for these two words also link elements for comparison. Check both elements to be sure that you are comparing equals. Errors most often involve the second element, not the first.

To correct faulty comparisons in your draft, you must truly compare like elements. Because most errors of this kind occur with the second element, you must do some revision:

> *Incorrect:* Joe wanted a *salary* higher than his brother Bill.

> *Revision:* Joe wanted a *salary* higher than his brother Bill's *salary.*

or:

> *Revision:* Joe wanted a *salary* higher than *that* of his brother Bill.

> *Incorrect:* America's foreign *policy* was every bit as complex as the *Soviet Union.*

> *Revision:* America's foreign *policy* was every bit as complex as the Soviet Union's foreign *policy.*

or:

> *Revision:* America's foreign *policy* was every bit as complex as the Soviet Union's.

This last version uses an *understood* construction because *foreign policy* is understood to follow the possessive form *Soviet Union's.*

Exercise 5.58   WRITING PARALLEL COMPARISONS

Each sentence below contains a faulty comparison because the items being compared are not equal (parallel) in nature. Rewrite each sentence, adding material that makes the comparison parallel. Use your own paper, and follow the examples provided earlier.

1. This Christmas, our budget was greater than last holiday.

2. The poetry of Robert Frost is written in a different style than Wallace Stevens.

3. Do you think that my *duck à l'orange* is as exquisite as Pierre?

4. Traveling by car is much faster than a bus.

5. The examinations in botany must be easier than physics.

6. My canary did not sing as often as Janet.

Faulty Parallel Structure

The second type of faulty parallelism involves balance and harmony in the way that sentence elements are presented. To get a feeling for structures that are or are not parallel, compare the sentences in the two columns of Table 5.2. Read them aloud, for problems in this area can be heard in much the same way that you might hear a singer sing the wrong note.

Parallelism is important because balanced sentence structures make ideas easier to understand. For example, in the first parallel sentence, *jogging* and *swimming* are indeed parallel because they are of the same grammatical type—gerunds with their *-ing* endings. Using *jogging* (a gerund) with *an occasional swim* (a noun preceded by two adjectives), however, mismatches the structures.

Table 5.2   Comparisons of Parallel and Unparallel Structures

Parallel Structures	*Faulty Parallelism*
Jogging and *swimming* are my favorite activities.	*Jogging* and *an occasional swim* are my favorite activities.
I wanted him *to respect my point of view* and *to recognize my independence.*	I wanted him *to respect my point of view* and *that I need my independence.*
Weeding the garden, doing the dishes, and *preparing meals* are relaxing activities for some people.	*To weed the garden, do the dishes,* and *preparing meals* are relaxing activities for some people.

Editing Your Draft for Faulty Parallel Structures

Focus on any sentence that uses the conjunction *and* to join two or more equal elements. Make sure parallel forms are used on either side of the conjunction. For example, if the first form has an *-ing* ending but the second does not, you must decide which form you prefer and change one of the two.

Dealing with faulty parallelism takes time, not only to locate the problem but to cure it. Try the following suggestions if your instructor notes an imbalance in parts of your sentences:

1. Read the draft aloud because lapses and changes in endings or construction can often be heard.

2. Be prepared to rewrite the sentence to bring all elements into balance. Read your revision aloud, too, to check its parallelism.

 Exercise 5.59   REWRITING FAULTY PARALLEL STRUCTURES

All of the six sentences in this exercise have faulty parallel structures. Read each sentence carefully to find the problem. Then, using your own paper, rewrite the sentence, making the various elements parallel.

1. Reading and writing papers are two important college skills.

2. I left him standing in the corner, and he muttered to himself.

3. There are two ways to solve a problem: the direct approach and doing it less directly.

4. Because my mind is sound and I have a healthy body, I don't think that I should visit a doctor.

5. Ending our relationship or possibly to continue it has me stymied at this moment.

6. Leopold was especially fond of roasted chestnuts, smoked almonds, and cashews.

 Exercise 5.60   LOCATING FAULTY PARALLELISM IN A TEXT

The following paragraph has four errors in parallelism. One involves a faulty comparison, and three involve imbalanced sentence structures. Mark **FP** above all of them. For easier viewing, circle or underline the faulty element. Use your own paper for any rewriting. (Try voicing sentences if you have trouble detecting imbalances.)

My "chic appeal" has never been as outstanding as Amanda. This stylish woman dresses well and also tends to exhibit good fashion judgment. On the other hand, I tend to be one or two steps behind. When I finally catch up to a current trend, it has been abandoned in favor of another. Amanda, however, is always in vogue. I have decided that the problem stems from a lack of interest and the fact that my time is limited. I would much rather read, garden, or go for a walk instead of evaluating and update my wardrobe. I have also learned that people should be careful when comparing themselves to others because everyone is an individual.

Exercise 5.61   LOCATING FAULTY PARALLELISM IN A TEXT

Locate the four parallelism errors in the following passage. One error involves a faulty comparison; three others involve faulty sentence structures. Write **FP** above the error; then circle or underline the faulty element for easier viewing.

I have always found the do's and don'ts sections of fashion magazines highly informative and memorable. Reading about what not to wear together is helpful, but to see a picture is much more dramatic. When the photographs are juxtaposed, it is even easier to see which way looks good and the one that doesn't. Sometimes I have actually laughed after seeing what some people wear. But when I spy one of my own fashion faults brought to light, I stop laughing and start to make mental notes to correct the problem. My fashion sense may never be as good as a professional model, but I have managed to improve over the years.

EDITING ERRORS IN GRAMMAR

The following exercises combine errors in grammar. Because there is more than one type of problem, you may need to read each paragraph several times. By all means, use your voice to help you detect problems such as fragments and verb tense switches, which can be heard with relative ease. Use the appropriate symbols or abbreviations to mark the errors. Place your notation as close as possible to the error so that it is clear where the problem occurs.

Exercise 5.62   EDITING ERRORS IN GRAMMAR

The following paragraph has four fragment errors and three subject–verb agreement errors. Enclose the fragments in brackets; write **S–V** directly above the site of the error. Then rewrite the entire paragraph, correcting the errors. Use your own lined paper.

Many colorful characters emerged from the American West in the 19th century. Largely because the law was not well established west of the Mississippi for many years. One of the attractions of the West for Easterners were the very fact that the place was so free. Without the many restrictions that was part of life in the developed East. Among the most colorful was the gangs that formed. Groups such as "The Hole-in-the-Wall Gang" or the James or Earp brothers. Many of their battles and those of other groups became legendary, and we still hear of the OK Corral. And places such as Tombstone, Arizona, and Boot Hill.

Exercise 5.63   EDITING ERRORS IN GRAMMAR

Find three fragments, two subject–verb agreement errors, and one comma splice *(CS)* in the following paragraph. Mark them as you did in the previous exercise. Then rewrite the entire paragraph with all errors corrected. Use your own lined paper.

Sometimes, a city develop a reputation just as a person does. To some people, especially Westerners, New Yorkers seems brash and aggressive. On the other hand, to many Easterners, residents of Los Angeles are often characterized as being too casual, self-involved, and "laid-back." A third place, Boston, Massachusetts, is known to some as a city with some of the least friendly people. And the worst possible weather. It is true that the weather can be fierce. But you will find that the average Bostonian often is very friendly. During a

recent snowstorm that closed businesses and schools. People made a
real effort to give help and look out for one another. They shared
what they had and opened their homes unselfishly. To others who had
been hurt or made homeless by this event of nature. Probably the best
lesson to be learned is not to label any group of people,
stereotyping of this kind can only lead to misunderstanding and
narrow-minded thinking.

Exercise 5.64   EDITING ERRORS IN GRAMMAR

Find and mark these errors in the following paragraph: three fragments, one run-together error,
two subject–verb agreement errors, one pronoun reference error, and three verb tense errors.
Enclose fragments in brackets; mark the other problems directly above the error.

A trip to any wine-growing area can be immensely satisfying.
Especially for someone who live in a metropolitan area. One of the
first things we notice is the amount of land devoted to the vines. Not
to roads, freeways, or parking lots! When my husband and I first
visit the vineyards, I was shocked. There was actually no high rises
or heavy blanket of smog to clog the air. Grape plants in every stage
of growth stretch before us we saw newly planted vines, which would
require years to mature. Then there were more mature plants, whose
branches were gnarled by comparison. All day long, we made leisurely
visits to various wineries. Sampling the various red and white
wines. I have never spent a more relaxing time! I would recommend to
anyone that they visit a wine-growing area and relax as we did.

Exercise 5.65   EDITING ERRORS IN GRAMMAR

Find and mark the following errors in the essay below remembering to enclose fragments in
brackets: four fragments, three comma splices, one subject–verb agreement error, one possession error, and two pronoun reference or agreement errors.

Many of our words have come to us from names of people. Both real and mythical. The word tantalize, for instance, is a verb, it signifies a teasing of some sort or a dangling of some desired object in front of someone to rouse the senses. Most use the word with food. Because the sight or smell of some succulent dish can truly get our attention and set our mouths to watering.

This special verb has come to us from Greek myth, Tantalus was a king who was punished by the gods. As a special form of punishment, he was kept bound with no way of using his hands. Periodically, a bunch of juicy grapes would appear above his head and get lower. Almost to the point of reaching his lips. When he strained to bite one, the grapes would move away, so Tantalus could never taste it. To add to his predicament was the presence of water at his feet. The water would flow near him, he would stoop to drink. Unfortunately, it would also move away, so neither of these nutrients were consumed.

In Tantalus case, the teasing was quite serious. As we use the word today. Its meaning revolves around the idea that temporarily, at least, a person is deprived of what they desire.

Exercise 5.66   EDITING ERRORS IN GRAMMAR

Find and mark the following errors where they occur in the essay below: three fragments, one run-together error, one comma splice, three subject–verb agreement errors, one possession error, two pronoun reference or agreement errors, and two verb tense errors.

Not only has poor King Tantalus given his name to a verb, his name is also used as a noun which refer to a very special type of holder for liquor bottles. A person might wonder how does liquor bottles and a special holder relate to Tantalus it does in an interesting way.

The tantalus was designed as a means of dealing with the problem of household servants who are in the habit of tippling. Or drinking the liquor of the masters' of the house. When liquor bottles were placed in the tantalus, a special bar was then lowered over the necks of the bottles and locked. In this way, the liquor could be displayed and not hidden away, but servants could not drink any of it. This time it is the servants being tantalized by the nearness of the drink.

Words such as tantalize and tantalus are indeed fascinating. Because it has a history and special background. The formal name for the study of words and their origins are etymology. A truly interesting and enjoyable area of study for any student of our language.

Exercise 5.67   EDITING ERRORS IN GRAMMAR

Find and mark these problems in the following paragraph; then rewrite the corrected paragraph on your own paper: one comma splice, one faulty comparison, one pronoun reference error, two fragments, one dangling modifier, two subject–verb agreement errors, one misplaced modifier, and one example of faulty parallelism.

My gardening ability was never as good as my neighbor. Max is able to grow any kind of plant which truly disturbs me. By contrast, I have had little success, this has been very frustrating! What is especially hard to accept is that I have read many books on the subject of gardening. Mainly because I want to know every fact possible. Max have never read any how-to gardening books to my knowledge. Perhaps he has indeed been blessed with the proverbial green thumb. Which allows him to plant anything successfully. Those of us with "blue thumbs" needs to have professionals to make our gardens grow. By carefully budgeting, the money for a gardener will be available. When I do have a gardener, I will have saved time, effort, and all sorts of frustration.

A GUIDE TO PUNCTUATION

INTRODUCTION

To understand better the role punctuation plays in language, try reading the following paragraph:

> One of my fondest memories is of a baby-sitter named Milly what a woman she let me do what I wanted to if my mother had known how much candy I could eat or how late I got to stay awake she would have been furious but Milly and I had a special understanding luckily for my young waistline and overall personality I wasn't left with sitters too often when I was I was always overjoyed to see Milly wouldn't you be too

The difficulty you have in reading this passage is normal because it has no guidelines for grouping words in an orderly fashion. This is exactly the function of punctuation: to keep some ideas separated while allowing others to stay together. The many punctuation marks at your disposal fall into two basic groups:

Marks that end sentences: the period, question mark, and exclamation point.

Marks that appear within sentences: the semicolon, comma, colon, parentheses, quotation marks, and dash.

END OF SENTENCE PUNCTUATION

The Period (.)

A period appears at the end of every sentence which is *not* a question or an emotional exclamation. A period is a full stop, ending the thought.

His temper bothered me.

Taking nineteen credits this term was not a good idea.

Taking nineteen credits this term was not a good idea because I also work twenty hours a week.

Although understanding what a period is is easy, many students are uncertain about what a sentence is. Because sentences come in all sizes from one word commands to extensive and complex units, review the definition of a sentence if you have trouble deciding where to put periods.

The Question Mark (?)

Question marks are used to end interrogative sentences, those that ask a question. Like periods, question marks end a sentence with a complete stop.

Who are you?

Can Dave go with us tomorrow?

Did the attempted political coup succeed?

Very few errors occur with this mark of punctuation. About the most serious, in fact, is accidentally leaving it out through inattention or misreading. Table 5.3 shows how direct questions require a question mark and indirect questions use a period.

Table 5.3   Punctuation for Questions

Direct Questions (?)	*Indirect Questions (.)*
What can be done to solve this dilemma?	What can be done to solve this dilemma is unknown at the present time.
Why do people hang on to their bad habits?	I cannot understand why people hang on to their bad habits.

Just as with any other mark of punctuation, don't overuse questions. A few well-placed questions are effective, but too many can weaken the entire effort.

The Exclamation Point (!)

Exclamation points bring dramatic or emotion-charged sentences to an end. These marks can also be used with short word groups to express strong emotion (interjections).

Before our very eyes, the plane plummeted to earth!

My God! Witnesses were stunned as they absorbed the sight.

In the more formal writing required in college classes, the exclamation point is unlikely to be used because it makes the writing and the writer appear less objective. However, in courses which require you to write about some of your own experiences or to generate short stories or poetry, you might well use the exclamation point to good advantage.

Exercise 5.68   END OF SENTENCE PUNCTUATION

Each sentence below should end with a period, question mark, or exclamation point. Add the necessary mark on the line after the last word.

1. I wonder if she can read my mind or if she is just a good guesser _____

2. Who has been sleeping in my bed _____

3. Get away from that cliff _____

4. In the course of American history, four presidents have been assassinated _____

5. Parents often worry about what the future holds for their offspring _____

6. What do you suppose Joe meant by that remark _____

Exercise 5.69   END OF SENTENCE PUNCTUATION

Follow the directions for each item, writing the answers on a separate sheet of paper.

1. Write a sentence which is a direct question.

2. Write an indirect question which would require a period, not a question mark.

3. Write an emotional, dramatic sentence.

4. Write an informative or descriptive sentence that is neither a question nor an emotional remark.

INTERNAL SENTENCE PUNCTUATION

Introduction

In addition to the full stops used to end sentences, there are punctuation marks used within sentences. Study the effects of these marks of internal punctuation in the following sentences:

When the dog howled, I woke up, but I could not get back to sleep.

After a thorough search, I found several possible sites for next year's conference: Dallas, San Diego, and New Orleans.

Peter the Great (1672–1725) was an impressive figure, for his height exceeded seven feet.

"Good heavens," Susan cried, "You are stepping on my skirt!"

I did not realize how hard I would work—and how exhausted I would be.

The Semicolon (;)

Semicolons usually serve to join complete and closely related sentences without a coordinator or a subordinator. They also block out larger units of a sentence which might otherwise confuse a reader. A semicolon represents a longer pause than does the comma but not the full stop of the period.

(sentence)   (sentence)

I love my cat Max; what a companion he is to me.

             ∧

(adverbial

(sentence)   conjunction)   (sentence)

I love my cat Max; consequently, I care for his needs.

            ∧

Note: Even though a semicolon can join two sentences, they are written with only one capital and one period.

Election of new officers resulted in the following slate: Sally Gwynne, president; Ted Collins, vice-president; Morris Katz, secretary; Alma Piretti, treasurer; and Vincent Brown, historian.

The previous two examples show the most common uses of the semicolon. The third, however, illustrates how this mark can keep a reader from being confused about who was elected to which office. The same cautionary note applies to semicolons as to other marks of punctuation that have special functions. Use the semicolon judiciously. Line after line of short sentences joined by semicolons, although technically correct, will be monotonous and choppy.

Exercise 5.70   APPLYING THE SEMICOLON

In each item below, add one or more semicolons where needed to separate sentences or avoid confusion within the sentence.

1. I refused his advances he made me nervous with his constant need for attention and approval.

2. I ordered coffee the waiter brought me tea.

3. Gloria couldn't believe her eyes the line stretched for blocks.

4. I wanted to buy a train, shoes, and a bike for Joey new skates, a paint set, and a dress for Mona and a mink coat for me.

5. Love can live on a person's lips and go no further it is best expressed in action.

6. More money was expended for parks and recreation therefore, many more citizens were able to use the facilities.

7. The fragrant aroma of curry filed the Indian restaurant I was in heaven.

8. Lisa felt she had enough cash however, when the bill arrived, she realized her mistake.

The Comma (,)

Commas are internal marks of punctuation representing a slight pause in the continuity of a sentence. They are *never* used to join full sentences.

As you will soon see, there are more rules for using the comma than for any other mark. Note the various ways commas are used.

1. To separate complete sentences joined by coordinating conjunctions.

2. To separate and equalize words or groups of words appearing in a series of three or more.

3. To separate coordinate adjectives or adjectives out of normal order.

4. To set off longer introductory groups of words including dependent clauses, modifiers, transitional phrases, parenthetical expressions, and absolute constructions.

5. To surround or set off nonrestrictive clauses or modifiers.

6. To separate elements that might otherwise be misleading or confusing.

7. To isolate or separate contrastive sentence phrasing.

Comma Rule 1

Commas separate complete sentences joined by the coordinating conjunctions: *and, but, for, or, nor, yet, so.*

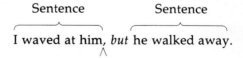

I waved at him, *but* he walked away.

She took that chance, *and* she is now very pleased.

She took that chance and now is very pleased.

This comma rule must be memorized, for there is no real difference in sound or pacing of the voice if a comma is left out. In the first two examples above, the coordinators *but* and *and* join what are two full thoughts, so the comma is placed before the coordinator. The third sentence has a coordinator, but the second part *is not a complete sentence.* The third example is, instead, a compound predicate— two verbs with the same subject.

Exercise 5.71   APPLYING COMMA RULE 1

After studying the discussion and examples above, read the following sentences; then add only those commas required by this rule.

1. Did he insult me or was I mistaken?

2. The archaeological dig yielded several valuable artifacts but none of outstanding quality.

3. I baked a chiffon cake but it tasted awful so I had to start all over again.

4. Janine went to the doctor for a checkup because she had a persistent pain in her back.

5. Should I take a bus or walk to the park?

6. Bob had to struggle in his accounting class yet he persisted and earned an A grade.

7. Getting up early seems quite normal to some people but not to those of us who are night owls.

8. I made my purchases carefully for I was on a restricted budget and couldn't overspend.

9. The home computer may make the typewriter obsolete since the former is more efficient and faster than the latter.

10. Some people can withstand high degrees of pain whereas others wince at the slightest little ache.

11. Rain usually freshens the air and generally improves the landscape.

12. My houseguests stayed for a month but were no trouble at all.

Comma Rule 2
Commas are used to separate and equalize words or groups of words appearing in a series of three or more.

> I prefer *bacon* and *eggs.* (only two nouns; no comma)

> I prefer *bacon, eggs,* and *toast.* (three nouns; two commas)

Rule 2 is one that you can hear, especially after the first of the three items in the series. A series, by the way, can list individual words or word groups.

1   **2**   **3**

The singer *walked on to the stage, smiled at the audience,* but *decided not to sing.*

Exercise 5.72   APPLYING COMMA RULE 2

Add commas where they are needed in the sentences below.

1. Boating hiking and fishing are Dick's favorite hobbies.

2. Would you want to see a movie or attend a live performance?

3. Having good basic skills in spelling punctuation and writing is valuable in college.

4. I could hardly understand his need to dominate others intrude into their private matters and then gossip about his findings.

5. He went to his mother's house took care of some chores but forgot to lock the door when he left.

6. I was allowed to choose from three dinner specials on a menu that included chicken fish and beef.

7. Writers need large supplies of paper pencils pens notebooks and patience.

8. Names such as Prudence and Patience are no longer popular ones for girls.

9. If I see one more inane situation comedy or another ridiculous commercial, I am going to scream.

10. My plumber electrician and doctor all charge too much.

Comma Rule 3

Use commas to separate coordinate adjectives or those adjectives out of normal order. *Coordinate adjectives* have equal weight with respect to the noun they describe. Because of this equal emphasis, a comma is required to show the pause between the two adjectives. The comma, in fact, replaces the conjunction *and*, which otherwise would join the two adjectives:

> Gregory was a *despondent, lonely* man.
> ⋀
> Physics demands *rigorous, dedicated* study.
> ⋀

Not all adjectives appearing before nouns are coordinate. In "I wore a green plaid coat," no comma is used between the two adjectives *green* and *plaid* because together they form the modifier. Use the following two-part test to decide whether adjectives require a comma:

1. Read the sentence with *and:* "Gregory was a lonely *and* despondent man." If this sounds good, move to the next step.

2. Reverse the adjectives and read the result: "Gregory was a *despondent* and *lonely* man." If the sense of the sentence is not altered, the adjectives are indeed coordinate and would require separation with a comma.

The normal position for adjectives is directly in front of the noun they modify. When adjectives appear directly behind the nouns they modify and are joined by conjunctions to form short phrases, they are set off by commas.

ADJ CONJ ADJ

Gregory, *lonely and despondent,* needed friends.

The island, *beautiful but dangerous,* lured many adventurers.

Exercise 5.73 APPLYING COMMA RULE 3

In the following sentences add a comma between coordinate adjectives or to set off adjectives that are out of normal order.

1. Writing a textbook is a grueling demanding activity.

2. That kind young woman gave me a ride during the storm.

3. My fingers stiff and cold needed immediate attention.

4. What was a shiftless no-account detective of Wally's sort doing on this case?

5. Would anyone like to own a soft cuddly puppy?

6. The sculpture curved and sensuous focused the light in a remarkably beautiful stunning manner.

7. Leafy green vegetables contain high amounts of vitamin A.

8. Can you imagine my surprise when that loud ill-mannered salesperson accosted me in the used-car lot?

9. She was a talented and lovely young woman.

10. Louise made an unforgettable entrance in an elegant evening gown.

11. Doing movie stunts is always dangerous, but in the early days of the industry, being a stunt man was an especially hazardous ill-paid job.

12. Few people venture into the sweltering inhospitable desert.

Comma Rule 4

Commas are used to set off longer introductory groups of words, including dependent clauses, modifiers, transitional phrases, parenthetical expressions, and absolute constructions.

Many sentences begin with introductory word groups. In such sentences, however, a comma is needed to separate the introductory unit from the main part of the sentence.

Dep. Clause
Because he was rude, the hostess asked him to leave.
                     ∧
Modifier: Participial
Swimming vigorously, I reached the island in an hour.
                      ∧
  Modifier: Adverbial
At the turn of the century, fashions changed dramatically.
                           ∧
                                        Transition
That man has dreadful table manners. *First of all,* he chews with an open
   mouth.   ∧

Parenthetical expressions consist of remarks or comments injected by the writer
or speaker. Often they effectively emphasize a point.

  Parenthetical
Without a doubt, Scrooge was a mean old fellow.

An absolute construction does not directly modify any word in the sentence, but
it is incomplete by itself.

  Absolute Constr.
Weather permitting, we shall have our picnic.

If you were to read these sample sentences aloud, you would hear pauses
where the commas are used. Transitional phrases, parenthetical expressions, and
absolute constructions may appear at other places in a sentence and require two
commas to set them off.

He said, *first of all,* that my manners were atrocious.
         ∧   ∧
Scrooge was, *without a doubt,* a mean old fellow.
            ∧   ∧
I will go to the picnic, *weather permitting,* and have a terrific time.
                        ∧   ∧

If you find this comma rule difficult, review material on transitional phrasing,
dependent clauses, and subordinating conjunctions in Unit IV.

Exercise 5.74   APPLYING COMMA RULE 4

Watch for dependent introductory elements, transitional phrasing, parenthetical expressions, and
absolute constructions in the following sentences. Read each sentence below aloud and listen
for the pause where a comma is needed. Add any comma which is required.

1. Because of its picturesque location and Old World charm the little town of Rothenberg is
one of the most popular tourist spots in Germany.

2. However there are many other German towns to attract a curious traveler.

3. Being a famous movie star has its rewards and its drawbacks.

4. While strolling through the park I spotted five graceful, elegant swans.

5. Chester would not buy any new clothes since current fashions did not suit his taste.

6. Offering a vast assortment of shops and services malls have become popular shopping areas in many cities.

7. Even if I had millions of dollars I would probably still want to work.

8. Jogging down some streets in metropolitan areas can be terribly hazardous.

9. As the end of the strike neared newsmen gathered to get the details of the settlement.

10. If you go to the store please get a carton of milk and a dozen eggs.

11. Turning fifty is truly a milestone in people's lives.

12. Therefore many people celebrate their fiftieth birthday by having a big celebration.

13. As a matter of fact Gerald is the ideal candidate for the post.

14. All else being equal we will try to meet you at the pier at noon.

15. Since my car was repaired it has performed admirably.

Comma Rule 5

Commas are used to set off nonrestrictive clauses or modifiers that add information of a secondary nature.

The terms restrictive and nonrestrictive can be illustrated by the following, almost identical sentences:

My sister, who lives in Philadelphia, has three children.

My sister who lives in Philadelphia has three children.

As you can see, the only difference between the previous two sentences is the inclusion of two commas to set off the clause "who lives in Philadelphia." Setting off this unit with commas indicates that it is information *not* crucial to the sentence's meaning. In other words, the relative clause could be removed without altering the meaning of the sentence or confusing the reader; the phrase contains merely supplementary information. This type of clause is *nonrestrictive*.

In the first example, the reader understands that the writer has only one sister and that she has three children. In addition, the reader knows that the sister "lives in Philadelphia."

However, when the relative clause *is crucial* to understanding the meaning of the sentence, it is said to be *restrictive*. That means it cannot be removed without altering the sentence's meaning or confusing the reader.

In the second example, the reader understands that the writer has more than one sister and is here referring to the one "who lives in Philadelphia." If this clause were removed, the reader might think the writer had only one sister or might be confused about which sister was being discussed. In this case the relative clause must remain close to the noun it modifies to restrict it and identify which sister the writer means. The second sentence, therefore, has no commas.

In the next examples, watch how the dependent clause appearing in italics in the last half of each sentence is punctuated:

I will wear the dress *when I lose ten pounds.*

The dependent clause is not punctuated because it tells us something vital: The writer will not wear the dress at all until a certain point is reached. This clause is thus considered restrictive and critical for understanding the situation. No comma is used.

I will wear the dress, *although it's tight in the hips.*

Here we have a different dependent clause situation. This person will wear the dress, no matter how it fits. The dependent part gives us extra—but not vital—information and requires a comma.

Comma rule 4 goes into effect whenever a dependent clause is placed at the front of a sentence; then a comma is *always* used:

When I lose ten pounds, I will wear the dress.

Although it's tight in the hips, I will wear the dress.

Another type of modifier that nearly always is nonrestrictive and requires commas is the *appositive.* An appositive phrase is a short group of words that is placed next to a noun and provides extra (nonrestrictive) details.

Ivan the Terrible, *Czar of Russia,* rivaled Henry VIII in marital adventures.

My cousin, *a former gymnast,* decided to major in business.

I could not tolerate Clint, *a rude and boorish fellow.*

Some short phrases used in apposition are restrictive and would appear without commas.

My Aunt *Mary* is a dear woman.

The letter *A* is the first of our alphabet.

Without the words *Mary* or *A,* a reader would not know which *aunt* or which *letter,* so they are restrictive and appear without commas.

Exercise 5.75   APPLYING COMMA RULE 5 TO NONRESTRICTIVE RELATIVE PRONOUN CLAUSES

Copy the following ten sentences on a separate sheet of paper. The relative clause in each sentence appears in italics; examine the adjacent noun and decide if it is specific in some way. Then examine what the clause adds to the noun. If the clause is nonrestrictive and just gives extra information, add commas to surround it. If the clause is restrictive and supplies vital information, write **NC** beside the sentence to indicate that no commas are needed.

1. A student *who wants to succeed* must be tenacious.

2. Peter the Great *who was Europe's tallest monarch* wished for the rapid Westernization of Russia.

3. Hanford's history class *which met every Thursday evening* was very popular with all of the students.

4. The candlesticks *which were our only pair* were nowhere to be found.

5. Medieval rulers *who taxed excessively or displayed unusual cruelty* were unpopular with the masses.

6. He took the road *that very few traveled.*

7. What do you feel should be done with people *who fail to pay their taxes?*

8. Sarah and Jane *who met in college* decided to start a business.

9. Beverly bought a car *that few could afford.*

10. The most popular actress in the early years of films was Mary Pickford *whom literally millions of moviegoers admired and emulated.*

Exercise 5.76   APPLYING COMMA RULE 5 TO NONRESTRICTIVE DEPENDENT CLAUSES

Copy the six sentences below onto a separate sheet of paper. Look at each of the italicized dependent clauses. If a clause provides extra information and is nonrestrictive, then add a comma to separate the clause. If, however, a clause provides vital information that defines the idea in the first half of the sentence, add no comma but write **NC** for no comma beside the sentence.

1. I decided to attend the meeting *although it was at an inconvenient time.*

2. My older brother promised to help me *if I would do his laundry for a week.*

3. My day begins at 6:00 AM *unless it is the weekend.*

4. I intend to change hairstyles *whether my husband approves or not.*

5. She started writing her examination *when several minutes had elapsed.*

6. This project will be funded *if the community supports it.*

Exercise 5.77   APPLYING COMMA RULE 5 TO PHRASES IN APPOSITION

Copy the eight sentences below onto a separate sheet of paper, adding either one or two commas to punctuate phrases in apposition. All sentences below will require some punctuation.

1. Marie my next door neighbor for five years moved to Ohio.

2. The television an idiot box to some actually can be quite useful and educational.

3. Tiger the children's cat liked to drink tomato juice.

4. Jim and Alan friends for years argued bitterly about the election.

5. I wanted to know more about Margaret a mysterious and exciting woman.

6. My U.S. history instructor lectured about the Gilded Age a time of great economic change.

7. Leonardo da Vinci a man of incredible genius remains a mystery to us in many ways.

8. My sister a poor disciplinarian had difficulties managing her young brood.

Comma Rule 6
Commas should be added to separate sentence elements that might otherwise be misleading or confusing.

> At fifty people sometimes start to worry about old age.

> At fifty, people sometimes start to worry about old age.

In the first example, without the comma, the eye of the reader automatically tends to group fifty and people together as if fifty people were being discussed. When this happens, the reader must stop and reread the sentence several times to see exactly what the writer wants to say. You can see the possible confusion and frustration this causes, especially if the trouble arises at an important point in the writing. The second example is punctuated properly so that the word "fifty" is separated from "people."

Exercise 5.78   APPLYING COMMA RULE 6

Each sentence below may confuse a reader. Each lacks a necessary comma to group words effectively. Copy all six sentences onto a separate sheet of paper, adding the comma.

1. When kissing people often close their eyes.

2. In the process of sampling diners ought to remember to eat only a little of everything.

3. When broiling cooks should not leave the kitchen for too long.

4. In the sport of shooting hunters often miss their targets.

5. If you do chew tobacco can stain your teeth and affect your breath.

6. At the crossroads signs point the way.

Comma Rule 7
Commas are required to set off or isolate contrastive phrasing.

> I wanted ravioli, *not lasagna.*

> Geology, *not geography,* was my choice of major.

A speaker reading such contrastive phrases would make a definite pause; therefore, reading your work aloud *may* help you hear where to place the comma in the first sentence or the two commas in the second.

Exercise 5.79   APPLYING COMMA RULE 7
_____

Copy the following sentences onto a separate sheet of paper; then examine each. (Watch for the word *not,* for example.) Add one or more commas as necessary. If possible, read the sentences aloud.

1. It was hard to understand why George not Arthur had answered the advertisement.

2. My choice of restaurant was Italian not French.

3. Multicolored bows not tinsel or bulbs festooned the huge Christmas tree in my grandparents' home.

4. Cats not dogs are ideal pets for people who prefer more independent animal companions.

5. Rubies not diamonds were his favorite gems.

6. It is said that perspiration not inspiration is the real source of human achievement.

Exercise 5.80   REVIEW OF COMMA RULES 1 THROUGH 7
_____

Copy the following sentences onto a separate sheet of paper. Read each carefully and aloud, if possible, for it may require one or more commas. Add any which are needed. If, however, a sentence is correct as written, write **NC** for no comma beside the sentence.

1. The oil painting faded for it had been in the hot punishing sun for too long.

2. Because of a receding gumline the dentist bonded several of my teeth and told me to brush less vigorously.

3. If you paint the brush should be held at a good angle.

4. Having gobbled up the last bit of turkey the guests sat back heaved sighs of relief and undid their waistbands.

5. All outdoor activity came to a halt on that hot sultry day in August when the mercury topped 105 degrees Fahrenheit.

6. Having twenty guests for dinner could make some people very nervous but my Uncle Elmo was always calm.

7. Stopping to appreciate some of the beauty around us is an inexpensive way to relax and calm down.

8. The person who took my shopping cart was unaware of the error but I ran to catch up with him.

9. Two of the record albums mine and yours melted in the sun.

10. When I smelled smoke I jumped up ran to the kitchen and turned off the oven.

11. The runner hot and tired headed for home.

12. Tahiti the island of my dreams is beyond my budget at this time.

13. The restaurant which is located at the center of town is extraordinarily costly don't you think?

14. My Aunt Effie who grew up in a small town has never made the adjustment to city life.

15. If you accept the job you must understand that it is temporary not permanent.

16. Whenever I write a paper I gather ideas choose a topic think of more ideas related to my choice and write a draft.

17. My spinach soufflé which looked strange actually tasted good so I attacked the plate with gusto.

18. Will the man who kicked me please apologize or do I have to get tough?

Exercise 5.81   USING COMMAS

Follow each of the directions given below. Write the sentences on your own paper.

1. Write a sentence that features three items or groups of words in a series. (Rule 2)

2. Write two sentences, joining them with the appropriate coordinating conjunction into one compound sentence. (Rule 1)

3. Generate a sentence which features a phrase in apposition to a noun. (Rule 5)

4. Begin a sentence with the words "My car," add either a restrictive or nonrestrictive relative pronoun clause afterward, and finish the sentence. (Rule 5)

5. Construct a sentence, featuring contrastive phrasing either at the end or in the middle. (Rule 7)

6. Finish the sentence which starts with these words: "Because he was so terribly rude" and add punctuation. (Rule 4)

7. Write a sentence in which you describe a person, place, object, or idea with coordinate adjectives. (Rule 3)

8. Write a sentence in which you describe a person, place, object, or idea with adjectives out of normal order. (Rule 3—Hint: you may restructure your sentence from item 7.)

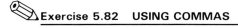

Exercise 5.82   USING COMMAS

The end punctuation of the sentence in the essay below is correct, but the essay has no commas. Read the essay carefully, decide where commas are needed, and place them in the text. There are 28 places for commas.

My friend who enjoys giving gifts with a personal touch has taught me the pleasure of giving baskets for the people on my birthday Christmas and anniversary gift lists. The kind of basket I assemble will depend on two factors: the occasion being celebrated and the person receiving the gift. All of the recipients of my baskets have I think been delighted.

When the occasion is an anniversary my baskets emphasize romance. A bottle of wine champagne or liqueur is the focal point of the basket but I also include two appropriate drinking glasses and some delicate appetizing treats for two. A box of crackers and a can of pâté are chosen to complement the wine or champagne. If I want to give a birthday gift to my youngest sister who happens to love toiletries I emphasize femininity. Last year for example I filled a special basket with bath articles: scented soaps bath oil and a special bath sponge. This year for Christmas gifts will be carefully chosen because I am on a budget but one basket for my neighbor is already forming in my mind. He enjoys gardening so his basket will include gloves small gardening shears and packets of various seeds.

There is something very satisfying to me about preparing these baskets. They do of course require a little more time to assemble but I am good about planning ahead. When emptied baskets are a bonus for they can be used in so many different creative ways in a person's home.

Exercise 5.83   USING COMMAS

The essay below has no commas although end punctuation is provided. Add whatever commas are needed directly to the text. Add 23 commas.

It would be an excellent practice in my estimation for secondary school districts to include one major excursion for each of its pupils prior to graduation. What I have in mind is a trip to Europe for not less than one month. The costs will be borne by the taxpayers and by the various government agencies now funding education because everyone benefits when young adults have been educated in a humane culturally tolerant manner.

A trip of this sort would occur in a student's sophomore or junior year and would feature a "Grand-Tour" type of itinerary. Europe is probably the most feasible because of its cultural ties to our country. First of all students would visit London to get a sense of a nation whose royal family is intact and flourishing. Then they travel to the continent to Paris the City of Lights for the beginning of a number of important visits. Any of a number of major cities such as Vienna Munich Amsterdam and Rome would be included on the travel agenda.

Can you imagine the influence a trip of this kind would have? History for example could take on new interest to a person who has visited an area not merely read of it. What of the magnificent priceless treasures stored in places such as the Louvre or the British Museum? No photographer however skillful could duplicate "the real thing." And what of the joy of meeting new people sampling new foods and dealing with all the day-to-day necessities of life in a different country? Although it is impossible to know if all

students would be positively influenced I think it is safe to say
that most would.

The students would of course resume their studies as either
juniors or seniors but they would be more well-rounded individuals
in numerous ways. Perhaps some would perceive the value of learning
a foreign language whereas others might decide that learning more
about the world was a good idea. If only a few students become a
little less egocentric and provincial in their thinking the cost of
the trip would have been justified. In our rapidly shrinking world
any practice which leads to communication and understanding could
only yield positive results for both the individual and for society.

The Colon (:)

Colons are used to indicate a major break in the continuity of a sentence and to introduce a list or series of items. The part of the sentence before the colon, however, must be complete.

Sentence→

Two artists emerged as Renaissance giants: Michelangelo and da Vinci.
∧
One worry kept nagging at me as I tried to sleep: the mortgage.
∧

Sometimes colons are used in the titles of papers or books to separate the subtitle from the main title; they follow the pattern shown above. The colon is also used to indicate a list or series.

The following are examples of semiprecious stones: garnet, amethyst, tourmaline, and topaz.

Exercise 5.84   APPLYING THE COLON

Each of the lines below needs a colon. Place it in the appropriate spot, making sure that a complete sentence precedes it.

1. Without a doubt, my favorite play is one of Shakespeare's gems "A Midsummer Night's Dream."

2. I never go to a department store when either of these events is going on white sales or month-end sales.

3. In our family we believe there is only one dessert worth eating fudge cake.

4. There are several people who make my life possible my mechanic, my tutor, my gardener, and my housekeeper.

5. To succeed in this class, you need do only two things read the material and do the assignments.

6. A recurrent thought haunted my mind what if I lose my job?

Parentheses (   )

Parentheses come in pairs and surround material that provides background information to the reader. If an entire sentence falls inside the parentheses, then the period is placed inside the parentheses.

> President John F. Kennedy (1960–1963) was the fourth American president to be assassinated in office.

The material in the parentheses gives the reader the specific dates of Kennedy's presidency to pinpoint his time in office.

> Wally's numerous patents (more than 1,000) brought nothing but exasperated sighs from his family.

Putting 1,000 into parentheses gives dramatic meaning to "numerous," so it is an effective piece of background information.

> Students should use their own lined paper and skip every other line as they write. Use ballpoint pens only. (Felt tips often smudge.) Turn in your paper at the end of the hour.

The example above shows how an entire sentence may be enclosed in parentheses. In this case, the sentence provides a reason for the instructor's directions.

Use parentheses judiciously. Used too often, they will suggest that you are unable to construct a solid statement, uncluttered by extra details. Pay close attention to your textbooks to see how material is enclosed and under what circumstances; be sparing in your use of these marks.

Exercise 5.85   APPLYING PARENTHESES

In order to follow the various directions given below, you may use a dictionary, encyclopedia, or any of your texts to supply the necessary information. Use your own paper to write your responses.

1. Construct a sentence that features the years of a famous person's life in parentheses.

2. Construct a sentence that encloses the term of office of one of the American presidents other than Kennedy.

3. Construct a sentence that tells of an imaginary person who had an unusual number of children. Put the number of children in parentheses to add dramatic meaning.

4. Write a brief series of instructions to someone to do a particular task. Be sure to put one bit of background information in parentheses just as in our third example.

Quotation marks ("   ")

Quotation marks occur in pairs and are used primarily to enclose a person's exact words. They are also used to highlight argot or slang, or a word or phrase used ironically. Quotations also are used around titles of short poems, short stories, television and radio programs, and articles appearing in newspapers, journals, or magazines.

> The President declared in his speech that he felt there was "a significant need for a lowering of the prime rate."

> "Thank you for the invitation," said Ms. Carnes, "but I am unable to attend your dinner party."

> CB radio users have given the term "Smokey" an entirely new meaning.

> Edgar Allen Poe wrote many memorable poems, including the classic "The Raven."

Using quotation marks becomes important in research papers, for most instructors require students to include direct quotations in their reports. The first example above uses the writer's words to provide a smooth transition into the direct language of the person quoted. The second example strictly quotes the speaker. Whether you are using the second form of quotation or the first, make sure that what lies between the quotation marks is exactly what the person said. With respect to the example about CB users, the marks allow the writer to highlight the CBer's unusual application (argot) of the word. Again, the caution: don't overuse this aspect of the quotation, for its effectiveness will be diluted.

 Exercise 5.86   APPLYING QUOTATION MARKS

Using the examples above as models, follow the directions below. Use your own paper to write out your answers.

1. Finish the following sentence by adding what the customer said; be sure to place quotation marks correctly.

The angry customer stormed out of the department store and bellowed out, _____ .

2. Supply the words that Mabel screamed. "_____," screamed Mabel.

3. Assume that you are the public affairs officer for the president of your college and make an announcement of something special that the president has decided to do. Use our first example as a model. Use *your* words first and gradually lead into the quoted material from the college president.

4. Now, assume that you are a television critic who is making a strong statement about a current television program. Express your opinion and be sure to give the program's title in quotation marks.

The Dash (—)

The dash is a single, long horizontal line appearing midway between the written or typed words. It is used to set off or dramatize a group of words in a less formal manner than a colon but with more force than a comma.

> I went to pay the traffic fine—and met my worst enemy!

> An old family friend had a fascinating way of talking—her arms flailed about erratically, her eyebrows lifted and dropped with unfailing regularity, and the hairy mole below her lower lip kept time with all the rest.

In most cases the dash should be used sparingly in college writing. Writing which is more personal does lend itself to an occasional dash. Unfortunately, some people use the dash to replace the colon, the period, and other marks of punctuation. This habit may be fine in personal letters but should be broken very quickly in more formal writing.

Guidelines for Editing Errors in Punctuation

If any or all of the rules of punctuation are new to you, try following the guidelines below to increase both your understanding of punctuation rules and your ability to punctuate your own drafts correctly.

1. *Review punctuation rules often,* especially those related to comma usage. You need not spend hours poring over this text; instead, review these rules two or three times a week or at least once a week for 15 to 20 minutes. Repeated reviews will help you remember the rules.

2. *Allow sufficient editing time* to search for and correct punctuation errors or omissions. This time is especially critical if you are already working on improving your spelling, grammar, and essay development. Each area of concern makes its own demands and will take time to do properly.

3. *Use any or all of your returned and marked papers as editing cues.* Even though many of us do not like to dwell on our errors, use whatever problems you experienced in earlier papers to guide your current editing.

4. *Be aware of the interrelationship between punctuation rules and areas of grammar.* Review The Parts of Speech in Appendix A at least once a week so that various terms become familiar to you. If you remember the comment made in the introduction to Unit V—that we need to focus our understanding of grammar so that it is clear, not vague—then make it a point to review additional material on a set schedule.

A GUIDE TO MECHANICS

INTRODUCTION

In addition to grammar and punctuation, a paper has other areas that fall within the category of *mechanics*. Examine the following areas of mechanical concern, for they, too, require attention and may prove helpful to you as a writer:

- Capitalization
- Italics
- Homonyms and sound-alike words
- Numbers
- Abbreviations
- Hyphenation

CAPITALIZATION

Use these two basic capitalization rules to guide you, for they cover the majority of your work in this area:

1. Always capitalize the first word of every sentence.

2. Capitalize all *proper* nouns because they refer to specific persons, places, things, or ideas (see Table 5.4, p. 334).

Your best source of reference when questioning whether a word should be capitalized is the dictionary.

Study the following situations, for you will probably encounter at least some of them during your time in college.

1. When you use the specific (exact) title of a book, magazine, journal, newspaper, play, or motion picture, capitalize the first word and every word of the title. (Major words are everything *except* prepositions, articles, and coordinate conjunctions, other than those appearing as the first or last word.)

Jaws	*A Guidebook for Romance*	*New York Times*
Dracula	*Architectural Digest*	*Light in August*

Table 5.4   Common Nouns *versus* Proper Nouns

Common	*Proper*
ocean	Atlantic; Atlantic Ocean
doctor, reverend	Dr. Harold Healer; Reverend Mr. Wilson
university, college	Princeton; Yale University
history, business	History 7B; Business I
language	English, Farsi, Spanish
theory	Theory of Relativity; Law of Diminishing Returns
high school	Jane Addams High School
religion	Buddhism, Catholicism, Protestantism, Judaism
day, month	Tuesday, March
planet, galaxy, star	Jupiter, Pluto, Sirius
company, firm	Stearns Aircraft Inc.

2. When you use the specific title of any article or chapter in a book, magazine, journal, or newspaper, capitalize the first word and every major word thereafter. Use quotation marks around this kind of title to distinguish it:

New York Times	"Inflation Hits Hard in State"
A Guidebook for Romance	"The First Date Jitters"
Modern American Poetry	"The Curtains in the House of the Metaphysician"

3. When you refer to a television or radio program, capitalize the first word and any other major word thereafter and enclose the words in quotation marks:

"A Prairie Home Companion"	"All in the Family"
"60 Minutes"	"All Things Considered"

4. When you create a title for your paper, capitalize the first word and all major words thereafter. Use no underlining or quotation marks.

My Favorite Month	Lost in Thought

Exercise 5.87   RECOGNIZING THE NEED FOR CAPITALS

Each sentence below requires the addition of at least one capital. In addition, some capitals may be unnecessary. Circle each letter which displays one of these problems. Rewrite the sentences correctly on a separate sheet of paper.

Example: I waited for the (B)us on Main (s)treet.

1. I love all of my Pets, but my dog fifi is especially dear to me.

2. When christmas is over, I always think of Taxes and the internal revenue service.

3. Brian studied portuguese in Summer School and did very well.

4. There are many Religions in the world, and one of the largest is roman catholicism.

5. I have always wanted to go to europe or to the orient.

6. I took several Business classes when I attended Princeton university, but the one I liked best was Industrial manufacturing.

Exercise 5.88   DEALING WITH CAPITALS IN SPECIAL SITUATIONS

Watch for different sorts of titles in the following items. When you have located a title, cross out the incorrect small letter and write the capital form above. You may also need to underline or to add quotation marks depending on what sort of title it is. Rewrite the corrected sentences on a separate sheet of paper.

Example: I read d̶racula because it is a classic.

1. One of Hemingway's most famous novels is for whom the bell tolls.

2. The newspaper article entitled ways to manage your money was highly informative.

3. I have always enjoyed the photography in the national geographic, a wonderful magazine.

4. I selected the poem my last duchess because of the personality of its narrator.

5. I subscribed to the ames country express for twelve years until the paper ceased publication.

6. A modern bestseller which popularized psychology for the masses was entitled games people play.

Exercise 5.89   EDITING CAPITALIZATION ERRORS

Read the following paragraph. At every place where you see the need for a capital, circle the letter or cross it out and place a capital above. If quotation marks are missing or underlining is required, add the necessary marks. There are 30 capitalization errors.

My sister jane has seen the movie, the mummy's curse, five times. The first time she saw it we were living in atlanta, georgia. Jane was only five years old at the time, and the movie really frightened her. Later, I read an article about horror movies in the reader's digest. The article was called how horror movies can harm your child. As jane got older, she insisted on watching the mummy's curse again and again and also, the bride of dracula. Even though the movies frightened her, she loved watching them. Each sunday she studied the television section in the local paper to be sure she wouldn't miss watching any of her favorite horror movies. Jane also has a big book called the world's greatest horror movies. Now that we live in los angeles, she has been able to visit some of the studios where her favorite movies were made.

Exercise 5.90   EDITING CAPITALIZATION ERRORS

In this exercise, some capitals are needed, but some of those which appear are used incorrectly. Seven capital letters must be added to the text. Thirteen capital letters are incorrectly used and should be deleted or circled. If any quotation marks are missing or underlining is needed, add these marks directly to the text.

A student's first Semester in College is probably the most difficult. First of all, the college is a new environment, and if it is a large Institution, there may be thousands of students from all over the World studying in the same place. The new sights and sounds can be distracting to the newcomer who must begin adjusting at the same time as he is taking classes and doing homework. A student's first few semesters are generally filled with required courses such as History, a Foreign Language, english, Psychology, and a Science or two. Professors bombard students with reading material in each class so that landmark studies or works are not overlooked. In

Economics, for example, Heilbroner's the worldy philosophers is

often assigned, whereas in History, a student might have to read

Hofstadter's anti-intellectualism in american history. The student

who can adjust to the Campus and to the Educational workload is the

one who will derive the most benefit and pleasure from the entire

experience.

ITALICS

Italics refers to a style of type with slanting letters used by printers for the titles of books, plays, magazines, newspapers, and any other formal publications. Foreign words or phrases that are not commonly used in English are also placed in italics.

Most writers do not have access to different typefaces when producing typed or handwritten material and, therefore, indicate italics by underlining.

She, written by H. Rider Haggard, is a popular adventure novel.

National Geographic has maintained a reputation for fine photography for many years.

Descartes's statement, cogito, ergo sum, takes an interesting point of view.

Printed material from publishing houses shows titles with a special slanted style of type.

She, written by H. Rider Haggard, is a popular adventure novel.

The article appearing in the *New York Times* was outstanding in style and content.

Many people now disagree with John Locke's idea that the human brain at birth could be likened to a *tabula rasa*.

Occasionally, you will write an essay that requires heavy use of italics. For example, if your instructor directs you to summarize, critique, or comment on a book or play, you will need to underscore every mention of the name of the publication. When using foreign words or phrases in your writing, consult a dictionary to determine if they have been accepted into English and, therefore, do not require italics.

Exercise 5.91   USING ITALICS

Follow the direction given in each of the items below. Write your answers on a separate sheet of paper.

1. Take the full title of any one of your textbooks and incorporate it into a full sentence. (If there is a subtitle, it should be included as part of the underlined title.)

2. Construct a sentence using the name of an encyclopedia; be sure that the name is spelled properly. To do so, check either the spine of the volume or open it to the title page.

3. Construct a sentence using the name of one of your local newspapers.

4. Write a sentence which expresses an opinion about one of the books you have read or plan to read. Use the title of the book in your sentence.

5. Consult a dictionary for the meaning of the foreign phrase *tempus fugit;* then use the phrase in a sentence.

HOMONYMS AND SOUND-ALIKE WORDS

Homonyms

Homonyms form a special category of words in English: words which are *identical in sound,* but different in spelling. Several examples are listed below:

to/too/two	there/their/they're	whose/who's
its/it's	I'll/isle/aisle	break/brake
hole/whole	your/you're	pale/pail
hale/hail	veil/vale	pier/peer
through/threw	wood/would	write/right
fare/fair	main/mane	pear/pare/pair
cite/sight/site	chute/shoot	red/read
reed/read	stair/stare	vein/vane
rein/reign/rain	blue/blew	tail/tale

You must be careful to use these homonyms correctly; carelessness can confuse your reader and affect the overall quality of your writing.

There is no magic method or quick way to cure homonym problems. But if you begin to pay attention to how the words in each pair or trio differ, you will be on your way to eliminating this error from your work. Another tactic is to edit your rough drafts with the particular type of problem in mind.

Listed below are four of the most commonly used and confused homonyms:

to/too/two   your/you're   its/it's   there/their/they're

To/Too/Two

to: a directional preposition or the sign of the infinitive.
  I want *to* go *to* the bank.

too: an adverb expressing an excess of something or meaning *also.*
  I ate *too* much.
  I, *too,* ate *too* much.

two: an adjective referring to number.
  Two polar bears were recently purchased for the Bronx Zoo.

Your/You're

your: a second-person possessive pronoun.
  Your mother is very special.

you're: the contraction of *you* and *are.*
  You're absolutely right!

There/Their/They're

there: an adverb used to indicate direction:
  There she is. Weeds grew *there.*

their: a third-person possessive pronoun.
  Their home was sold.

they're: the contraction of *they* and *are.*
  They're wrong.

Its/It's

its: a third-person possessive pronoun.
  The group lost *its* sense of direction.

it's: the contraction of *it* and *is* or *it* and *has.*
  It's raining.
  It's been wonderful.

Exercise 5.92   DISTINGUISHING CORRECT HOMONYM FORMS

Number a separate sheet of paper from 1 to 8. Select the correct homonym from those in the parentheses, and write it on your paper.

1. I wanted (to, too, two) much from him.

2. The Grant family sold (its, it's) ranch and moved (to, too, two) the big city.

3. Whose idea was it (to, too, two) finish this project when (there, their, they're) is so much more to be done?

4. (There, Their, They're) not going to like the fact that this house is (to, too, two) small.

5. The park system is at (its, it's) busiest during the summer.

6. If (your, you're) sure of (your, you're) material, then go ahead and present it (to, too, two) him.

7. I (to, too, two) wish I were a millionaire because I could go through life without a worry.

8. (There, Their, They're) livelihood depends on cattle.

Sound-Alike Words

A number of words are often categorized with homonyms because they are similar, but not identical, in sound. Technically, they are not homonyms, but their pronunciations are often slurred so that they sound identical. The frequent result is that they are spelled incorrectly. Here are a few examples:

accept/except	are/our	an/and
lose/loose	idea/ideal	affect/effect

If a speaker pronounces these pairs identically, then he or she is very likely to be confused about them. For this reason, pay very close attention to the suggestions for pronunciation in each of the groups below. And remember, here again a dictionary can be a great help with any word about which you may be confused.

Accept/Except

accept: a verb, pronounced ACK-cept, meaning to receive or agree to.
Will you *accept* my apologies?

except: a preposition, pronounced ECK-cept, meaning with the exclusion of.
We all went in *except* him.

Lose/Loose

lose: a verb, pronounced looze, meaning to fail at or mislay something (rhymes with snooze).
Harold will *lose* if he doesn't try harder.

loose: a verb or adjective, meaning not tight (rhymes with goose).
After my diet, all my dresses were *loose*.

Are/Our

are: a plural form of the verb *to be,* pronounced as one syllable, exactly as the letter *R.*
Are you coming with us or not?

our: a first-person possessive pronoun, pronounced as two syllables, exactly as the word *hour.*
Our team is the best!

Idea/Ideal

idea: a noun, *pronounced in three* syllables: *i-dee-uh;* plural—i-dee-uhz.
That is a great idea!
His ideas were useless.

ideal: an adjective or noun, *pronounced in two* syllables exactly as you if said "I-DEAL a deck of cards;" plural—ideals.
He aspired to his *ideal* of elegant behavior. (noun)
An *ideal* gift for her would be a home computer. (adjective)

An/And

an: an adjective, pronounced as the name *Ann* or *Anne.*
I have *an* idea for your composition.

and: a conjunction, rhymes with band.
Typing *and* notetaking are useful skills.

Affect/Effect

affect: verb, meaning to influence (pronounced uh-FECT).
His remarks *affected* me.

effect: a noun or verb, meaning the consequence of or to cause (pronounced Ei-FECT).
The *effect* (noun) of her words upon the audience was incredible.
The president *effected* (verb) a change in policy.

Almost always when you require a noun, you need *effect,* and almost always when a verb is called for, you need *affect.*

Exercise 5.93   DISTINGUISHING BETWEEN THE NEAR SOUND-ALIKES

Copy each of the sentences below onto a separate sheet of paper. Supply the proper word from those in parentheses.

1. The first tranquilizer dart had no (affect, effect) on the elephant.

2. (Accept, Except) for my neighbors, all my party guests responded to my invitation.

3. Justice is a lofty and fine (idea, ideal) to which we should all strive.

4. My filling came (loose, lose) after I bit into some caramel corn.

5. Your negative behavior will (effect, affect) everyone if you don't restrain yourself.

6. Do you have any (ideal, idea) how much this room addition is going to cost?

7. We could not believe (are, cur) ears when we heard the announcement.

8. Lacking sleep and food, I began to (lose, loose) my ability to concentrate.

9. I cannot (except, accept) your excuse.

10. In (and, an) instant, I lost sight of my small niece.

11. (Our, Are) you going to donate any of your time?

12. I bought several suits (an, and) blouses for my new job.

Exercise 5.94   LOCATING HOMONYM ERRORS

There are 11 homonym errors and errors with closely related words in the following paragraph. Write **H** above each incorrect word; rewrite the corrected paragraph on your own paper.

Are next-door neighbors are very fine people. We get along well accept for one minor problem: there five cats. As a matter of fact, we own a cat, but she is very quiet and spends most of the day sleeping in the bushes. The five neighbor cats, however, are very outgoing an loud. Its not unusual for several too meow for half an hour at a time. One especially likes too tease are dog, which has the affect of making him bark uncontrollably. I try not to loose my patience or temper, but its hard sometimes.

Exercise 5.95   LOCATING HOMONYM ERRORS

There are 8 homonym errors in the paragraph below; write **H** above each one that you locate. Then rewrite the paragraph on your own paper, correcting each of the errors.

A camera buff would probably find the zoo a good place too shoot many exciting and colorful photographs. The zoo is and ideal place because its been carefully landscaped and designed to show its animal guests in the best possible environment. Of course, their is also an advantage to photographing a rhino or elephant when each is safely enclosed. The animals can't get lose and are often very interesting subjects. Of course, the weather will effect the outcome of many photographs, but as long as its clear, they're is an excellent chance that the snaps will be visually delightful and full of color.

NUMBERS

Numbers are dealt with differently depending on the circumstance. Spell out numbers of fewer than three digits or large round numbers of four or more digits.

> She gave a party for *twenty* people.

> More than *two thousand* soldiers and civilians arrived.

Always spell any type of figure or number that appears as the first word in the sentence.

> *Five hundred* dollars was too much for that tie.

Use numerals in these cases:

1. fractions such as this: (1⅓)

2. units of currency when the figure does not appear at the start of a sentence: $38.52

3. dates: August 24, 1946

4. street numbers: 2219 Albion Way

5. page references: page 39

6. percentages: 11 percent

7. hours of the day when written with A.M. or P.M.: 9 A.M.

ABBREVIATIONS

Many abbreviations have become acceptable by themselves: some as names (UNICEF, UCLA), some as standard titles (Mr., Mrs., Ms., Dr.), and others as standard references (B.C., A.D., A.M. and P.M.).

Be careful to avoid using shortened forms in other areas. For example, in formal papers don't write psych for psychology, econ for economics, PE for physical education, govt. for government, or LA for Los Angeles.

Although these short forms are perfectly acceptable for everyday speech, they do not operate to your advantage in formal writing. You will give the impression that you either do not know how to spell these words (and did not wish to use your dictionary) or that you simply did not want to take the time necessary to write them out.

HYPHENATION

Some words, combinations called compound words, are hyphenated when written:

It was an *age-old* conflict.

It was written in *two-part* form.

After some *self-analysis,* she apologized.

Your dictionary is your best reference if you are unsure about whether a hyphen is needed.

In other instances, hyphens are used to break or divide words when you reach the right-hand margin when typing a paper.

I wanted to take a good look at the photograph, but my mother simply refused to let me.

You can only hyphenate words of *two or more* syllables: con-vict; in-vi-si-ble; in-flec-tion. Never try to align a margin so perfectly that you either split too many words or split words of only one syllable. Your best source to check for breaking points is the dictionary. Even before a word's meaning is given, the proper division (syllabication) is provided.

If You Are Using a Word Processor

In this unit on grammar, punctuation, and mechanics, you may make some notations in the text. However, in most of the exercises, sentences or paragraphs must be rewritten, and you can do all of these on the word processor.

Grammar

You will find word processing useful for rewriting flawed sentences in the grammar exercises. For instance, if a sentence has a misplaced modifier, you can try out different placements of the modifier until you are certain you have it in the right spot.

Consider making a special grammar file to list frequent errors your instructor notes on your papers. Update this file often, and type in the correct grammar rule under each of your mistakes. Then, print out a copy of your list when you sit down to edit a paper so that you can check for specific recurring errors.

Punctuation

You will find that word processing is especially helpful for rewriting punctuation exercises. Often, when commas, semicolons, or periods are applied by hand, they are not written clearly and are misread by the instructor. The word processor, like the typewriter, makes each mark clear and easy to read. Also, when you work on the processor, you have the chance to reread your work and change the punctuation easily. This saves time because you do not need to rewrite the sentence and risk making new mistakes.

Consider making a personal file on punctuation, too. As you look over the papers your instructor has marked, note any punctuation errors and include them in your file with the correct rule underneath the error. When you have mastered a form of punctuation and it no longer appears as an error on your papers, delete it from your file.

Mechanics

Making these corrections allows you to use many of the editing features which make writing on the word processor a pleasure. However, you will need to spend a little extra time on hyphenation. Because most software provides the word-wrap feature, you probably will get little practice in correctly hyphenating words. Nevertheless, you will benefit from learning how to hyphenate for those times when you are handwriting papers, letters, forms, and so on.

APPENDIX: THE PARTS OF SPEECH

The parts of speech form a system for classifying words, the building blocks of sentences. There are eight parts of speech, but only seven will be highlighted. The eighth type, *interjection*, consists of words or expressions delivered with strong emotion—*Mercy! Oh, no!*—and are not usually a part of expository writing.

If you need to review the parts of speech, keep this thought in mind—Words are like people in that both are able to *assume a number of different roles*. Therefore, never memorize a particular word as, for example, a noun or an adjective. Many words can perform different roles:

> **N**
> My *time* is valuable.
> (*Time* labels an idea.)
> **ADJ**
> Your *time* sheet has been lost.
> (*Time* now describes sheet.)
> **V**
> I *will time* your test.
> (*Will* plus *time* now work together to express action in the future.)

If you learn the definition of each part of speech, then you will have fewer problems determining the functions of words, especially those which can assume various roles.

NOUNS

A noun is any word that names or labels people, places, objects, ideas, emotions, or activities. This is a huge category of words, for we need many labels to account for (name) all elements of our physical, emotional, intellectual, and spiritual worlds. Study the following sentence in which nouns are identified:

			name for an abstract idea	name for an activity
name of a person	name of an activity			

My *mother* enjoys *swimming* while I enjoy a less strenuous *form* of *exercise*.

346

Useful Facts about Nouns

1. Three words *(a, an, the)* called noun indicators or article adjectives, always mark the approach of nouns.

An apple *a* day keeps *the* doctor away.

2. Collective nouns are those such as *team, jury, family,* and *group.* Usually these are treated as singular, rather than plural, if the emphasis is on the unit, not the individuals.

The *team* is on the field.

3. Proper nouns are capitalized, for they label specific entities:

New Mexico, Susan, Labor Day. (Common nouns are general and not capitalized: state, woman, holiday.)

4. Gerunds are *-ing* words which look like verbs but which behave as nouns in sentences.

Straining your voice can be harmful to your throat.

In Sentences, Nouns Play a Number of Roles

My *cat* became ill yesterday.
(*Cat* is the doer, the subject.)

I took the *cat* to the vet.
(*Cat* now receives action and is the direct object.)

I had trouble (with the *cat*).
(*Cat* is the object of the preposition *with* in a prepositional phrase.)

He is my favorite *cat.*
(*Cat* renames the subject *He* but in the predicate; therefore, it is a predicate nominative.)

The vet gave my *cat* a shot.
(The *shot* is the direct object, but the *cat* is now the indirect object and receiver of the shot.)

PRONOUNS

A pronoun either replaces or refers to a noun. A smaller group than nouns, pronouns have critical uses in communication. They allow us to simplify messages, combine ideas, and express a type of ownership.

The *replacement* function of pronouns is shown in these pairs:

Gloria gave a gift to the Judsons.

She   gave   it   to   them.

The *reference* function of pronouns is shown by these examples:

N   PRO

Susan wanted a meal *that* was filling.

That refers to *meal*, a noun, and paves the way for more information about the kind of meal wanted: the relative pronoun clause—*that was filling.*

My mother helped *her* friend solve a problem.

My refers to *mother*, telling whose mother she is—the speaker's; *her* refers to *friend* and indicates that this person "belongs to" the mother, not the speaker.

Useful Facts about Pronouns

1. The personal pronouns include *I, me; you; he, him; she, her; they, them; we, us;* and *it.*

2. The indefinite pronouns are not quite as specific in nature: *someone, anyone, everybody, anybody, somebody, each, all, most, some, few, several, both, any, neither, either, one.*

3. Relative pronouns include *who, whom, which,* and *that* and form relative pronoun clauses when placed next to nouns. Most of the time, *which* and *that* are used interchangeably with nouns not relating to people; however, *that* can be used for people.

People that are too materialistic are often unhappy.

People who are too materialistic are often unhappy.

4. Possessive pronouns derive from personal pronouns and allow us to express ownership: they are *my, her, his, our, their, your,* and *its.* (These possessive forms will always appear before a noun, indicating ownership of some kind.)

In Sentences, Pronouns Have the Same Role as Nouns

I love ice cream.
(*I* is the doer, the subject.)

Ice cream pleases *me.*
(*me* receives action and is the direct object.)

He gave *me* the ice cream.
(*ice cream* is the direct object, but *me* is the indirect.)

I gave the ice cream to *her.*
(*her* is bonded to the preposition *to* in a prepositional phrase.)

It was *she* who ate the ice cream.
(*she* renames the subject *it* and is the predicate nominative.)

In sentences, some pronouns exhibit *case,* a term that indicates how the pronoun is used. When personal pronouns serve as subjects or predicate nominatives, they are in the *nominative* case.

He wanted to borrow my car.

When personal pronouns are direct or indirect objects of the verb or preposition, they are in the *objective case.*

I would not lend it (to *him*).

The pronouns *you* and *it* do not change from nominative to objective case. But case is present in the relative pronoun *who* and *whom.*

He is the man *who* sent me flowers.

The form *who* is used because it functions as dual subject of the verb sent: *who* sent or *(man) who* sent.

He is the man *whom* I admire.

In this situation, the objective form *whom* is used because this word is no longer the subject but the object of the verb admire: I admire *whom.* Although the word *whom* refers to *man,* it is not the subject of the relative clause as *who* was in the previous example. This is the important thing to remember when deciding whether to use *who* or *whom:* How does the pronoun function in the relative clause? Ignore the function of the relative clause in the context of the sentence.

ADJECTIVES

An adjective describes a noun or pronoun. Adjectives form an enormous group of words that allow us to talk about persons, places, things, and ideas in greater detail. Watch how adjectives work in the following sentence, and imagine how uninformative writing would be without this type of word:

Those new swimming suits are very daring, but they are *cute.*

Useful Facts about Adjectives

Adjectives fall into many categories, for they have many descriptive functions:

> **article:** *a* gorilla, *an* ape, *the* monkey
>
> **numerical:** *one* dog; *two* horses; *several* animals
>
> **demonstrative:** *this* person; *that* idea; *those* shoes
>
> **interrogative:** *which* people? *what* ideas?

The list of adjectives that generally *describe* qualities is huge and includes words such as *tall, short, beautiful, sensual, expressive, enormous, smooth, rough, difficult,* and so on.

The participle is a verbal, a word formed from a verb but used as an adjective. Participial endings include *-ing, -ed, -en*. Participles may consist of one word or of a phrase held together by a participle:

> My *swimming* suit is *daring.*
> (Two single-word participles are describing the suit.)

> *Driven by passion,* the countess raced to her love.
> (*Driven by passion* describes the countess and forms a participial phrase.)

In Sentences, Adjectives Are Positioned Near Nouns and After Pronouns

Most often, they appear directly in front of the noun modified.

> *The last sirloin* steak was eaten by *the hungry* dog.

They may also appear after nouns in one of two ways:

> The man, *tall and handsome,* came into my room.
> (These adjectives appear directly behind the noun.)

> The man is *tall* and *handsome.*
> (These adjectives appear in the predicate.)

Adjectives will appear after pronouns.

> She is *clever.*

VERBS

Most verbs express action in relationship to the present, past, and future. Other verbs express the fact of being or existence.

The verb category is far more complex than any of the other parts of speech, for it functions to express a basic human capacity for action or existence within the setting of time. If you have ever tried to learn a foreign language, you have probably found the verbs to be the most difficult to learn, particularly because they often consist of more than one word and have different forms.

My mother *has been swimming* for many years because she *is* an active woman who *enjoys* sports.

Useful Facts about Verbs

All verbs can be divided into two large categories, depending on the patterns or the forms they use to express different times *(tenses)*:

1. *Regular verbs* behave in a predictable manner, using an *-ed* ending to denote the past and continuous past tenses.

Today I *play;* yesterday I *played;* I *have played* baseball often.

2. *Irregular verbs* change form internally (no *-ed* endings) and tend to cause many problems, especially for people learning English.

Today I *see* him; yesterday I *saw* him; I *have seen* him here many times.
(A more extensive list of irregular verbs is featured on pp. 356–357.)

In expressing many actions or states of existence, verbs often need help from words called helpers or auxiliary verbs. Essentially, helpers include any word or words which serve along with the main verb in a sentence; the main verb is the one holding the key to the actual activity.

An important category of helpers comes from the verbs *to have* and *to be*.

I *have studied* math for years.

I *am studying* calculus right now.

She *has been* a student for one semester.

The main verb in each example appears as the second in the pair with the helper preceding it. The helper assists specifically to indicate time and how the action or existence occurs.

Other standard groups of helpers include *do, does, did, can, may; will* and *shall* for the future; *could, would, might* for the conditional; and words such as *should, must* for indicating judgment.

I *may go* to the store.

Mike *could go* tomorrow.

I *will go* to the store.

Mike *should go* tomorrow.

The largest possible number of words grouped as a single verb (helpers and main) is four, as in these examples:

I *will have been studying* Spanish for four years next August.
An action is literally projected and completed in the future.

I *must have been dreaming* last night.
An action takes place over a period of time in the past, but the author of the statement is not entirely sure *(must)*.

Transitive verbs are all those which take objects or receivers of their action:
                        D.O.
I *took* a break. (Took what? A *break*.)
Intransitive verbs, a category that includes linking verbs, do not take objects. Instead, other word groups such as prepositional phrases or predicate nominatives or adjectives appear after the verb.

　V　PN
I *am* tired.
　V　Prep Phrase
I *fell* (on the stairs.)

In Sentences, Verbs Behave in Certain Ways

They form the main part of the *predicate*. They must agree in number with the subject. In the majority of sentence patterns, the verb appears after the subject in the sentence. In questions, however, the pattern changes. Verb constructions can be interrupted by various elements such as adverbs and negative elements.

　V　　ADV　　V
I *do* occasionally *exercise*.
(The adverb *occasionally* appears between the two parts of the verb.)
　V　NEG　V
She *does* not *exercise* often.
(The negative element *not*, which allows us to negate an action, will break in if the verb has 2 or more parts.)

ADVERBS

The adverb can describe a verb, an adjective, or another adverb. Although adverbs share a descriptive function with the adjective, the adverb associates itself only with the three groups above, not with nouns or pronouns. Adverbs allow us to refine meaning even further.

> V   ADV
> We *often* ran *vigorously* in the *very* early hours of the day.

Useful Facts about Adverbs

Most adverbs are formed by adding *-ly* to the adjective form: strong, *strongly;* beautiful, *beautifully.* However, a number of important adverbs show no *-ly* ending: *very, often, quite, rather, well, too, just.*

Adverbs provide information in these categories: *where, when,* or *how* an action occurred; or *to what extent* a description is to be understood:

>   V   V
> *Tomorrow,* I will *probably* sunbathe *outside.*

(Here, we have one adverb to tell us when the action will occur *(tomorrow),* one to modify the action *(probably),* and the third to tell us where the activity will occur *(outside).*)

>   ADJ   N
> She wore an *exceptionally* beautiful dress.

(Now we know to what extent the dress is beautiful—to a great extent or *exceptionally.* This is the pattern that occurs when adverbs modify adjectives.)

>   ADV   V
> I *very nearly* lost my balance.

(The first adverb next to the verb *lost* tells how the action occurred *(nearly),* but the adverb that modifies *nearly* tells to what extent—*very.* This construction would indicate that this was a "close call" in some way.)

In Sentences, Adverbs Will Show These Characteristics

1. Adverbs modifying verbs will usually appear close to or within the actual verb construction:

>   V   V
> I can *hardly* see.

2. They may be used at the beginning of sentences, especially to indicate *when* an action occurs:

Sometimes I enjoy daydreaming.

3. Adverbs such as *often, frequently,* or *occasionally,* when placed in the mid-part of a sentence, may create a *squinting modifier,* an adverb that is ambiguous in its reference. (See dangling modifiers, page 297.)

4. Watch out for the misuse of the adverb *well* in your sentences:

Incorrect: I did *good* on my test.
(*good* is an adjective and cannot describe a verb or tell how you did.)

Correct: I did *well* on my test.
(*well,* the adverbial form of *good,* is correct.)

PREPOSITIONS

A preposition is a word whose primary function is to form phrases with nouns, pronouns, and verbs. We could use the term *gregarious* to describe this category of word, for prepositions do not like to be alone. In combination with nouns and pronouns, they form prepositional phrases; with verbs, the preposition *to* forms the infinitive. Some verbs also require this preposition as part of the actual verb: She *put up* some preserves for the winter. (*Put up* indicates the action of canning food.) Study the following example which has three prepositional phrases and one infinitive phrase: The prepositional phrases are enclosed within parentheses (   ); the infinitive phrase is within brackets [   ].

I went (with him) [to see] (about a job)(at the bank).

Useful Facts about Prepositions

1. Prepositions include these words, many of which show direction: *in, at, on, over, above, beyond, between, among, out, of, with, to, under, beneath, during, except, for, from, by, near, beside, along, through, around, about.*

2. When prepositions combine with nouns, the nouns are bound to the preposition in a unit called the prepositional phrase: *out the door; to the classroom; from my mom; between friends.*

3. Adjectives may appear between the preposition and the noun or an adverb to modify the adjective: *with a very dear friend;* no verbs appear in the phrase.

4. When prepositions bond with pronouns, they form two-word phrases: *to him, to her, with them, of us, above you;* pronouns will take the objective case in these instances.

5. The only preposition which can form the infinitive is *to;* it will bond with any verb to form units such as these: *to be, to go, to spend, to live.* These phrases usually appear in the predicate to influence action; the phrase itself is not, however, part of the main verb:

V
I *wanted* [to go].

(*Wanted* is the verb; *to go* adds important information in the predicate but is not part of the action because this person only *wants* and has not actually gone.)

In Sentences, Prepositional Word Groups Can Behave in These Ways

1. Prepositional phrases can appear in either the subject or the predicate parts of the sentence and may even be stacked one next to the other.

(*On Friday*), some *(of the people) (in my office)* enjoy a visit *(to the local restaurant) (for the seafood special).*

2. Infinitives will tend to appear near the verb in the predicate; however, infinitive phrases may serve as the subject of a sentence:

  S   **V**
To see that movie was a waste of time.

3. In most sentences, the nouns and pronouns appearing in the prepositional phrase will not be eligible to serve as subjects, for they are bound to the preposition:

 S   **V**
Two (of my sons) *are going* to be married this year.
two: simple subject; *are going:* complete verb
(*Sons* cannot serve as the subject, for it is grammatically tied to its preposition *of.*)

CONJUNCTIONS

Conjunctions are able to join words, groups of words, or whole sentences. Conjunctions are the joining words we use every day to connect related ideas or elements. The single most important and perhaps most widely used conjunction is *and.*

Ice cream *and* cake are my favorite desserts *because* they are delicious, *but* they are often fattening.

Useful Facts about Conjunctions

There are three types of conjunctions.

1. Coordinating: *and, but, for, or, yet, so, neither–nor; either–or.*

2. Subordinating: *because, since, after, if, although, when, unless, as, though, that.*

3. Adverbial: *however, therefore, moreover, consequently, thus, in fact.*

In Sentences, Conjunctions Perform These Functions

1. Most coordinators join all types of word groups and sentences.

   Bacon and *eggs* are tasty.

   I enjoyed his slides but *not his lecture.*

   He took fine pictures, but *he spoke badly.*

   Punctuation of coordinators used to join sentences is shown in Comma Rule 1, pages 316–317.

2. Subordinating and adverbial conjunctions serve primarily to join larger word groups and sentences. When a subordinator joins an idea to another related thought, a complex sentence is formed.

   Dependent Clause

   I stepped forward *when my name was called.*

   Review punctuation for both subordinate and adverbial conjunctions on pages 214–216.

SOME COMMON IRREGULAR VERBS

Table A.1 is a listing of common irregular verbs which form the simple past and continuous past tenses other than by adding *-ed* to the present tense. The first two on the list are shown in greater detail so that you can get an idea of how these verbs function.

Table A.1   Common Irregular Verbs

Infinitive	Present Tense	Simple Past	Continuous Past
to be	I *am;* you *are;* he, she, it *is;* we, they *are*	I was; you *were;* he, she, they *were*	I *have been;* he, she, it *has been;* they *have been*
to break	I *break;* you *break;* he, she, it *breaks;* we, they *break*	I *broke;* you *broke;* he, she, it *broke;* we, they *broke*	I have broken; you *have broken;* he, she, it *has broken;* we, they *have broken*

Table A.1 Common Irregular Verbs

Infinitive	Present Tense	Simple Past	Continuous Past
to bring	bring, brings	brought	have, has brought
to buy	buy, buys	bought	have, has bought
to catch	catch, catches	caught	have, has caught
to cling	cling, clings	clung	have, has clung
to draw	draw, draws	drew	have, has drawn
to drink	drink, drinks	drank	have, has drunk
to drive	drive, drives	drove	have, has driven
to eat	eat, eats	ate	have, has eaten
to fly	fly, flies	flew	have, has flown
to freeze	freeze, freezes	froze	have, has frozen
to grow	grow, grows	grew	have, has grown
to hang (an object)	hang, hangs	hung	have, has hung
to have	have, has	had	have, has had
to hold	hold, holds	held	have, has held
to know	know, knows	knew	has, has known
to lay (to put)	lay, lays	laid	have, has laid
to lie (to recline)	lie, lies	lay	have, has lain
to rise	rise, rises	rose	have, has risen
to set	set, sets	set	have, has set
to sit	sit, sits	sat	have, has sat
to steal	steal, steals	stole	have, has stolen
to swim	swim, swims	swam	have, has swum
to teach	teach, teaches	taught	have, has taught
to tell	tell, tells	told	have, has told
to throw	throw, throws	threw	have, has thrown
to write	write, writes	wrote	have, has written

INDEX

Student Questionnaire

In preparing the second edition of RE: WRITING, we would appreciate your evaluation of the present edition. Please return this questionnaire to the English Editor, College Division, Holt, Rinehart and Winston, 111 Fifth Avenue, New York, New York 10003

Name _____ Date _____

School _____

Course
Title _____

Instructor's Name _____

1. Did you find this book too easy? _____ too difficult? _____ about right? _____

2. Which sections were most helpful? Which sections were least helpful?

	Helpful	Not Helpful
UNIT I GETTING STARTED		
Overview	_____	_____
Introduction	_____	_____
Beginning a Writing Project		
Understanding the Assignment	_____	_____
Time and the Writing Process	_____	_____
Clarifying the Writing Process		
The Larger Picture: The Dynamic Process	_____	_____
Completing the Picture: Your Audience	_____	_____
Using Prewriting to Get Started		
An Introduction to Prewriting	_____	_____
A Prewriting Model	_____	_____
Some Prewriting Alternatives	_____	_____
Effective Data Gathering	_____	_____
Choosing Your Topic	_____	_____
Gathering Data for Your Topic	_____	_____
Developing Analytic Techniques	_____	_____
Generating a Strong Thesis Statement	_____	_____
Preparing for the Rough Draft		
Suggestions for Drafting	_____	_____
A Model for Grouping Ideas	_____	_____
If You Are Using a Word Processor	_____	_____
UNIT II WRITING THE PARAGRAPH		
Overview	_____	_____
Introduction	_____	_____
Analyzing the Paragraph		
Paragraph Structure	_____	_____
Paragraph Content	_____	_____
Topic Sentence Placement	_____	_____
Evaluating the Paragraph	_____	_____
Writing a Paragraph		
A Prewriting Model	_____	_____
A Rough Draft Model	_____	_____
An Editing Model	_____	_____
The Final Copy	_____	_____